Edinburgh German Yearbook

Edinburgh German Yearbook

General Editor: Peter Davies

Vol. 1: Cultural Exchange in German Literature
Edited by Eleoma Joshua and Robert Vilain

Vol. 2: Masculinities in German Culture
Edited by Sarah Colvin and Peter Davies

Vol. 3: Contested Legacies: Constructions of Cultural Heritage in the GDR
Edited by Matthew Philpotts and Sabine Rolle

Vol. 4: Disability in German Literature, Film, and Theatre
Edited by Eleoma Joshua and Michael Schillmeier

Vol. 5: Brecht and the GDR: Politics, Culture, Posterity
Edited by Laura Bradley and Karen Leeder

Vol. 6: Sadness in Modern German-Language Literature and Culture
Edited by Mary Cosgrove and Anna Richards (forthcoming 2012)

Edinburgh German Yearbook

Volume 5

Brecht and the GDR:
Politics, Culture, Posterity

Edited by
Laura Bradley
and
Karen Leeder

Camden House
Rochester, New York

First published 2011
by Camden House

Camden House is an imprint of Boydell & Brewer Inc.
668 Mt. Hope Avenue, Rochester, NY 14620, USA
www.camden-house.com
and of Boydell & Brewer Limited
PO Box 9, Woodbridge, Suffolk IP12 3DF, UK
www.boydellandbrewer.com

ISSN: 1937-0857

ISBN-13: 978-1-57113-492-9
ISBN-10: 1-57113-492-1

This publication is printed on acid-free paper.
Printed in the United States of America.

Edinburgh German Yearbook appears annually.
Please send orders and inquiries to Boydell & Brewer at the above address.

Edinburgh German Yearbook does not accept unsolicited submissions:
a Call for Papers for each volume is circulated widely in advance of publication.
For editorial correspondence, please contact either the General Editor,
Professor Peter Davies, or the editor(s) of individual volumes, by post at:

Edinburgh German Yearbook
German Section
Division of European Languages and Cultures
59 George Square, Edinburgh, EH8 3JX
United Kingdom

or by email at: egyb@ed.ac.uk.

Contents

III. Creative Responses to Brecht's Work

Abbreviations

BAP   *Brecht on Art and Politics*, translated by Laura Bradley, Steve
           Giles, and Tom Kuhn, edited by Tom Kuhn and Steve Giles
           (London: Methuen, 2003)

BBA   Bertolt-Brecht-Archiv, Berlin

BFA   Bertolt Brecht, *Große kommentierte Berliner und Frankfurter
           Ausgabe*, 30 vols., edited by Werner Hecht, Jan Knopf, Werner
           Mittenzwei, Klaus-Detlef Müller, and others (Berlin and
           Frankfurt a.M.: Aufbau and Suhrkamp, 1988–2000)

BT   *Brecht on Theatre: The Development of an Aesthetic*, edited and
           translated by John Willett (London: Methuen, 1964)

Journals   Bertolt Brecht, *Journals 1934–1955*, translated by Hugh Rorr-
           ison, edited by John Willett (London: Methuen, 1993)

Letters   Bertolt Brecht, *Letters 1913–1956*, translated by Ralph Man-
           heim, edited by John Willett (London: Methuen, 1990)

n.p.   no pagination

Plays   Bertolt Brecht, *Collected Plays*, vols. 1–8, translated by various
           hands, edited by John Willett, Ralph Manheim, and Tom Kuhn
           (London: Methuen, 1970–2003)

Poems   Bertolt Brecht, *Poems 1913–1956*, translated by various hands,
           edited by John Willett and Ralph Manheim (London: Methuen,
           1976, 1979)

trans. mod. translation modified

Other abbreviations are explained in the essays in which they appear.

Editors' Note

Where dates are given in parentheses in the main text, they refer to the
genesis rather than the publication of the works in question.

Introduction

Laura Bradley, University of Edinburgh

BERTOLT BRECHT HAS come to exemplify the dilemmas faced by German socialists of his generation. The popular revolution he fought for failed to materialize, and when the opportunity arose to create a socialist state in the ruins of the Third Reich, the project did not command the support of the majority of its citizens. In the years that followed, Brecht struggled with the challenge of defending and improving a socialism that was ordained from above and implemented by politicians who did not necessarily view him as an ally. The question of the compromises that he may have made, both politically and personally, has drawn other writers to his life in the GDR as a subject for new literature. Günter Grass depicts Brecht as a hypocritical theater director, whose obsession with the politics of the playscript blinds him to the needs of workers on the streets, while Jacques-Pierre Amette presents him as an aging Lothario caught in a web of Stasi intrigue.[1] These fictional responses to the GDR Brecht share similarities with the accounts offered by anticommunist critics, who have displayed a tendency to cast him in what Loren Kruger calls a "cold war melodrama,"[2] a term which captures the rhetorical excess that characterizes some discussions. Tony Calabro goes so far as to compare Brecht with Adolf Hitler and Erich Honecker, while Oliver Kamm describes him as a propagandist "for an orthodox Communism that followed every twist of Stalin's whims,"[3] a view that would have surprised the East German cultural politicians who dealt with Brecht in the early 1950s. While anticommunist criticism of Brecht can be traced back through the Cold War to the Weimar Republic,[4] these critics are intervening in a debate about what becomes of the socialist icon after the end of the socialist state. This is one of the questions that the present volume seeks to address.

Brecht's decision to settle in East Berlin clearly had major consequences for the ways in which his legacy was constructed and mediated over the following forty years, and it continues to influence international perceptions of his work in the twenty-first century. Even so, we need to be careful not to project the state's cooption of Brecht as an orthodox socialist icon back onto him as a historical individual. Brecht lived through just seven years of the GDR, long enough to witness the revelations about Stalin's crimes at the Twentieth Congress of the Communist Party of the Soviet Union, yet not long enough to see the show trials of Wolfgang Harich and Walter Janka, or the construction of the Berlin Wall. His relationship with the GDR authorities was complex: he was awarded the National Prize for Literature, but only second class; he was given the Theater am Schiffbauerdamm for his theater, the Berliner Ensemble (BE), but the authorities did not want his methods to catch on.[5] It was only after Brecht's death that the regime sought to elevate him to the status of a socialist classic, and this shift came at the price of the selective appropriation of his legacy and the development of authorized modes of interpretation and performance. Poets, theorists, dramatists, and directors soon reacted against what they saw as the stagnation of Brecht's critical impetus: they began to subject his work to his own treatment, taking his methods to more radical conclusions and often using non-canonical texts as a source of material and inspiration. For writers such as Wolf Biermann and Volker Braun, Brecht's oeuvre provided tools that could be used to recuperate the aspirations of socialism from the political reality of the GDR state, both during its lifetime and after its collapse.

This volume provides the first overarching study of Brecht's work and legacy in the GDR, examining his theatrical, literary, and political activities in the 1950s; the posthumous management of his legacy; and creative responses to his works in literature, music, and theater. It thus seizes an opportunity to focus on a cohesive set of themes in one context: the GDR marked a crucial and distinctive phase in Brecht's career, when he was contributing to the construction of a new theater and a new society, testing out his ideas and plays, and investing in a place where he hoped to leave a permanent artistic and political legacy. But the volume also broadens the focus from Brecht as a historical individual to the construction of his public image and his reception. By investigating the roles of his heirs, collaborators, and artistic successors, it extends the debate beyond the question of Brecht's own loyalty and dissent in the 1950s,[6] and explores a cultural field that was always broader and more complex than the question of Brecht's relationship with officials in the ruling Socialist Unity Party (SED). The collection is not conceived as a comprehensive history, but as a series of soundings and tests, rather in the spirit of Brecht's title for his series of publications: *Versuche* (Experiments).

Brecht in the GDR

On 10 February 1948, in the Soviet sector of Berlin, the Deutsches Theater hosted a "Brecht Evening" in honor of Brecht's fiftieth birthday. It featured the Weimar Republic stars Ernst Busch, Kate Kühl, and Gerda Müller, who performed a cross-section of Brecht's works.[7] Brecht himself was in Switzerland at the time, watching events in Germany from a position of relative proximity and distance, as he had done in exile in Svendborg. His supporters used the occasion to campaign for him to come back to Germany: Herbert Ihering, who had backed Brecht ever since the 1922 premiere of *Trommeln in der Nacht* (Drums in the Night, 1919–22), called on him to return to Berlin where he was needed.[8] This view was echoed by Slatan Dudow, who had worked with Brecht on *Die Maßnahme* (The Measures Taken, 1930) and *Die Mutter* (The Mother, 1932), and also by Heinz Lüdecke, who had reviewed Brecht's work — not uncritically — for the communist press in the Weimar Republic.[9] The press coverage of Brecht's birthday indicates that critics pinned their hopes on him as a writer; the articles show little awareness of his potential to change theater practice. While critics attempted to reconnect the public with the avant-garde culture of the Weimar Republic by telling anecdotes about their previous encounters with Brecht, their articles simultaneously conveyed a sense of rupture and loss.[10] As one critic explained, those who had remained in Germany had no knowledge of his exile works, while the younger generation was entirely unfamiliar with his oeuvre.[11]

Brecht came back to the Soviet occupied zone of Germany in October 1948, returning to Switzerland in February 1949, before settling permanently in East Berlin in May. This move entailed a shift from working in political opposition to advocating change from a position of support, from within prestigious institutions such as the Academy of Arts. For all Brecht's disagreements with the SED — particularly over cultural policy — his commitment to the socialist project was never in doubt. At the same time, his poems and journals show he was acutely aware of the hold that Nazi attitudes still had on the population, and of the unpopularity of the occupying Soviet forces (*BFA* 12:312, 314; *BFA* 27:283, 285, 315). His decision to keep his exit route open — with his Austrian passport, Swiss bank account, and West German publisher — needs to be seen as a reaction to this precarious political situation, not just to his relationship with the SED. And while Brecht did have advocates such as the Soviet cultural officer Alexander Dymschitz, it is easy to see why SED politicians were suspicious of him: he had spent his exile in

Scandinavia and the USA rather than the Soviet Union, flaunted his lack of Party membership when summoned before the US House Committee on Un-American Activities, and now took his Marxist instruction from Jacob Walcher, who was expelled from the SED in 1951.

What was at stake in the cultural battles that ensued was not simply Brecht's status in the GDR, but the national culture of the new state. From the perspective of the SED leadership, it was vital to forge a distinct identity for the GDR, given that it was in direct competition with the Federal Republic. Brecht was used to establish the cultural line on key issues: on the Party's relationship to the agitprop tradition (*Die Mutter*), the treatment of history and the cultural heritage (*Urfaust*), pacifism (*Lukullus*), and modes of representation in theater (the Stanislavsky Conference). These contests were played out in public, presenting artists and audiences with a simplified set of choices that often bore little resemblance to the reality of Brecht's work.[12] At the same time, the Party's hard line against Brecht was a response to the extent of his ambition. From his arrival in Berlin, he made it clear that he was aiming to change the national theater culture and that he espoused a far broader concept of the cultural heritage than SED politicians were willing to countenance. Individuals who had opposed Brecht in the debates over realism and aesthetics in the exile journal *Das Wort* now wielded political power in the GDR; they perceived Brecht as a loose canon, and argued that he needed to be brought under control.

During the 1950s, the cultural climate became increasingly inhospitable to Brecht. He complained that his productions were having barely any impact in the press (*BFA* 27:346), and that GDR theaters were among the few worldwide that did not perform his plays. In fact, he famously advised aspiring writers to found their own theaters, arguing that this was the only way he was able to secure productions of his texts (*BFA* 23:367–68). Yet Brecht did publish more contributions in *Sinn und Form*, the journal of the Academy of Arts, than any other writer, and he even had an issue of the journal published in his honor when he returned to the GDR. He thus experienced an exclusive form of marginalization: he was confined to an elite journal and an elite theater, tolerated at least partly because of his international standing. Werner Hecht aptly describes this as a form of "Gestattungsproduktion" (permitted production), a term used to describe goods produced in the GDR primarily for Western export, but sold in small quantities to the domestic market.[13] This model would become useful for many nonconformist writers in later years.

Brecht reacted to the SED's cultural policy with scathing criticism, and not just in private.[14] After the failed uprising of 17 June 1953, he resumed his work on *Turandot oder Der Kongreß der Weißwäscher* (Turandot or The Whitewashers' Congress, 1953), a satirical attack on the opportunism and false consciousness of intellectuals, whom he nicknamed "Tuis." Brecht had begun working on this material in the Weimar Republic, and he developed it further in exile to include allusions to Hitler and National Socialism, Adorno and the Frankfurt School, intellectuals in the Soviet Union, and conflicts among anti-Nazi exiles, before adding a thinly-veiled critique of GDR bureaucracy in the 1950s.[15] In scene 9 (*BFA* 9:182–88), Brecht intervened in the debate on the cultural heritage, bringing together allusions to the Nazi campaign against "degenerate" art, the attacks against avant-garde artists in the Soviet Union, and the Formalism Campaign in the GDR. The scene shows how, after the gangster Gogher Gogh — a failed artist like Hitler — has come to power, Tuis rescue works of art and store them for safekeeping in a swordsmith's home. The house becomes so overcrowded that the swordsmith can barely fight his way through to his forge, which he needs in order to supply weapons to the poor who are engaged in a popular uprising. Brecht thus continues his satirical attack on the false priorities of the Tuis and their understanding of what is worth saving; the peasant Sen jokes that a Tui is probably leading an invisible god to a place of safety at that very moment (*BFA* 9:184). Yet Brecht simultaneously uses the Tuis to smuggle a defense of avant-garde art into his play. The works that the Tuis rescue suggest a broad definition of the cultural heritage: they include a picture of blue hills, possibly an allusion to Franz Marc's painting *Turm der blauen Pferde* (Tower of Blue Horses, 1913), a painting that Brecht had defended in an essay of 1937–38 (*BFA* 22.1: 350). Sen accepts the painter's non-realist approach (*BFA* 9:186), endorsing the rescue and thereby rejecting not just National Socialist cultural policy but also the SED's prescriptive Socialist Realism. Read as a critique of SED cultural policy, the scene implies that the formalism debate is a distraction from the current needs of the class struggle.

Unlike the pseudo-intellectuals in *Turandot*, Brecht continued to seek critical dialogue with the authorities. The poem "Die Wahrheit einigt" (The Truth Unites, 1953) begins "Freunde, ich wünschte, ihr wüßtet die Wahrheit und sagtet sie!" (*BFA* 12:315; Friends, I'd like you to know the truth and speak it, *Poems* 441). According to Käthe Rülicke, who worked as a dramaturge at the Berliner Ensemble, Brecht commissioned her to send this poem to Prime Minister Otto Grotewohl, with the request that he should read it out at a meeting of the Council of

Ministers.[16] Yet even though Brecht had called for open dialogue about
the causes of the June uprising and published poems that were critical of
cultural policy in the *Berliner Zeitung*,[17] he did not attempt to publish
the poem that he sent to Grotewohl. Brecht's restraint in withholding a
poem that criticized the Party leadership was closely related to his fears
about the resurgence of fascism, and to his determination not to give
ammunition to the Federal Republic. In another of his late plays, *Die
Tage der Kommune* (Days of the Commune, 1948–49), we see him
thinking through the measures needed to safeguard socialism, and his
awareness of the uncomfortable measures that its supporters might be
prepared to sanction. The Communard Langevin comes to regret having
listened to the people and argues that the Commune should have
suspended democratic rights in the interests of its survival. His key criticism is: "Wir waren noch nicht bereit [. . .] auf die persönliche Freiheit
zu verzichten, bis die Freiheit aller erkämpft war." (*BFA* 8:301; We were
not yet prepared [. . .] to forgo personal freedom until the freedom of all
had been achieved, *Plays* 8:111, trans. mod.) It is surely significant that
Brecht originally planned to open the Berliner Ensemble with this combative play (*BFA* 8:507–10).

The four essays in part 1 of this volume deal with Brecht's experiences in the early GDR. David Barnett focuses on Brecht's production
practice at the Berliner Ensemble, presenting some of the initial findings
of his research for a two-volume monograph on the company's history.
Barnett shows that Brecht was experimenting not just with production
aesthetics, but with the organization of theater itself. He empowered the
staff to make positive contributions to rehearsals, reducing their alienation from the production process and enhancing the quality of productions in a "virtuous circle." Barnett examines Brecht's work on two
productions: his socially critical comedy *Herr Puntila und sein Knecht
Matti* (Mr. Puntila and His Man Matti, 1940), and Johannes R. Becher's
tragedy *Winterschlacht* (Battle in Winter, 1942), which is set during the
Battle of Moscow in 1941–42. Barnett emphasizes that Brecht was
staging political theater but not propaganda; his productions opened up
the plays to dialectical investigation, resisting the temptation to point to
a definite synthesis.

While it was Brecht's theater work at the Berliner Ensemble that initially attracted worldwide attention, his poetry has often been
considered his most significant new writing in the GDR. Brecht's postwar poetry, particularly the *Buckower Elegien* (Buckow Elegies, 1953),
has been classified as "late" or "old-age" work, yet his death at the age of
just fifty-eight has led some recent commentators to challenge such

notions of biographical lateness. In her essay, Karen Leeder reads Brecht's last poems in the light of theories of lateness, old-age literature, and late style. She focuses particularly on Brecht's preoccupation with illness, death, memory, wisdom, and classical forebears, but also on the link with epochal lateness — despite the strong sense of beginning associated with the young GDR state — and finally on an aesthetics of lateness or "late style." Here, Leeder shows that the poems fit the categories set out in Edward Said's volume *On Late Style* (2006) — intransigence, anomaly, discontinuity, untimeliness, and irony — with striking consistency. Through this discovery, she offers a way out of the longstanding stalemate between interpretations of the *Buckower Elegien* that foreground political aspects and those that see the poems as more private and introspective.

During his research for a new biography of Brecht, Stephen Parker has uncovered fresh material on Brecht's medical history in the early GDR, which he presents here. Parker shows that Brecht was more seriously ill when he settled in East Berlin than critics have hitherto suspected; a urological condition compounded the long-term effects of his childhood illnesses. Parker uses evidence of Brecht's failing health to provide new perspectives on his cultural and political battles with the SED: he was hospitalized during the first crucial phase of the Formalism Campaign of 1951, and again in early 1953. Parker examines Brecht's health as he worked on the plays *Katzgraben* (1953) and *Turandot*, concluding that by 1954 his extraordinary intellectual energy was nearly spent. In Parker's view, the political intrigue of the SED accelerated this aging process.

The controversy surrounding Brecht's reactions to the uprising on 17 June 1953 has been compounded by rumor, speculation, and contradictions between the versions of different eyewitnesses. Patrick Harkin re-examines the evidence, constructing an account of Brecht's actions on 17 June and assessing his responses in newspaper articles, letters, journal entries, and poetry. Brecht has been judged in the West on the basis of his statement of support to the First Secretary of the SED Central Committee Walter Ulbricht (*BFA* 30:178), but Harkin shows that Brecht rushed off this statement before he had witnessed events on the streets. His more considered responses identified government mistakes as a key cause of the uprising and advocated communication between workers and the government as the solution. Both Harkin and Parker single out Brecht's journal entry stating that "der 17. juni hat die ganze existenz verfremdet" (*BFA* 27:346; 17 june has alienated the whole of existence, *Journals* 454–55). Yet Harkin reads the entry more positively than Parker, seeing it through the lens of Brecht's aesthetic theory, where *Verfremdung* (estrangement) functions as a process that yields new understanding. In Harkin's view, Brecht settled into a frame of mind that was at times optimistic and at times pessimistic, with pessimism as the dominant force.

The Management of Brecht's Legacy

It was not just Brecht who chose to settle in the GDR, but some of his key collaborators from the Weimar Republic and his years in exile. In fact, his letters show that he worked hard to ensure that Elisabeth Hauptmann, Paul Dessau, and Caspar Neher would join him in Berlin (*BFA* 29:467–68, 473, 475). At the Berliner Ensemble, Brecht and his wife Helene Weigel soon recruited new collaborators who were starting out on their careers in the GDR, such as the directors Benno Besson, Peter Palitzsch, and Manfred Wekwerth. After Brecht's death in August 1956, his former collaborators helped to manage his legacy and to disseminate his works and staging methods. Their roles in the co-creation of works — whether literary texts or theater productions — gave them the authority to represent Brecht and his ideas. Yet tensions would soon emerge: while Weigel and Hauptmann focused on the preservation and transmission of Brecht's methods, Brecht's younger collaborators began to seek the freedom to experiment and develop these methods in different directions. Besson was the first to leave the BE after Brecht's death.

The state ceremony at Brecht's funeral and the eulogies in the press marked the start of his incorporation into the GDR cultural heritage: Walter Ulbricht and the Minister of Culture Johannes R. Becher were among the funeral guests. The process of canonization was concluded on the first anniversary of Brecht's death, when his image appeared on commemorative postage stamps, marking his new status as a figurehead for the GDR state [Fig. 1]. The quotation on the first-day issue of these stamps was taken from Brecht's affirmative poem "Die Erziehung der Hirse" (The Rearing of Millet, 1950), which tells of a nomad from Kazakhstan who pioneers new methods of improving grain yields, thereby ensuring that the Red Army can be supplied with food during its fight against Hitler.[18] During the years that followed, Brecht began to play an increasingly important role in public discourse, and politicians used quotations from his works as a source of rhetorical authority and legitimation.[19] His plays were even treated as a vehicle for cultural diplomacy: the Berliner Ensemble represented the GDR abroad, and GDR

Fig. 1: First-day issue of the earliest postage stamps commemorating Brecht. The quotation translates as: "The earth as she is / Need not so remain. / Through research and work / Extend your domain."[20]

directors staged his works in other socialist states, from Cuba to Afghanistan.

Brecht's rapid elevation to the status of a national cultural icon relied on the propagation of a certain vision of the writer and his works. As the poet Johannes Bobrowski put it in his poem "Berliner Ensemble": "diesen richtigen Brecht gibt's ja erst jetzt: weil er tot" (this correct Brecht only exists now: because he's dead).[21] In schools, pupils first encountered Brecht through *Die Gewehre der Frau Carrar* (Señora Carrar's Rifles, 1937), a play that poses few challenges to "dramatic" theater. In fact, Wolfgang Conrad concludes that a large proportion of Brecht's innovative force, which was connected to the theory and practice of epic theater, was simply banished from the literature curriculum for years.[22] While theater repertoires were more varied, *Die Gewehre der Frau Carrar* was still the most frequently performed of Brecht's plays in the GDR, and audiences had to wait until 1971 to see *Im Dickicht der Städte* (In the Jungle of the Cities, 1922) and until 1973 to see *Turandot.* Even then, the plays were staged partly because the BE was running out of "new" Brecht material.[23] In the 1960s, Brecht's "model" productions were revived at the BE and used as a rigid template for stagings elsewhere in the GDR, closing down the dialectic that Brecht had — as Barnett argues — striven to keep open.[24]

The three essays in part 2 focus on the management of Brecht's legacy in the GDR. Erdmut Wizisla, the director of the Bertolt Brecht Archive in Berlin, uses new material to examine key moments in the archive's history, a history that has yet to be written. Wizisla pays tribute to Helene Weigel's energy and commitment in establishing the archive and increasing its holdings. While other collaborators such as Hauptmann and Wekwerth argued for the censorship of particular works, Weigel and her daughter Barbara Brecht-Schall fended off state demands for censorship, with the result that Brecht's texts were barely censored in the GDR. The role of Brecht's heirs in the history of the Brecht Archive thus challenges assumptions that public ownership is to be preferred to private. Wizisla argues that "in circumstances in which 'public' had the same meaning as 'state-controlled,' a private set-up may well have been the more democratic principle." After Weigel's death in 1971, the authorities sought to confiscate Brecht's estate and strip his heirs of any real power. Yet Brecht's heirs succeeded in retaining possession of the original documents until 1992, ensuring that the precarious balance between public and private was maintained throughout the GDR.

Helene Weigel was justly proud of having ensured that the texts of the Suhrkamp and Aufbau editions of Brecht's works were identical. Yet she was less sanguine regarding the situation at the Berliner Ensemble. On 16 November 1969, she told Werner Hecht: "My biggest concern is that I wasn't able to have a similar success in the theater."[25] This may sound odd given the theater's international renown, but from the late 1960s the BE was struggling to redefine its identity now that it had staged most of Brecht's plays and his methods had entered mainstream theater. This difficulty was particularly acute during the BE's large-scale commemorations for Brecht, as Laura Bradley shows in her examination of the seventieth, seventy-fifth, and eightieth anniversaries of his birth. These occasions were not just about celebrating the theater's past, but about reaffirming its identity and setting goals for the future. In 1968, as crisis loomed, different groups at the BE pulled together to stage the first international "Brecht Dialogue." The situation had changed by 1973: the GDR's leading Brecht experts were located outside the BE and were critical of developments under Weigel's successor, Ruth Berghaus. The run-up to the 1978 anniversary was characterized by panic at the BE, and the deadlock between the company's artistic management and Brecht's heirs was only resolved when Manfred Wekwerth was appointed as the new manager. By this time, anniversaries had come to exert immense pressure on the theater, dictating decisions over the repertoire and spurring the authorities into action.

Whereas the other contributions in part 2 focus on institutions and the individuals working within them, Paula Hanssen's essay examines Elisabeth Hauptmann's role in the GDR. Hauptmann is best known for her collaboration with Brecht in the Weimar Republic and for editing his works in the GDR, but Hanssen shows that she also continued to contribute significantly to new works created for and at the Berliner Ensemble. She worked with Brecht's young collaborators on new plays and productions, advised on management and pedagogical issues, and dealt with royalties and performance rights in her correspondence with foreign theaters. Like Wekwerth, Hauptmann was a partisan defender of both Brecht and the GDR: she knew that he had withheld certain texts from publication in the 1950s, and she chose to exercise "responsibility" in editing his texts for the public. This editorial approach reflected the sense of authority that derived from Hauptmann's status as a co-creator of key works. She carried out much of this work behind the scenes, and Hanssen suggests that her full contribution to Brecht's legacy has yet to come to light.

Creative Responses to Brecht's Work

While Brecht has attracted an unusually broad international reception, it is still possible to identify specific strands and preoccupations in GDR artistic responses to his work. In the 1950s and 1960s, some writers returned to his works in order to affirm the GDR's achievements. Helmut Preißler's cycle of poems *Stimmen der Nachgeborenen* (Voices of Those Born Later, 1961) expressed the view that the state had realized Brecht's hopes and overcome the class divisions of the past.[26] These poems had their dramatic equivalent in plays by Helmut Baierl, notably his socialist adaptations of *Mutter Courage* (Mother Courage, 1939) and *Die heilige Johanna der Schlachthöfe* (Saint Joan of the Stockyards, 1932). The new versions, *Frau Flinz* (1961) and *Johanna von Döbeln* (1968), accepted the SED line that the antagonistic conflicts of capitalism no longer existed in socialism, weakening the dramatic force of the plays. The affirmative function of Baierl's work can be seen from the weeks after the construction of the Berlin Wall, when the Berliner Ensemble staged an election rally based on its production of *Frau Flinz*. When asked how Frau Flinz would have reacted to the Wall, Helene Weigel reportedly replied with a mischievous smile: "Das hätt euch auch früher einfallen können."[27] (You could have thought of that earlier.)

Criticism — or even resentment — of Brecht's authority is concentrated particularly in GDR literary responses to his works, and this concentration can be seen as a reaction to the status and function accorded to him by the regime. The singer and poet Wolf Biermann sought to recuperate Brecht from the heritage industry that promoted him; in poems from the 1960s, he is critical of Weigel's role at the BE, and he imagines Brecht gently mocking the industrious scholars at the Brecht Archive.[28] Yet Heiner Müller traces the problem of Brecht's authority back to his own work, as we can see from his response to the poem "ich benötige keinen Grabstein" (I need no gravestone, 1933). In Brecht's poem, the speaker claims not to need a gravestone, only then to ask that if his readers need one for him, it should record that he made suggestions, which they have accepted (*BFA* 14:191–92). The speaker's professed modesty is disingenuous, and while the poem demonstrates a desire for reciprocity, it positions posterity as the junior partner. Müller responds with a relentless attack on his own authority as a writer:

> Aber von mir werden sie sagen Er
> Hat Vorschläge gemacht Wir haben sie
> Nicht angenommen Warum sollten wir[29]

> [But of me they will say He
> Made suggestions We did not
> Accept them.
> Why should we]

Yet even as Müller rejects Brecht's ideas for an epitaph, the poem employs the fractured syntax and rhythms that are so characteristic of Brecht's poetry, acknowledging and demonstrating what he has learned from Brecht — even if Müller dispenses with the punctuation that Brecht would have used. We find a similar explicit quoting of poetic strategies in Volker Braun's reflection on the way in which Brecht is officially remembered:

> Wer wohnte unter dem dänischen Strohdach?
> Auf der Bronzetafel steht der Name des Dichters.
> Wem außer ihm
> Bot sich der Unterschlupf?[30]

> [Who lived under the Danish thatch?
> On the bronze plaque there's the name of the poet.
> To whom other than him
> Did the house offer refuge?]

Here Braun uses the strategy of critical reading advocated in "Fragen eines lesenden Arbeiters" (Questions From a Worker Who Reads, 1937) to coolly question the image of Brecht as lone genius. It is the skeptical, questioning Brecht that Braun takes as his inspiration; in his journal, he explains that for him Brecht's photograph has taken on the function of "Der Zweifler" (The Doubter), a reference to Brecht's 1937 poem about the image of a figure who forces the speaker and his colleagues to question whether their work has succeeded.[31] Removed from his pedestal, Brecht is able to function for Braun as a critical sounding board, as an ally and confidant.

Artists' relationships with Brecht, and their attitudes toward the authority that he has accrued, figure prominently in the first essay in part 3 of this volume, in which Joy Calico examines how two of Brecht's most important collaborators, Hanns Eisler and Paul Dessau, responded to his death. Both composers marked Brecht's death by returning to texts that he had written in exile, following Brecht's own practice of repurposing and reworking material. But their responses were different: Eisler's was characterized by a despair and nostalgia that can be traced back to his disappointments in the GDR, where his libretto for *Johann Faustus* (1951–52) came under fierce attack. In contrast, Dessau's symphony *In memoriam Bertolt Brecht* (1957) was deeply ambivalent, and Calico reads it as a modern elegy that incorporates disagreement, accusation, and disaffection. She concludes that the composers' responses proved prophetic: when Eisler died in 1962, he had composed relatively little since Brecht's death, whereas Dessau was galvanized by the new critical course of *In memoriam*, away from vocal music to full-scale orchestral works.

In the second essay on post-Brechtian poetry and music, David Robb examines how members of new generations of GDR artists sought to revive a vibrant relationship with Brecht. Robb focuses first on Wolf Biermann's poetry from the 1960s to his expatriation in 1976, and then examines the attempts of Hans-Eckardt Wenzel and Steffen Mensching to create a new *Liedertheater* (song theater) in the 1980s and beyond. The essay highlights the appeal of the grotesque in Brecht's early work, which offered GDR writers an opportunity to reconnect with a profane poetic tradition reaching back through Brecht to the fifteenth-century poet François Villon. Biermann, Wenzel, and Mensching projected an image of Brecht that clashed with the SED-approved icon, and material from Brecht's works served as a provocative tool that could be used to expose the stagnation of revolutionary ideals in the GDR.

It was not just the plebeian tradition that GDR poets returned to in Brecht's oeuvre; his works offered a rich fund of material, motifs, and techniques, and his experience of exile offered critical intellectuals a

means of registering their own sense of displacement in the GDR. Karen
Leeder has shown the international range of poets who have taken up the
challenge of Brecht's most famous exile poem, "An die Nachgeborenen"
(To Those Born Later, 1934–38), to test their own times against
Brecht's standards.[32] Yet this urge had a particular force and relevance in
the GDR, as the state in which Brecht subsequently invested his hopes
for the future. East German writers such as Peter Huchel and Wolf
Biermann have used phrases from the poem as a critical yardstick for state
socialism.[33] Biermann's direct response, "Brecht, deine Nachgeborenen"
(Brecht, Your Posterity, published 1972) functions as a palimpsest, in
which the original shows through the surface text. Where Brecht and his
generation went through exile "öfter die Länder als die Schuhe wechselnd" (*BFA* 12:87; changing countries more often than our shoes,
Poems 320, trans. mod.) the GDR's bureaucrats are described as "öfter
noch als die Schuhe die Haltung wechselnd" (changing convictions more
often than their shoes).[34] And where Brecht's generation was hoarse
from anger against injustice, Biermann's bureaucrats simply have nothing
more to say. The distortion of their erstwhile ideals is reflected in the way
in which the language twists in the poem, as the "Träume" (dreams) laid
out before the speaker morphs into "Trümmer" (rubble).[35] What makes
Biermann's poem stand out is his ability to inhabit the rhythms and
cadences of Brecht's elegy, and to turn them back on the bureaucrats
who claim the writer as their own. By rewriting and estranging Brecht's
verse, Biermann lays his claim to Brecht's legacy.

In drama, the SED's acceptance of Brecht opened the way for playwrights to experiment with self-conscious theatricality and challenge the
limits of Socialist Realism, in ways that would not have been available to
Brecht in the 1950s. But two of the GDR's leading dramatists, Heiner
Müller and Volker Braun, became increasingly skeptical of the pedagogy
and dramaturgy of Brecht's Marxist plays. After attending the first performance of *Die Maßnahme* in the GDR, Braun noted in his journal:

> das dilemma die endlichkeit seiner fabeln: man kapiert die kausalität.
> müller der phänomenologe und somit ein großer dichter, der auf
> unendlichkeit reitet. nach der hellen die schwarze kunst.[36]
>
> [the dilemma the finite nature of his plots: we understand the causality.
> müller the phenomenologist and for this reason a great poet, riding on
> infinity. after the light art the black.]

The reference to phenomenology highlights Müller's attention to subjective experience, in contrast to what Braun sees here as the restrictive
Enlightenment rationality of Brecht's plays. In Müller's later work, his

reaction against the author as controlling super-ego takes the form of an increasingly radical rejection of the Brechtian *Fabel*, which Brecht used — particularly in his work at the BE — to plot the course of plays and productions. Where Brecht used the *Fabel* to connect the episodes in his plays, Müller's late works assault the audience with fragments, forcing spectators to make connections between them and increasing the likelihood that spectators will make connections that the producers have not foreseen. This is still political theater, but one that Helen Fehervary describes as a theater of inundation and entanglement.[37]

While Müller initially turned to the *Lehrstücke* (learning plays) as an alternative to Brecht's parable plays, he became increasingly fascinated with Brecht's play *Der Untergang des Egoisten Johann Fatzer* (The Downfall of the Egotist Johann Fatzer, 1926–30). Moray McGowan's essay shows how important *Fatzer*, its absence and presence on the GDR stage, and its championing and adaptation by Müller are for our understanding of Brecht's reception in the GDR. Brecht's dramatization of the energies of anarchic refusal and the emergence of the new as an inchoate, pre-ideological process driven by and experienced with fear ran counter to the bland confidence of the sanctioned, superficially Marxist historiography of progress. For Müller, *Fatzer*'s strengths lay precisely in its unfinished and unfinishable form, its starkness, and its staging of the emergence of the new as a moment of terror. In the transmutation, from draft to draft of Brecht's *Fatzer*, of the figure of Koch, the character who most strongly opposes Fatzer's asocial anarchy, into the figure of Keuner, the rationalist, Müller saw the essence of the decay of revolutions into bureaucracies, and thus the stagnation and failure of the GDR as a utopian socialist project. This links to the sustained and even growing interest in *Fatzer* in the two decades since the GDR's collapse, as the play now resonates with the new forms of resistance and refusal in the age of globalization.

Loren Kruger's essay opens up further perspectives on the post-GDR Brecht, showing that the collapse of state socialism has opened up space for the revival of Brecht's anticapitalist plays, including *Die heilige Johanna der Schlachthöfe* (Saint Joan of the Stockyards, 1932). GDR theaters struggled to deal with this play; it was rarely performed and never became part of the standard Brecht repertoire in East Germany. Yet the fact that it has been staged more than a dozen times between 2003 and 2010 indicates that the play commands attention now, due to its treatment of speculation, profiteering, and market manipulation. Kruger examines productions at two of the GDR's former flagship theaters. Claus Peymann's 2003 production at the BE targeted both capitalism and the difficulty of fighting it. At the Deutsches Theater in 2009, Nicolas Stemann applied deconstructive techniques associated with the ex-GDR director Frank Castorf, introducing quotations from pop culture, scrambling text, characters, and the legacies of East and West. While some critics have written off *Johanna* as simplifying the struggle between labor and capital, Kruger argues that it offers a powerful antidote to free-market fundamentalism. Her essay offers a forceful riposte to commentators who argue that the collapse of the GDR has invalidated Brecht's socialist critique.

Brecht's socialist convictions ensured that he split audiences in his lifetime, and he continues to do so today. While he has achieved a remarkable international impact and has entered into the very language of poetry, theater, and even film and politics, he remains a contested classic — contested in the sense that some commentators argue that his reputation is too high. This view recurs in the feuilletons when Brecht's plays are premiered,[38] and it was perhaps reflected in the slimness of the volume representing his place in the German literary canon in the

Fig. 2: Sculpture Der moderne Buchdruck
(Modern Book Printing) *on Bebelplatz, Berlin (2006).*
This was one of six sculptures in the "Walk of Ideas." © Lyn Marven.

sculpture displayed in 2006 on Bebelplatz in Berlin. The volume was held in place by the far larger books representing Goethe and Mann — presumably Thomas rather than Heinrich [Fig. 2]. This somewhat grudging acknowledgment contrasts with Brecht's institutional presence elsewhere in Berlin, in the Brecht Archive, Berliner Ensemble, and Brecht House. These institutions can be seen as a lasting legacy of his heirs and the GDR, a legacy that has now been integrated into the fabric of the reunified city. But it is Brecht's works themselves that continue to provoke creative responses and to reward critical re-reading. Their reception in the GDR shows that they offer the tools to resist even the most sustained and determined attempts at assimilation, enabling artists to play Brecht off against Brecht, Fatzer against Keuner. This ongoing dialogue suggests that the GDR sculptor Fritz Cremer may have got it right with his monument outside the Berliner Ensemble: it invites passers-by to sit down with "the man on the bench who / Doubted so much" (*Poems* 270–71) and continue the discussion.[39]

Fig. 3: Fritz Cremer's sculpture of Bertolt Brecht on Bertolt-Brecht-Platz, Berlin. The sculpture was erected in 1988, in honor of the ninetieth anniversary of Brecht's birth. © Tom Läßig.

Notes

¹ Günter Grass, *Die Plebejer proben den Aufstand* (Neuwied: Luchterhand, 1966); Jacques-Pierre Amette, *Brecht's Mistress*, trans. Andrew Brown (New York and London: The New Press, 2005). See also the film *Abschied: Brechts letzter Sommer* (The Farewell: Brecht's Last Summer), dir. Jan Schütte, 2001. On the relationship between the "Boss" in Grass's play and Brecht, see Patrick Harkin's essay in this volume.

² Loren Kruger, "'To Those Born Later': Brecht's Centenary and Other Commemorations," *Rethinking Marxism* 11, no. 2 (1999): 67–79, here 67.

³ Calabro argues that "Honecker's betrayal of his people was no greater than Brecht's, and perhaps less significant" and suggests that "the most striking parallel with Brecht's demagoguery might be with Hitler." Tony Calabro, *Bertolt Brecht's Art of Dissemblance* (Wakefield, NH: Longwood Academic, 1990), 16 and 17; Oliver Kamm, "A Quiet Smile at Absolute Folly," *The Times* (London), 3 January 2006.

⁴ See e.g. Hannah Arendt, *Men in Dark Times* (New York: Harcourt, Brace & World, 1968); Martin Esslin, *Brecht: A Choice of Evils* (London: Eyre & Spottiswoode, 1959).

⁵ *"Die Regierung ruft die Künstler": Dokumente zur Gründung der "Deutschen Akademie der Künste" (DDR) 1945–1953*, ed. Petra Uhlmann and Sabine Wolf (Berlin: Henschel, 1993), 171.

⁶ Discussions of Brecht in the GDR have tended to focus on this aspect. See e.g. James K. Lyon, "Brecht in Postwar Germany: Dissident Conformist, Cultural Icon, Literary Dictator," in *Brecht Unbound*, ed. James K. Lyon and Hans-Peter Breuer (London: Associated University Presses, 1995), 76–88; Matthew Philpotts, *The Margins of Dictatorship: Assent and Dissent in the Work of Günter Eich and Bertolt Brecht*, British and Irish Studies in German Language and Literature 34 (Frankfurt a.M.: Peter Lang, 2003).

⁷ Deutsches Theater, "Brecht-Abend zum 50. Geburtstag des Dichters" [theater program], in Berliner Ensemble Archive (henceforth BEA), "BRECHT: Internationales Brecht-Colloquium 70. Geburtstag Februar 1968."

⁸ Eh, "Bert Brecht und Ernst Busch," newspaper and date unknown, in BEA, "BRECHT: Internationales Brecht-Colloquium."

⁹ Slatan Dudow, "Der denkende Dichter: Zum 50. Geburtstag Bertolt Brechts," newspaper and date unknown; Heinz Lüdecke, "Ein deutscher Aufklärer: Bert Brecht zum 50. Geburtstag," newspaper and date unknown. Both in BEA, "BRECHT: Internationales Brecht-Colloquium." Lüdecke would be among those who criticized *Lukullus* in 1951. See *BFA* 23:486.

¹⁰ See e.g. Lüdecke, "Ein deutscher Aufklärer."

¹¹ D. F., "Bert Brecht 50 Jahre," newspaper unknown, 10 February 1948. In: BEA, "BRECHT: Internationales Brecht-Colloquium."

¹² For the way in which the controversies surrounding *Urfaust* and *Johann Faustus* simplified and obscured Brecht's relationship to the classical tradition, see Stephen Parker, Peter Davies, and Matthew Philpotts, *The Modern Restoration: Re-thinking*

German Literary History 1930–1960 (Berlin and New York: Walter de Gruyter, 2004), 283–84.

[13] Werner Hecht, "Brechts Gestattungsproduktion in der DDR," in *Gelegentlich: Brecht*, ed. Birte Giesler, Eva Kormann, Ana Kugli, and Gaby Pailer, Beiträge zur neueren Literaturgeschichte (Heidelberg: Universitätsverlag Winter, 2004), 63–74.

[14] For details of critical poems that Brecht published in the GDR press, see the essays by Stephen Parker and Patrick Harkin later in this volume.

[15] See Klaus-Dieter Krabiel, "Turandot oder Der Kongreß der Weißwäscher," in *Brecht-Handbuch*, ed. Jan Knopf, vol. 1, *Stücke* (Stuttgart: Metzler, 2001), 597–612, here 600; Tom Kuhn, "Editorial Notes," in *Plays* 8, 250–55, here 250.

[16] Hans Bunge, "Gespräch über Bertolt Brecht mit Käthe Rülicke am 13. Dezember 1958," Bundesarchiv (henceforth BArch) DY 30 IV 2/2.024/49, 28.

[17] See the essays by Stephen Parker and Patrick Harkin later in this volume.

[18] While Western critics were highly critical of the poem, it was welcomed in the GDR and taught in schools. See *BFA* 15:450 and David Caute, *The Dancer Defects: The Struggle for Cultural Supremacy during the Cold War* (Oxford: Oxford UP, 2003), 300.

[19] The BE participated in this process. When Palitzsch chose not to return to East Berlin after the construction of the Wall, the BE condemned his decision in an open letter that quoted lines from Brecht's *Leben des Galilei* (Life of Galileo, 1938–39): "Jemand, der die Wahrheit nicht kennt, ist bloß ein Dummkopf. Aber jemand, der die Wahrheit kennt und sie eine Lüge nennt, ist ein Verbrecher. Gehen Sie hinaus aus meinem Haus!" (A person who does not know the truth is just a fool. But a person who knows it and calls it a lie is a criminal. Get out of my house!) The BE thus invoked Brecht's patriarchal authority against his former protégé and assistant. See Kurt Bork, "Klare Verhältnisse — saubere Atmosphäre," *Theater der Zeit* 16, no. 11 (1961): 8–12, here 10; *BFA* 5:248–49.

[20] Bertolt Brecht, "The Rearing of Millet," trans. Robert C. Conard in collaboration with Ralph Ley, *New German Critique* 9 (Fall 1976): 142–52, here 144.

[21] Johannes Bobrowski, "Berliner Ensemble," in *"O Chicago! O Widerspruch!" Hundert Gedichte auf Brecht*, ed. Karen Leeder and Erdmut Wizisla (Berlin: Transit, 2006), 131.

[22] Wolfgang Conrad, "Das Brecht-Bild im Literaturunterricht der DDR: Zum Wirken institutioneller Rahmenbedingungen," in *Deutschunterricht in der DDR 1949–1989: Beiträge zu einem Symposium in der Pädagogischen Hochschule Freiburg*, ed. Kurt Abels (Frankfurt a.M.: Peter Lang, 1992), 335–46, here 337.

[23] Even then, the decision to stage these plays encountered resistance in some quarters. Manfred Nössig suggested that the restaging of "well-known and important works" should take priority over attempts to extend the repertoire by including plays that had not previously been performed in the GDR. See Manfred Nössig, "Brecht: *Herr Puntila und sein Knecht Matti* — Dresden, Gera," in *Die Schauspieltheater der DDR und das Erbe (1970–1974): Positionen — Debatten — Kritiken*, ed. Manfred Nössig (East Berlin: Akademie-Verlag, 1976), 184–90, here 186.

[24] See Laura Bradley, *Brecht and Political Theatre: 'The Mother' on Stage* (Oxford: Clarendon, 2006), 88–91.

[25] Quoted in Werner Hecht, "Farewell to Her Audience: Helene Weigel's Triumph and Final Exit," trans. Theodor F. Rippey, *Brecht Yearbook* 25 (2000): 317–27, here 318.

[26] See Malcolm Humble, "Brecht and Posterity: The Poets' Response to the Poet," *Modern Language Review* 74, no. 1 (1979): 97–116, here 100–101; Karen Leeder, "Those Born Later Read Brecht: The Reception of 'An die Nachgeborenen,'" in *Brecht's Poetry of Political Exile*, ed. Ronald Speirs (Cambridge: Cambridge UP, 2000), 211–40.

[27] "Frau Flinz 1961: Notizen von einem Wahlforum mit Schauspielern, Regisseuren und Kritikern," *Neues Deutschland* (East Berlin), 14 September 1961.

[28] Wolf Biermann, "Frau Brecht," in *Alle Lieder* (Cologne: Kiepenheuer & Witsch, 1991), 61; Biermann, "Herr Brecht," in *"O Chicago! O Widerspruch!,"* ed. Leeder and Wizisla, 140. In an interview with Henry Schmidt and Helen Fehervary, Biermann claimed: "gemessen an dem Meister sind wir alle zwergig" (measured against the Master, we are all like dwarves). Henry Schmidt, Wolf Biermann, Helen Fehervary, "Dokumentation: Wolf Biermann," *German Quarterly* 57, no. 2 (1984): 269–79, here 276.

[29] Heiner Müller, "Aber von mir werden sie sagen," in *"O Chicago! O Widerspruch!,"* ed. Leeder and Wizisla, 119; Heiner Müller, "But of me they will say," in *After Brecht: A Celebration*, ed. Karen Leeder (Manchester: Carcanet, 2006), 80. Volker Braun has also responded to Brecht's poem, writing: "vorschläge hat er gemacht? wir werden sie säuberlich prüfen. / eh die entscheidung nicht fällt, bleibt unbeschrieben das grab" (he made suggestions? we will check them carefully / until the decision has been reached, his epitaph will remain unwritten). See Volker Braun, *Werktage 1: Arbeitsbuch 1977–1989* (Frankfurt a.M.: Suhrkamp, 2009), 514.

[30] Volker Braun, "Wer wohnte unter dem dänischen Strohdach," in *"O Chicago! O Widerspruch!"*, ed. Leeder and Wizisla, 27; Volker Braun, "Who lived under the Danish thatch," trans. David Constantine, in *After Brecht*, ed. Leeder, 6 (trans. mod.).

[31] Braun, *Werktage 1*, 131.

[32] See Leeder, "Those Born Later Read Brecht"; "'B.B.s spat gedenkend': Reading Brecht in the 1980s and 1990s," *Brecht Yearbook* 24 (2000): 111–26; "'Des toten Dichters gedenkend': Remembering Brecht in Contemporary German Poetry," in *"Verwisch die Spuren": Bertolt Brecht's Work and Legacy; A Reassessment*, ed. Robert Gillett and Godela Weiss-Sussex (Amsterdam: Rodopi, 2008), 277–93.

[33] Peter Huchel, "Der Garten des Theophrast," in *"O Chicago! O Widerspruch!,"* ed. Leeder and Wizisla, 70.

[34] Wolf Biermann, "Brecht, deine Nachgeborenen," in *"O Chicago! O Widerspruch!,"* ed. Leeder and Wizisla, 125–27; Wolf Biermann, "Brecht, Your Posterity," trans. Karen Leeder, in *After Brecht*, ed. Leeder, 87–89, here 88.

[35] Biermann, "Brecht, deine Nachgeborenen," 125.

[36] Braun, *Werktage 1*, 674.

[37] Helen Fehervary, "Enlightenment or Entanglement: History and Aesthetics in Bertolt Brecht and Heiner Müller," *New German Critique* 8 (1976): 80–109.

[38] See e.g. Nick Cohen, "Time for Curtain to Fall on Brecht," *The Observer* (London), 18 May 2008; Charles Spencer, "The Good Soul of Szechuan: Brecht's Cruel Punishment," *The Daily Telegraph* (London), 16 May 2008. For a critique of Cohen and Spencer, see Mark Ravenhill, "Don't Bash Brecht," *The Guardian* (London), 26 May 2008.

[39] This is a quotation from Brecht's poem "Der Zweifler" (The Doubter, 1937). The original German reads: "der Mann auf der Bank, der / So sehr zweifelte" (*BFA* 14:376).

I. Brecht in the GDR

Undogmatic Marxism: Brecht Rehearses at the Berliner Ensemble

David Barnett, University of Sussex

T HE FOUNDATION OF the Berliner Ensemble (BE) on 1 September 1949 in East Berlin gave Brecht the resources he needed to develop approaches to making theater: approaches that, for the most part, it had only been possible to theorize during his fifteen years in exile. According to the contract between the Soviet occupying authorities and Brecht's wife Helene Weigel, the BE was to receive just over one and a quarter million marks in its first year, despite the fact that the BE was a theater company that did not have its own theater building.[1] Initially, the BE was only a guest at the Deutsches Theater (DT) and had to wait until 1954 to gain full control over its means of production when it finally moved to the Theater am Schiffbauerdamm. The financial security guaranteed by the state, however, gave Brecht the freedom to experiment, not only with production aesthetics but also with the very way that a theater could be organized.

This essay is concerned with the ways in which Brecht realized his ideas with the BE. Some critics have been keen to suggest that Brecht's managerial and directorial work owed nothing to his theories of theater. John Fuegi writes that for Brecht theory "had a valuable place outside the theatre but almost none in actual day-to-day staging practice."[2] The curious basis for this assertion is that Brecht rarely used the term *Verfremdung*[3] in rehearsal, a point W. Stuart McDowell also makes. McDowell goes on to claim that "theories such as *Verfremdung* and *Gestus* become academic exercises and not effective processes to realize the text [. . .]."[4] At the heart of both commentators' arguments is a determination to de-politicize Brecht the theater practitioner by suggesting that his productions tell us more about the richness of a timeless human condition than the political realities of the moment. Brecht refuted this formulation in a text published posthumously that describes the work at the BE as focused on showing human nature as both changeable and dependent on social position.[5] On one of the last pages of Fuegi's book, he writes with respect to the productions of *Edward II* in 1924 and *Galileo* in 1957: "from first to last, essentially Brecht had remained the same" (185). This simplistic, convenient, and ahistorical conclusion, which classes Brecht as an unchangingly great director, will be challenged in this essay. I shall be examining how Marxist theory suffused Brecht's approaches to staging at the BE, and how its tenets could produce quite varied results while ultimately remaining close to a dialectically materialist understanding of the world. First, however, I shall consider the ways in which Brecht sought to realize his politicized practice by radicalizing the organization of the BE along more democratic lines.

From the very beginning of the enterprise, Brecht was keen to turn the BE into an institution that empowered as many of its workers as possible to make positive contributions to the rehearsal process. This extended all the way from the creative staff via the actors to the technicians and even more tangential figures, like Brecht's driver.[6] While Brecht's word was usually final, it was important to him to allow constructive debate that would influence the way productions took shape. This attempt to undermine traditional hierarchies, or at least to open them up, had ideological roots whose benefits were twofold: cultural workers could become less alienated, in the Marxist sense, from the production process; and their contribution could ultimately lead to a better quality in production. That is, the ideological drive to empower as many as possible had the practical advantage of serving the theater in a virtuous circle.

The desire to enfranchise the company's creative staff can be seen clearly in a document circulated barely two weeks after the first rehearsals began at the BE. The young assistant directors and dramaturges were required to attend special lectures and to make active contributions to the company. Further suggestions were "erwartet [. . .], die [. . .] das theoretische Handwerkzeug der Einzelnen bereichern und gebrauchsfähig machen" (expected [. . .], which [. . .] enrich the individuals' theoretical "toolkit" and make it serviceable).[7] This short quotation shows how important the dynamic and reciprocal relationship between theory and practice was at the company. The pedagogical thrust casts Brecht more as a teacher than a theater-maker determined willfully to push through his ideas and monopolize the limelight. Instead he sought to expose his practice to other influences and to discuss it with other people in a bid to test its efficacy and, if necessary, modify or adapt it. The impulse to let others take charge was realized remarkably early, too. Brecht was quick to promote his protégés, entrusting Egon Monk, who was just twenty-three at the time, with directing what was only the company's sixth production, *Biberpelz und roter Hahn* (The Beaver Coat and the Red Hen) in 1951. However, often without taking credit directly, Brecht supervised almost all BE productions and so his imprint was always clearly visible.[8]

Brecht's own directorial practices, bolstered by the input from and debate among his collaborators, demonstrate how a common approach to making theater politically can produce divergent results. As will be shown, Brecht's Marxist aesthetics did not make for propagandistic productions but were concerned with opening up the dramas in question to dialectical investigation. I have chosen two contrasting productions for analysis in this essay, *Herr Puntila und sein Knecht Matti* (Mr. Puntila and His Man Matti) of 1949 and *Winterschlacht* (Battle in Winter) of 1955. They are taken from the beginning and the end of Brecht's short directorial career at the BE, not only to understand a sense of development in his practice, but also to examine how two contrasting genres were treated.

Puntila was the very first production by the BE and is subtitled "ein Volksstück," a genre for which there is no adequate translation in English. This term, meaning roughly "play of/for the people," was a nineteenth-century coinage and it was primarily intended to entertain. In an essay, Brecht associated the "krudes und anspruchsloses Theater" (crude and unambitious theater) of the *Volksstück* with a similar view of the common people handed down by the ruling classes.[9] His aim was to write a play that represented the spectrum of social classes in such a way that entertainment could be combined with class analysis and the study of social contradiction. The play itself can equally be called a comedy, due to the humor evinced by the conflicts. *Puntila* was directed by Brecht and Erich Engel. Engel staged the world premiere of *Die Dreigroschenoper* (The Threepenny Opera) at the Theater am Schiffbauerdamm in 1928, the production that would make the play an international hit. It should be noted here that although Engel co-directed the production, he was responsible more for the delivery of the lines than the innovative visual practices that Brecht sought to introduce.[10]

Winterschlacht by Johannes R. Becher, on the other hand, is unmistakably a tragedy. It is set during the battle of Moscow (1941–42) and follows Johannes Hörder, a middle-class soldier whose experiences of Nazi aggression finally drive him to disobey a barbaric order to bury pro-Soviet partisans alive and to shoot himself dead instead. Tragedy was, in a way, an illusory genre for Brecht, as can be seen from the following extract from the *Messingkauf* (The Messingkauf Dialogues, 1939–55):

Philosoph: Die Ursachen sehr vieler Tragödien liegen außerhalb des Machtbereichs derer, die sie erleiden, wie es scheint.

Dramaturg: Wie es scheint?

Philosoph: Natürlich nur wie es scheint. Menschliches kann nicht außerhalb des Machtbereichs der Menschen liegen, und die Ursachen dieser Tragödien sind menschliche.[11]

[Philosopher: The causes of a lot of tragedies lie outside the power of those who suffer them, so it seems.

Dramaturge: So it seems?

Philosopher: Of course it only seems. Nothing human can possibly lie outside the powers of humanity, and such tragedies have human causes.]

The tragic therefore requires qualification and relativization in a theater concerned with the potential for change rather than the inevitability of disaster. *Winterschlacht* was staged by Brecht and Manfred Wekwerth in 1955, a year and a half before Brecht's death. It should be noted that Wekwerth played the role of the apprentice here, as evidenced by the production's rehearsal records. And while he certainly was not a silent partner, Brecht was the main creative force in the relationship.

I shall be exploring Brecht's approaches to staging these contrasting plays with a view to showing how a common theoretical position might generate very different types of performance while nonetheless adhering to a Marxist understanding of reality.

Undogmatic Marxism

It is worth understanding an important distinction in terminology from the outset: Meg Mumford notes that while "contradiction was a vital feature of Brecht's theatre [. . .], as he became increasingly familiar with Marxism he came to view the idea of contradiction in accordance with the philosophy of dialectical materialism."[12] This distinction moves Brecht the director away from a broad notion of conflict, common to all productions of drama, to a more nuanced understanding of contradiction. The dialectic is a specific form that articulates contradiction and is Hegel's model of how change occurs: a thesis meets its contradiction in an antithesis; when the tension between the two becomes too great, elements of both sides form a new entity, the synthesis. This process never stops, as the synthesis in turn becomes a thesis itself, against which a new antithesis will emerge, and so on in perpetuity. While the process may appear mechanical or deterministic, this is not the case at all. If one considers how complex each aspect of a dialectical tension may be, it is impossible to predict which elements will combine to form a synthesis. The classical Marxist dialectic concerns the contradiction between labor and capital, yet syntheses of this tension were quite different in different parts of the world where different conditions dominated. In Russia, for example, a revolution took place, whereas in Britain the tension led to the establishment of a welfare state. Brecht was clear about the non-deterministic nature of the dialectic in a note: "zu der ent. idealisierung [*sic*] der dialektik gehört es auch, dass der versuchung, ein system zu bilden, widerstanden wird" (part of the de-idealization of the dialectic involves resisting the temptation to create a system).[13] Here the "system" is the attempt to predict the outcome of the dialectic, since its productive strength, according to Brecht, lies in presenting contradictory material on stage without pointing to a definite synthesis. That task was passed on to the audience and made them co-producers of meaning.

The dialectic is also, in Marxism, materialist, which effectively means that what happens on stage cannot flout the laws of society or history at any given time. In Brecht's theater, materialism was guaranteed by a concept of realism that departs from the more common one in theatrical aesthetics and that may broadly be described as an accurate copy of what one finds in everyday life. The prerequisite for Brecht's writing and directing practice was an idea of realism that is defined in *Theaterarbeit* (1952), the book that documents the first six productions at the Berliner Ensemble, in a quotation from Friedrich Engels, as "die Wiedergabe typischer Menschen unter typischen Umständen" (the representation of typical people under typical circumstances).[14] This postulate is placed in contradistinction to an unashamedly partisan definition of naturalism as a "Kunstrichtung, die bei der Wiedergabe der Naturerscheinungen nach peinlichster Genauigkeit strebt, jedoch bei der pedantischen Anhäufung zufälliger Details oft alle Sinnzusammenhänge zudeckt" (an artistic direction that strives for the most painstaking accuracy in the reproduction of natural appearances but that often smothers any meaningful connections by pedantically accumulating arbitrary details).[15] It is clear from the two definitions that realism has a special meaning in Brecht's theater because it includes a generalizing principle that goes beyond the superficial imitation of reality. It is a philosophical rather than a purely aesthetic category. Realism here is something that applies to a given society as a whole because it reproduces the laws under which the dialectic works, regardless of apparent differences between individuals.

Human beings are in constant dialogue with their environment, which means that they, too, are always in dialogue with the dialectic. They have the power to make decisions but not to stand outside the dialectical process. Consequently, characters on stage have to show their connection with greater social, political, or historical formations, and this is where Brecht's powerful tools for performance play a central role.

What connects bodies on stage to their fictional but materialist society is the untranslatable term *Gestus,* which is a central part of Brecht's theatrical arsenal. As Laura Bradley writes, *Gestus* "is best understood as a physical action or a spatial configuration which reveals the ideological, social and economic relations between two or more characters."[16] While one might want to expand this definition to include the relationship between one person and his or her sociopolitical context, the term nonetheless articulates how actors' physicalities can be used to go beyond the individual and connect him or her to the social. That contexts change suggests that the actor also changes between and/or during the scenes themselves at particular turning points. *Gestus* thus becomes a readable index of a character's status at any given time. And *Gestus,* unlike *Verfremdung,* was a term that was frequently used in rehearsal and concretely tied Brecht's practices to dialectical materialism.

The undogmatic quality of Brecht's direction, as we shall see, is rooted in the non-determinism he identified in the processes of dialectical materialism. There was no definitive solution to staging the dialectic; it was more a question of how contradictions could best be articulated from a complex set of theses and antitheses. As Brecht put it in another note: "es handelt sich nicht darum, [. . .] die aufführung zu fixieren — sondern im gegenteil darum, änderungen zu provozieren, die eine entwicklung der spielweise bewirken und wahrnehmbar machen können" (it isn't a question of turning the production into something fixed — on the contrary, it's about provoking changes that can influence the development of the mode of performance and make it perceptible).[17] The idea, then, of a "finished" production was profoundly undialectical, and Brecht was keen to play with the different aspects of the dialectical elements in a bid to make them as striking and effective as possible. While he viewed the dialectic in partisan terms and clearly loaded it in the favor of the proletariat, he sought any dialectical means necessary to effect a richness of contrast that would astonish and galvanize the audience into seeing the relations on stage with fresh eyes.

Puntila as the Comic Raising of Class Consciousness

Brecht had already directed *Puntila* in Zurich in 1948, although for legal reasons he was not allowed to be credited as director at the time.[18] He was therefore very familiar with the play in performance and decided to open the BE's tenure at the DT with a new production. He was able to persuade Leonard Steckel, who played Puntila, to reprise the role in Berlin, although, as Steckel was to discover, important changes were to be made in order to improve the dialectical impact of the character.

Puntila deals with the tensions between the property-owning middle class and the working class in a variety of ways, because the *Volksstück* form allows for the inclusion of characters from all walks of life. The central tension, however, is focused, as the title suggests, on Puntila, the landowner, and his chauffeur Matti. The central conceit of the play is that Puntila is a brutal exploiter when sober but a perfectly reasonable person when drunk, which he is for much of the play. From this simple contrast, Brecht explored the very question of what it meant to be a human being in a class society. In the opening scenes of the play, production notes establish how "merkwürdig" (strange) Puntila is in that he becomes a "Mensch" (human being) when drunk [Fig. 1]. In addition, Eva, Puntila's daughter, makes "die merkwürdige Entdeckung" (the strange discovery) in the second scene that Matti is also "ein Mann" (a

Fig. 1: Establishing strangeness visually:
Matti treats Puntila's apparent "humanity" with skepticism.
Photo: Ruth Berlau, Hainer Hill, Percy Paukschta. BBA 005/015.

man) and not just a servant.[19] These apparently self-evident qualities required special theatrical measures to reveal that the definition of what it means to be human varies between different social classes. As a result, the first meeting between Matti and Puntila was to suggest a "Begegnung zweier Patrouillen, Erkundung im fremden Gebiet" (meeting of two patrols, reconnaissance on *terra incognita*).[20] Brecht was fond of using analogies to suggest the gestic situation; this image evokes mutual suspicion and asks the actors to investigate each other, rather than to treat the first encounter as something self-evident. This *Verfremdung* of the meeting is also comic; the put-upon worker does not merely accept his employer's humanity but treats it as a remarkable trait.

Brecht had discovered from the Zurich production that Puntila ran the risk of being perceived as a mainly sympathetic character "mit einigen üblen Anwandlungen im Zustand der Nüchternheit" (with some nasty traits when sober) and thus set about keeping the character in check through the application of dialectical tension.[21] His humanity when drunk could thus be rendered not as in some way natural but as a particular behavior that worked to his advantage. Steckel wore a bald cap in the BE production and this allowed him, an actor who was well known to the theatergoing public, to appear more grotesque, with a hint of "Genghis Khan."[22] His drunken self, while ostensibly friendly, took on the qualities "eines Krokodils" (of a crocodile) charming its prey.[23] Steckel consciously performed pleasantness for the BE production; here the characteristic was no longer merely humanizing but suggested invitation and threat, a dialectic that the audience could then trace back to Puntila's social position. In other words, the friendliness was subjected to *Verfremdung*, and the familiar became strange, as a way of suggesting that drunkenness was a refuge from Puntila's viciousness rather than a state of natural affability.

Matti, on the other hand, was presented as a likeable working man, but this, too, could simply have offered the audience an undialectical presentation, ignoring the fact that a proletarian is also a social being. Matti was not constructed in the same grotesque fashion as Puntila, although Brecht had also experimented with furnishing him with a prosthesis. Erwin Geschonneck, who played Matti, reports that a large ear was tried but discarded during rehearsals.[24] Instead, Matti was dialectically integrated into the production through *Gestus*, best understood in the scene in which he is offered Eva's hand in marriage. Here Matti takes from Eva a platter of herrings that are meant to be served to other guests. His contemplation of one herring among the many connects him to the fish in an unexpected way: "wie in der griechischen Tragödie, Matti erkennt den Hering. Einer hat den anderen immer für einen fremden Mann gehalten, nun erkennt er: er ist ein naher Verwandter" (as in Greek tragedy, Matti recognizes the herring. One who has always considered the other a stranger recognizes: he's a close relative).[25] The unexpectedness of the *anagnorisis*, in which two previously unequal parties are revealed as exploited equals, is funny. Having established the equivalence, Matti then serves the fish to the other guests, who come from different social classes. Their gestic response to the fish, which is now a symbol of the downtrodden, tells the audience more about social attitudes. Puntila, for example, eats the fish with great curiosity, reminding the audience of his attitude to Matti in his drunken state; Laina the cook shows how familiar she is with the fish after years of service in the kitchen. All the characters betray something about their social position and thus suggest the ways in which their society has affected them. Matti, who experiences the epiphany, examines the responses as a transformed man in possession of new knowledge.

The scenes themselves were divided up into sections to help the actors negotiate their turning points. For Brecht, a lack of clarity spelled doom for a sequence — he had no problem with complexity, but that complexity had to be broken down into its constituent parts in order for the audience to follow the dialectical unfolding of events. The scene in which Eva initially toys with Matti, for example, was plotted precisely, based on the contradictions of social interaction between the classes. Here Eva becomes bored with Puntila and decides to amuse herself with Matti as someone she assumes she can net with ease. Matti recognizes the maneuver and puts her off; the rebuttal leaves her nonplussed. She has intended to embark upon a romantic adventure but is not prepared for the resistance she encounters. Each section of the story was told as an image and changed only when the situation demanded it. Every movement had to serve the social development of the action and visually the scene unfolded with the utmost clarity. Similarly, in the scene in which Puntila sobers up before dismissing the four women to whom he has previously proposed marriage, the stages of his sobriety had to be clearly shown in order for the audience to note his gradual change from kindness to nastiness.

As is clear from the above descriptions and analyses, actors found that characteristics stemmed from situations, from action, and not vice versa. This is typical of the *Fabel* in Brecht's directorial work. The *Fabel* is the term Brecht favored as a paraphrase for "the action," but it suggests more than this. The *Fabel* is the control element in the analysis of a play; it reveals the rules under which a particular society functions and how they affect the characters. In an early note on the rehearsals, an anonymous assistant quotes Brecht's instruction: "wir wollen jetzt nur den Text lesen und uns bemühen seinen Sinn zu erfassen" (at present we only want to read the lines and try to discover their meaning). The assistant explained that the aim was to find out "wie die Sätze am einfachsten, am natürlichsten klingen, noch nicht auf die Charakterisierung der Person eingehend" (how the words sound simplest, most natural, not yet considering how to portray the character).[26] The quotation tells much about the inductive approach Brecht took. The rehearsal itself was a "Stellprobe," literally a "placement rehearsal." Actors were positioned on stage so as to make their relationships, in response to the *Fabel*, as clear as possible. The lines were a tool in this process, and Brecht, despite being the author of the text, had no monopoly on interpretation; the process of realization was open to all involved.

The quest for clarity pervaded every aspect of the production. A suggestion from Geschonneck, for example, was turned down "weil die gewünschte Wirkung durch ein Zuviel von Nebenbedeutungen verwischt worden wäre" (because the desired effect would have been blurred by too many secondary meanings).[27] The opposing sides of the dialectic had to be clearly articulated and a muddling of the terms would obscure its mechanism for the actors and the audience. The kind of input Brecht welcomed can be seen in a suggestion by Engel that was adopted. He wondered whether a fence could be placed on stage as "Zeichen des begrenzten Besitzes" (a sign of the limits of wealth), that is, that despite his onstage dominance, Puntila's power was not unbounded and there were others like him abroad.[28]

The production was a great success. A typical response may be found in a comment from Susanne Hess-Wyneken, who wrote:

es [gibt] keine Vernebelung der Gesinnungen; deutlich und streng trennt [Brecht] die Schichten, die sozialen und die menschlichen. In grossartige Breite baut Brecht kein Drama, sondern eine Zustands-schilderung, in der ein scharf beobachteter Realismus zur Kritik wird und aus übersteigerter Groteske alle Humore blitzen.[29]

[there is no confusion in the politics; Brecht clearly and strictly divides the classes, both social and human. With wonderful breadth, Brecht constructs not a drama, but a depiction of conditions in which a sharply observed realism is treated critically and heightened grotesquery gives rise to all manner of humor.]

The primacy of social conditions over human drama noted here is a tribute to Brecht's attempts to emphasize the process and not the end point of the scenes, social mechanisms rather than their localized vicissitudes. The reviewer identifies a distinction between the clarity of the action and questions it left open. While other reviews drew attention to the occasional caricatures of some of the characters, the production nonetheless achieved many of its aims by moving away from character-based theater into one firmly rooted in the social context and the actions it brought forth.[30]

Historicizing *Winterschlacht* away from Tragedy

Johannes R. Becher had been a member of communist organizations since 1917, and fled the Nazis in 1933. On returning to the Soviet-occupied sector after the Second World War, he began to play a major role in the cultural life of the sector and, after 1949, the GDR itself. He co-founded the influential literary magazine *Sinn und Form*, and became the GDR's first Minister of Culture upon the formation of the Ministry in 1954. Becher's play offered something of a contrast to the critical mirth of *Puntila*. Initially, though, Brecht had not planned to direct it at all and had invited the Czech Emil Burian to restage the play, which Burian had successfully produced in Prague in November 1952. Burian was a committed communist, yet his approach to directing the play demonstrated the differences between a director who emphasized the inherent political qualities of the characters and one who, like Brecht, derived these qualities from the characters' social contexts.

In a rehearsal on 1 November 1954, Burian instructed: "der Schauspieler muss tief in die Person eindringen, wenn er sie begreifen will" (the actor has to plumb the depths of the character if he is to understand it).[31] The problem with this point of departure was that it led to a number of imputations that did not correspond to the material reality of the play. One of the smaller characters in the play is a Russian Prince who had gone into exile in Paris but is now enlisted in the German army in a bid to regain the rank and privileges lost after the Russian Civil War. Burian was reported to have imputed a "Dostojewski'sche Emigranten-Sentimentalität" (Dostoevskian sentimentality of an émigré) to the Prince when he remembered his time working as a chauffeur in France.[32] The notes from Brecht's production include the following one by Heinz Kahlau:

Der Fürst hat ein stärkeres Klassenbewusstsein als die deutschen Offiziere. [. . .] Wenn er auch in Paris als Chauffeur war, dann gerade deshalb. Er hatte diese revolutionären Leute kennen gelernt [*sic*], denen man nichts nachweisen kann, [*sic*] und die so gefährlich sind.[33]

[the Prince has a stronger class consciousness than the German officers. [. . .] Even if he's been a chauffeur in Paris, then precisely because of this. He's seen these revolutionaries up close, who won't be told anything and who are therefore dangerous.]

In Brecht's production, the Prince's characteristics are located more concretely in his bitter experiences. In addition, the Prince was positioned relationally to the action, as notes of a rehearsal on 20 November 1954 report: "Der Fürst will die Deutschen benutzen, damit er seinen Grundbesitz wieder bekommt. Die Deutschen wollten den Fürsten benutzen, um in der Heimat Stimmung zu machen. Jeder will jeden für sich benutzen" (the Prince wants to use the Germans to regain his estates. The Germans want to use the Prince to blow their trumpet in his homeland. Everyone wants to use everyone else for their own ends).[34] In this way, a dialectical relationship was established in which competing political objectives could be shown in tension on stage, something that clearly contrasts with Burian's speculative psychologism. It is also worth noting just how much care was taken with such a minor character.

The move from Burian to Brecht was not simply a case of rejecting everything that had gone before. Brecht observed: "Jede unserer Neuerungen soll man nach der Burian'schen Anlage auswerten und ihr gegenüberstellen" (each one of our new ideas is to be evaluated and compared with Burian's plans).[35] Even here one notes how the team proceeded dialectically by adopting the productive material and rejecting the rest.

Becher often uses monologues in his play but these presented Brecht with an ideological and aesthetic problem. While Brecht was used to writing direct addresses to the audience in his plays as a way of either moving the action forward or articulating social pressures affecting a character, Becher's monologues ran the risk of entering the realms of the naturalism criticized above. The danger of straying into the private, something that could exclude the social dimension, was addressed in a rehearsal note entitled "Vorschläge, [. . .] den Monolog aufzumachen" (suggestions to open up the monologue . . .).[36] One suggestion that won out here was for an actor to imagine he was in dialogue with his image of Germany's grandeur itself. In his reflections on the production after its premiere, Brecht noted: "Das Monologisieren [. . .] zeigt die Zerrissenheit der Gesellschaft, die Isolierung des Einzelnen" (the monologues show the shattered society, the isolation of the individual).[37] By contextualizing the potentially private moment, Brecht was able to give the speeches a social dimension rather than allow them to stand as individual contemplations divorced from the outside world.

While *Puntila* played in a version of the present, *Winterschlacht* had a concrete historical frame and this allowed Brecht to shift the emphasis from tragedy to history. He called the play "die ideologische Abrechnung mit der Nazizeit" (the ideological reckoning with the Nazi period).[38] This meant that the action and characters portrayed could be faced with insoluble contradictions because their circumstances, rather than innate character flaws, were to blame for the catastrophes that run through the play. The ideological dimension could be found at all turns and was not merely restricted to the Nazis on the battlefield. Much action takes place on the home front where a socialist alternative, as represented by working-class soldiers and partisans, is not present. In a scene between Hörder's father and mother, Brecht worked on presenting a clash of rigid Prussian morality in the mother and a more pragmatic Nazi morality in the father, "die bequemer und nützlicher ist" (which is more convenient and useful).[39] The two ways of thinking helped to define the two characters in dialectical fashion, but because neither offered a solution, the production's suggestive techniques were able to indict both positions.

Brecht pointed to his protagonist's historical constriction and lack of agency in the following metaphorical sketch of his character's arc: "Hörder ist zu Anfang des Stückes blind, als er sehen [*sic*] wird, werden ihm die Augen gewaltsam geschlossen" (at the beginning of the play, Hörder is blind; when he does start to see, his eyes are violently closed).[40] The short description traces a line of development that is progressive, born of experience, but that is prematurely cut short by the brutality of his situation. The tragedy is therefore one of its time; Hörder is unable to realize his insights because of historical circumstances that need to be changed.

The relativization of the characters' agency was brought about by a constant play of individual and society, something encapsulated in another telling line from Brecht: "wir können keinen Klassenkampf darstellen, ohne die Sitten und Gebräuche der Klassen zu zeigen" (we can't depict the class struggle without showing the customs and habits of the classes).[41] Customs and habits are developed over time, and betray an interdependency between people and their social environment. Brecht differentiated the social from the apparently natural in instructions given to the Nazi officers when they got drunk, for example. On the surface, actors playing characters under the influence might see this as a purely physiological transformation, but Brecht insisted that officers got drunk in a different way from the rank and file, in that they tended to stiffen up with more drink as a way of showing their discipline [Fig. 2].[42]

Brecht also saw the necessity of depicting the soldiers in such a way that put across their commitment to the Nazi cause. Originally, the actors, pursuing a most Brechtian impulse, ironized the fascist and militarist lines as a way of opening them up to criticism. However, this lessened their realistic force. It was only when Wekwerth directed the actors to drown out the sound of their vehicles' engines on stage by barking their lines that they achieved "den überzeugten Ton" (the tone of conviction) for which the production was striving.[43] Thus, rather than exacting a critique on stage through irony, the directors confronted the audience with realistic fanaticism, against which Hörder's drama took place.

A key to unlocking the historicized tragedy was to be found in the actors themselves. Possibly the greatest virtue a Brechtian actor could demonstrate was the difference between him- or herself and the role. (For example, at Regine Lutz's audition, Brecht asked her to recite a poem but was more interested in her ability to recite it as if she had never seen a poem before.[44]) Brecht emphasized the quality of difference in an exchange with the actress Carola Braunbock:

Fig. 2: Class-conscious drunkenness: the officer in the middle retains the stiffness expected of him after several stiff drinks. Photo: Vera Tenschert, Percy Paukschta. BBA 005/002.

B[recht]:	Sie müssen eine feine Dame spielen.
Braunbock:	Dann bin ich falsch besetzt.
B[recht]:	Gerade Sie können das besser als die wirklich feinen Leute.[45]
[B[recht]:	You're to play a well-heeled lady.
Braunbock:	Then I'm the wrong person for the role.
B[recht]:	You of all people can play her better than the real upper crust.]

Showing social construction by contrasting the actor with the role was a crucial way of de-naturalizing what was seen on stage. This could also, however, be achieved by the careful contrast of attitudes as a way of opening up the contradictory forces acting upon a character. In a letter of praise to Ekkehard Schall, who played Hörder, Brecht wrote that he enjoyed "das widerspruchsvolle Entsetzen zur Eingrabung der Partisanen [. . .]: Entsetzen über die Barbarei und über die eigene Insubordination zugleich" (the contradictory horror at burying the partisans alive [. . .]: horror at the barbarity and at his own insubordination at the same time).[46] The split showed Hörder at the point of traditional tragedy, just before he takes his own life. He was torn between a revulsion at what he had been asked to carry out, which would denote a very human response, and the social anxiety that he was disobeying an order. Hörder's death was a tragedy, but a political one — he had been put in an impossible position from which, under the prevailing circumstances, there was no escape.

The Possibilities of Dialectical Performance

Brecht's rehearsal practices were materialist and dialectical; without either of these he felt that he would be offering unrealistic theater that would have no political function for his audience because the performances would be removed from its experiences of the world. Reality, however, was something he acknowledged as complex and contradictory, and he claimed no sovereign right to play its flawless interpreter. Rehearsals, conducted in an air of constructive criticism, were concerned with identifying dialectical conflicts, firstly by constructing a text's *Fabel*, and then by articulating its terms on stage. This process was not a science but a series of attempts at understanding how characters related to their circumstances. There was nothing mechanical about the procedure, as different aspects of the dialectic were teased out, emphasized or sidelined over the whole rehearsal period. The "virtuous circle," mentioned earlier, in which ideological imperatives concerning democracy in the workplace led to an actively open invitation for input from those involved in the productions themselves, was a crucial prerequisite for the development of the BE's stagecraft. The perspectives offered by the creative team, the actors, and the technical staff called existing theatrical solutions into question and provoked new approaches to staging the dialectic. While critics often praised BE productions for their ensemble playing, they were unable to observe just how collective the realization process was, and how the productions they lauded owed so much to the formal organization of the company.

Neither production discussed above was considered finished once it had been premiered, and both were given new productions in the years that followed their respective premieres. Leonard Steckel, who played Puntila in 1949, departed, for example, and was replaced by the popular comic actor Curt Bois. The difference between the two was great in terms of their physicality: Steckel was a large man, while Bois was slight and wiry. The association of Steckel with a well-fed landowner was relatively straightforward but Bois had to develop his own way of fleshing out the character and establishing its authority. As a result, all the scenes needed to be rethought and restaged to integrate a very different human being into the dialectics of the production. The problem with Bois was that his lean body often brought an unwelcome haste to the scenes, something that Brecht's famous rehearsal technique, in which actors play their parts in the third person and in the past tense, sought to correct.[47] Bois's nervousness disappeared when the actor concentrated on the actions that drove the scene forward, and when it was replayed in the present, gestural clarity trumped nervous energy. That said, the majority of reviews reproached Bois for weakening the contrasts between the drunk and the sober Puntila, arguing that he was not able to go beyond his own well-developed physical comedy.[48]

The complexity of the components of the dialectic meant that the search for contradictory representations could produce a variety of solutions. Brecht and his team sought contrasts that would provoke the audience to produce meaning from the open questions articulated on stage. As a result, the productions, with their orthodox Marxist inflection, cannot be called propaganda; they are dialectical explorations of a complex of problems. By the end of *Puntila* and *Winterschlacht*, the contradictions that force Matti to leave his master's service and Hörder to take his own life remain. And while a socialist revolution may well seem to be suggested as the implicit answer to the global problems of the plays, the complexity of the relationships in the productions themselves show that this is no simple matter. Brecht was aware that the GDR's socialism was imposed from "above" and that there had been no popular workers' movement in the wake of the Second World War. (Indeed, the BE's third production, an adaptation of J. M. R. Lenz's 1774 play *Der Hofmeister* [The Tutor] was a critique of the failure of Germans to carry off a revolution of their own.)

The BE's productions, aside from their specificities, were attempts at offering spectators a dialectical view of the world. Brecht's method had the effect of shifting plays away from their original genres into presentations of situations, opened up for the dialectical insights they could produce. *Puntila* lost some of its drama in favor of the depiction of dialectically constructed characters whose contradictions were humorous; *Winterschlacht* lost some of its emotional bleakness in favor of a historical analysis of Hörder's position as soldier on the "wrong" side. Yet both productions attained a liveliness drawn from the well-honed and precisely presented contradictions of the plays. The shift from unreflected emotional effects (mindless laughter or humanist pity) to considered examinations of the comic and the tragic marks the Brechtian turn in performance. This turn, however, cannot be pinned down to any specific individual effects in isolation: Brecht's undogmatic pursuit of his own method continually sought new insights into the workings of the stage and the world.

Notes

I should like to thank the British Academy for its Research Development Award and the Humboldt Foundation for supporting the research for this essay.

[1] Contract between Helene Weigel and the Verwaltung für Volksbildung (Office for Education), 24 September 1949, in BBA, uncatalogued file "Aktuelles." The contract, as the date of signing shows, actually came into effect after the BE had been founded.

[2] John Fuegi, *Bertolt Brecht: Chaos according to Plan* (Cambridge: Cambridge UP, 1987), xiii.

[3] The term for "making the familiar strange," to which I shall return, is often mistranslated as "alienation." While "defamiliarization" is a closer rendition, I shall retain the untranslatable German. It is well documented that Brecht rarely used the term in rehearsal.

[4] W. Stuart McDowell, "*Verfremdung* be Damned! Putting an End to the Myth of Brechtian Acting," *Communications from the International Brecht Society* 38 (2009): 158–68, here 160–61 and 165.

[5] See Brecht, "[Die Eigenarten des Berliner Ensembles I]," *BFA* 23:311.

[6] See the report of the driver, Werner L., that Brecht encouraged him to attend rehearsals and offer opinions, in *Erinnerungen an Brecht*, ed. Hubert Witt (Leipzig: Reclam, 1964), 228–29.

[7] Anon., "Pflichtbesuch," 25 September 1949, Berliner-Ensemble-Archiv (henceforth BEA), File 2. All translations from the German are mine unless otherwise acknowledged.

[8] The one exception was the BE's second production, which was directed by Brecht's friend Berthold Viertel. Even the two productions credited to actors Therese Giehse — Heinrich von Kleist's *Der zerbrochne Krug* (The Broken Urn, premiered 23 January 1952) — and Ernst Busch — Nikolai Pogodin's *Das Glockenspiel des Kreml* (The Kremlin Chimes, premiered 28 March 1952) involved much input from Brecht.

[9] Brecht, "Anmerkungen zum Volksstück," *BFA* 24:293.

[10] Helene Weigel said that she could not have played Mother Courage in the production of 1949 if Brecht had not co-directed with Engel. Quoted in Werner Hecht, *Helene Weigel: Eine große Frau des 20. Jahrhunderts* (Frankfurt a.M.: Suhrkamp, 2000), 28–29. This is not to deny the importance of Engel's contribution, something Weigel affirmed: see 77–78.

[11] Brecht, "[*Messingkauf*: Fragment B 13]," *BFA* 22:711; *The Messingkauf Dialogues*, trans. John Willett (London: Methuen, 1965), 32.

[12] Meg Mumford, *Bertolt Brecht* (Abingdon: Routledge, 2009), 85.

[13] Brecht, "[Notizbuch 48–50]," BBA 814/52.

[14] Ruth Berlau, Bertolt Brecht, Claus Hubalek, Peter Palitzsch, and Käthe Rülicke, eds., *Theaterarbeit: 6 Aufführungen des Berliner Ensembles* (Dresden: VVV Dresdner Verlag, 1952), 434.

[15] *Theaterarbeit*, 433.

[16] Laura Bradley, *Brecht and Political Theatre: "The Mother" on Stage* (Oxford: Oxford UP, 2006), 6.

[17] Brecht, "[Notizbuch 48–49]," BBA 811/32.

[18] See Werner Hecht, *Brecht Chronik* (Frankfurt a.M.: Suhrkamp, 1997), 823. Brecht did not possess a Swiss work permit.

[19] Anon., untitled, undated, BBA File 2.

[20] Anon., "*Puntila* — Stellprobe — 1. Bild, 19. 9. 49," undated, BEA File 2.

[21] Brecht, "Steckels zwei Puntilas," *BFA* 24:310.

[22] See Anon., "*Puntila* — Stellprobe — 1. Bild, 19. 9. 49," undated, BEA File 2.

[23] Anon., "*Puntila* — Stellprobe — 1. Bild, 19. 9. 49."

[24] See Geschonneck in *"Denken heißt verändern. . ." Erinnerungen an Brecht*, ed. Joachim Lang and Jürgen Hillesheim (Augsburg: Maro, 1998), 51. The ear was supposed to signify Matti's sensitive perception of situations but was considered crass and was rejected.

[25] Anon., "Freitag 28. Oktober 1949. BB EE CN. VIII," undated, BEA File 2.

[26] Anon., "*Puntila* VIII. Bild, Stellprobe. 23. 9. BB und Assistenten. P/K," undated, BEA File 2.

[27] Anon., "*Puntila* Donnerstag, 22. September 1949. BB EE + Assistenten," undated, BEA File 2.

[28] Anon., "Stellprobe 4. Bild *Puntila* 21. 9. 1949 (B. E. N.)," undated, BEA File 2.

[29] Susanne Hess-Wyneken, "Bert Brechts *Herr Puntila und sein Knecht*," *Berlin's* [*sic*] *Modenblatt* 1 (1950): 22.

[30] See, for example, Hans-Ulrich Eylau, "*Herr Puntila und sein Knecht Matti*," *Berliner Zeitung*, 13 November 1949.

[31] Anon, "Notate *Winterschlacht*," undated, 15 pages, here p. 7, BEA File 18.

[32] Anon., "Notate," 4.

[33] Heinz Kahlau, "Notate *Winterschlacht*," undated, 35 pages, here p. 29, BEA File 18.

[34] Anon., "Notate *Winterschlacht*," undated, 14 pages, here p. 2, BEA File 18.

[35] Kahlau, "Notate," 30.

[36] See BBA 940/11.

[37] Brecht, "Zur Aufführung der *Winterschlacht* beim Berliner Ensemble," *BFA* 24:444.

[38] Brecht, *BFA* 24:444.

[39] Kahlau, "Notate," 13.

[40] Kahlau, "Notate," 8.

[41] Anon., "Notate," 4.

[42] See Kahlau, "Notate," 14.

[43] Heinz Kahlau, "*Winterschlacht* Notate," undated, n.p., BEA File 18.

[44] See Monika Buschey, *Wege zu Brecht* (Berlin: Dittrich, 2007), 37–38.

[45] Anon., "Notate," 3.

[46] Brecht, "Brief an den Darsteller des jungen Hörder in der *Winterschlacht*," *BFA* 23:408.

[47] See Brecht, "Kurze Beschreibung einer neuen Technik der Schauspielkunst, die einen Verfremdungseffekt hervorbringt," *BFA* 22:644; *BT* 138.

[48] See, for example, Lothar Kutsche, "Ein entschärfter *Herr Puntila*," *Die Weltbühne*, 30 January 1952.

Lateness and Late Style in Brecht's Last Poetry

Karen Leeder, New College, Oxford

T HE WORK WRITTEN by Brecht in the last decade of his life has
often been classified in the secondary literature as "late" work or
the work of the "late Brecht." Walter Hinck's volume of 1959
Die Dramaturgie des späten Brecht (The Dramaturgy of the Late Brecht)
set the tone; many standard critical works then followed in pinpointing
the end of the Second World War as the caesura marking the beginning
of a discrete period in Brecht's aesthetic thinking and practice, a period
that they label "late."[1] This understanding has come to dominate the
reception of Brecht's work in the GDR — especially of the *Buckower
Elegien* (Buckow Elegies, 1953) and the poems written in the last years
before his death — for reasons that are partly to do with the prejudices
surrounding the lyric genre as one of inwardness, but also hinge on the
contested reception of the *Buckower Elegien* in particular. However, the
question of what "late" work might be has scarcely been addressed.
When does late work begin and how is it defined? And what does the
label mean for understanding the work in question? Studies have varied
in when they define the precise beginning of Brecht's late phase: favoring
the beginning of his period of exile in 1938, at one extreme, or Brecht's
move to the newly founded GDR in 1949 at the other. But the approach
has been remarkably consistent. The notion of late work (*Spätwerk*) has
been uncritically merged with the notion of the work of old age
(*Alterswerk*). Any form of theoretical understanding of what these might
entail is absent. Instead, both have been caught up within a longstanding
critical debate about whether Brecht's poetry of the GDR years became
more inward-looking or remained politically oriented.

In 1966, Alexander Hildebrand confidently claimed Brecht's post-
1948 poetry as "Alterslyrik" and adumbrated what he called a "late
style" focused on the compression of the poetry and what he saw as the
classicism of the form.[2] Twenty years later, Jan Knopf's pioneering

complete edition of the *Buckower Elegien* (1986) also took as its starting point "die Klassizität des Texts" (the classicicity of the text). In it, Knopf asserts straight out: "Die *Buckower Elegien* sind, obwohl Brecht so alt nicht geworden ist, typische Alterslyrik: weise, distanziert, lakonisch und im klassischen Sinn 'naiv', innerhalb der deutschen Literatur vergleichbar nur mit Goethes *West-östlichen Diwan*."[3] (Despite the fact that Brecht did not live to old age, *The Buckow Elegies* are typical old-age poetry: wise, distanced, laconic, and "naïve" in the classical sense, only comparable within German literature to Goethe's *West-Eastern Divan*.) Here certain characteristics are mentioned that are often associated with old-age poetry, but the analysis is overtaken by a comparison with a great late work by Brecht's great model (and rival) Goethe. In one of a number of articles from the 1990s on the theme Helmut Koopmann classifies the *Buckower Elegien* not as "Alterswerk an sich" (old-age work per se) but rather, and on the face of it curiously, as "Alterswerk des Exils" (old-age work of exile). Here, despite the identification of this late poetry with the GDR, Koopmann foregrounds what he sees as the lasting experiences of exile as pivotal for an old-age aesthetic.[4]

However, in 2001 Jan Knopf, the author of the section in the *Brecht-Handbuch* on the poems that Brecht wrote between 1947 and 1956, made short shrift of these interpretations. Contrary to his earlier position, Knopf argues: "Ein früher Tod — B[recht] wurde ja nur 58 Jahre alt — macht aber ein Werk, das die Jahre vor ihm entstanden ist, keineswegs zum Alterswerk." (His premature death — Brecht died at only 58 — certainly does not make the work that came into being during the years before that into *Alterswerk*.) For Knopf this would mean using an inappropriate yardstick to judge Brecht's output, since in fact it was written at a time when a man of Brecht's age might be considered to be middle-aged. He concludes "erst ab 60 pflegen wir das Seniorenalter anzusetzen" (we tend not to define someone as a senior citizen until the age of sixty)[5] and sets about systematically rebutting Koopmann's delineation of aspects of old-age work. Jörg Wilhelm Joost, who wrote the introductory section on the *Buckower Elegien* themselves, is similarly dismissive. Despite citing a number of critics who do make the notion of *Alterswerk* central to their interpretation, he is caustic about the thesis in general, and Koopmann's work in particular, judging it to be part of an "anachronistic" return to an unreflective biographical reading of the poetry that sidelines the political content.[6]

What is striking in these discussions is the lack of a serious engagement with lateness as a category. There is no distinction between old age and lateness, no methodological underpinning to the concepts, and no attempt to formalize what might distinguish an aesthetic of lateness. This is curious in some respects since a discourse of old age and late work was well established by the time even the earliest of these critics were considering Brecht's late work. Moreover, it originated precisely in the German tradition. This essay seeks to read Brecht's late poems, especially the *Buckower Elegien* and poems associated with it, in the light of theories of lateness, old-age literature, and late style. In doing this it will shed new light not only on the poems but also on the very predictable critical debates that have surrounded the *Elegies* up to now. Firstly, it offers a way out of the stalemate between interpretations that privilege the political agenda and those that focus on the poems as intimations of idyll — readings that have resulted from very partial examinations of the poetry.[7] Secondly, it examines how use of some of Edward Said's terms can answer the bewilderment critics face when confronted with the very diverse modes of poetry that Brecht wrote during his last years. Finally, it aims to explore the relationship of Brecht to the GDR.

On Creativity and Lateness

It has been claimed that the relationship between biography and artistic creation may be clearer in late works than in any other phase of life; and the self-exploration that is often prompted by the confrontation of an artist with old age or death can be deeply human but also surprising, initiating new phases or modes of creativity.[8]

The notion of "late style" is part of a characteristically German discourse that has determined the canonical view of late work in the early twentieth century: the decisive break of a mature and exceptional (male) artist with his previous style in favor of a mode more serene, often more autobiographically inflected, sometimes primitive or childlike, but in any case effortlessly transcendent and sublime. The privileged place that late work occupies in the critical imagination does not only, however, rest on its biographical force, but rather on a more complex relationship between the artist and his or her era. This is particularly evident in Adorno's thinking on the subject. As early as the 1930s he had taken up the concept of "Spätstil," approaching it from an aesthetics grounded in Marxist thought rather than individual biography.[9] In his influential writings on late Beethoven, for example, he suggested that the key to late works lay not in any psychological or organic life trajectory of the artist or composer but in the relation of art to its historical context. Beethoven, he claimed, used the conventions of the bourgeois era in his late works, but in doing so he was able to express a more fundamental negation of its values. Late style was thus no longer interpreted merely as the discordance of the artist with his era; it had become instead a product of the era's own inner contradictions, and its governing aesthetic was now one of fragmentation and dissonance.[10]

Sixty years later, and explicitly following Adorno, Edward Said, in his own late (indeed posthumously published) work *On Late Style* (2006), also rejected the notion that reconciliation and serenity were hallmarks of late works.[11] Asking how bodily condition impacts upon aesthetic style and how both interact with the historical moment, Said explores not only the work produced by mature artists, but also their relationship with their own times. With reference to various writers and musicians, but centrally Adorno and Beethoven, he highlights the fundamental "untimeliness" of late works, which he describes in various different ways: following Adorno, as a kind of exile; an irascible gesture of leave-taking; a nostalgic awareness nevertheless preternaturally aware of the present. Or, as Said, pithily puts it: "Late style is *in*, but oddly apart *from* the present" (24). Death in the works is represented in a refracted mode, as allegory, anachronism, anomaly, or irony. Instead of harmony and resolution, the privileged style of artistic lateness is, according to Said, "intransigence, difficulty, and unresolved contradiction" (7). As he summarizes: "This is the prerogative of late style: it has the power to render disenchantment and pleasure without resolving the contradiction between them" (148).

Said's provocative formulation of the problem has been closely followed by several important publications that draw on his ideas. However, the idea of "late style" as set out by Adorno or Said is only one facet of discourses of lateness more generally and is in itself a problematic one. Their shared notion of a canon of great male geniuses across history reveals universalist, transhistorical, and gendered assumptions about lateness that deserve to be challenged in a number of ways. Also their very particular notion of an "aesthetic of lateness," while usefully pitched against older, flawed understandings, does not itself present a universal answer and relies heavily on the biographical. In particular Gordon McMullan's work on Shakespeare has reminded us of the potential of such transcendent models to deliver a handful of dominant archetypes that function as transhistorical, transcultural phenomena and eclipse the historical specificity of the individuals or historical moments concerned. McMullan also introduces the useful notion of writing "in the proximity of death" to address the historically-determined question of when lateness or old age might begin.[12] Nevertheless, no one has as yet examined Brecht's work in this context. My project is not, especially within the scope of this essay, to map ideas of lateness one to one onto Brecht's GDR poetry, but rather to suggest ways in which such theories might offer a productive way of reading what is, in some respects at least, a difficult and controversial body of work.

Brecht and Lateness

There are a number of reasons why Brecht's poetry might be thought to lend itself to a reading in terms of lateness quite apart from the simple fact of his biography. These rest partly on the conscious thematization of different aspects of old age, death, elegy, exile, and epochal lateness in his work, and partly on the basis of what might be termed a "late style" of the kind already adumbrated here, encompassing aspects of (apparent) naivety, simplicity, and classicism, but also self-citation, irony, anachronism, discontinuity, and anomaly. There is the fact too that the *Buckower Elegien* as a collection became known only piecemeal and was finally published in a comprehensively annotated form, based on archive manuscripts, a full thirty years after Brecht's death.[13] In particular the delay — "Verspätung" (*Brecht-Handbuch* 2:452) — before the publication of the more explicitly political poems caused a rupture in the reception of this phase of Brecht's work. According to Jan Knopf, this still impacts on the way they are read today and has accorded the poems a special status as myth.[14] This essay will offer a first attempt to reflect on some of these things.

The sense that lateness might embrace both an individual biography and its relation to the historical moment is important in approaching Brecht's late work. Moreover, this understanding is in tune with Brecht's own thinking. In September 1938, reflecting on decadence and decline, Brecht compared his 1927 collection of poetry, *Die Hauspostille* (Domestic Breviary), with the *Svendborger Gedichte* (Svendborg Poems) of 1937 and famously noted what bourgeois critics would judge as an aesthetic impoverishment. However, he went on to reject what he called the outdated images associated with such a judgment — the notion of the organic flowering of a work or an aesthetic — and insisted instead that such things were the product of their material context: "Abstieg und Aufstieg sind nicht durch Daten im Kalender getrennt. Diese Linien gehen durch Personen und Werke durch" (*BFA* 26:523; withdrawal and advance are not separated according to dates in the calendar. they are threads that run through individuals and works, *Journals* 17; lower case in the published translation). Similarly, his famous hymn to posterity "An die Nachgeborenen" (*BFA* 12:85–87; "To Those Born Later," *Poems*

318–20) deplored the dark times in which it had been written and the delinquencies forced on those who struggled within them. It looked forward to a time after the flood when "der Mensch dem Menschen ein Helfer ist" (*BFA* 12:87; man is a helper to man, *Poems* 320). This would be an era in which new possibilities for humane existence and the writing of poetry would exist and presumably also a new aesthetic could prevail. His return to Germany, and particularly his move to Berlin and the young socialist state, demanded that these new possibilities be put into practice. As he faced the "travails of the plains" (*BFA* 15:205; *Poems* 415–16), a new energy was called for that would rally the socialist reconstruction. Certainly the poems testify to that sense of youth, newness, and regeneration: Brecht celebrated his arrival in the poem "Ein neues Haus" (*BFA* 15:205; A New House, *Poems* 416), wrote declamatory poems to comrades, and set to work on a cycle of "Neue Kinderlieder" (New Children's Songs), even producing a "Kinderhymne" (*BFA* 12:294; Children's Anthem, *Poems* 423) as a candidate for a new national anthem.

Nevertheless, an acute awareness of mortality hangs over Brecht's years in the GDR, exacerbated by his failing health, the difficult political situation, and in particular the events of June 1953.[15] Research has only recently begun to examine the full significance of Brecht's medical records for his work in the GDR.[16] Numerous letters and journal entries throughout the 1950s present a catalogue of Brecht's ailments, as well as his struggle against signs of physical deterioration. At Buckow in 1952, for example, Brecht initially threw himself into working on Erwin Strittmatter's *Katzgraben* (Katzgraben, 1953) with his assistant Käthe Rülicke (*BC* 1021–22). However, it was not long before she noticed how "gray and broken-down" he looked and concluded that he seemed "prematurely old" (*BC* 1025). Stephen Parker among others makes the point that the toll Brecht's ongoing illness and frequent hospitalization were taking on his day-to-day life was made worse by his frustration at the political situation and a concerted campaign by the authorities against him. His famous comment recorded on 20 August 1953 that the Workers' Uprising of 17 June had "alienated the whole of existence" (*Journals* 454; den ganzen Existenz verfremdet, *BFA* 27:346) could be understood as a caesura in this respect. Certainly after this point the intensity of the feeling of decline and dissatisfaction increases.

In 1954, for example, Brecht acknowledged explicitly for the first time that his creative powers were deserting him (*BFA* 27:362). His diary from this time frequently reports that work remains unfinished or that he is too exhausted to continue. The preoccupation becomes more marked in his final two years, in almost every aspect of his existence. In a letter to Peter Suhrkamp in March 1954, he comments on his last Berlin apartment in Chauseestrasse 125 with all its windows facing down onto the graveyard: "Er ist nicht ohne Heiterkeit" (*BFA* 30:231; It's not without its cheerful side, *Letters* 528). Koopmann is not the only one to reflect that this was a symbolic place for Brecht at that time.[17] But Brecht also began to think of the public and official aspects of his death. Before flying to Moscow on 15 May 1955 he wrote a last will and testament and left instructions for the Academy of Arts regarding his burial (*BFA* 30:342). And many letters and journal entries from 1955–56 demonstrate an encroaching feeling of finality that manifests itself quite literally in notes about his medication or hospital visits, but also symbolically. "Hier wird es grau und kälter," he reports to Ruth Berlau in December 1955 (*BFA* 30:397; Here it's getting grey and colder, *Letters* 551): a reflection that does not only concern the weather.

In 1952–53 Brecht began to reflect on impending death, as the following note records: "Ich, Bertolt Brecht, Sohn bürgerlicher Eltern / Hab diesen Sommer im Gefühl, die Zeit sei knapp / Durchblättert mein Gewissen" (*BFA* 15:263; I, Bertolt Brecht, the son of bourgeois parents / Have leafed through my conscience this summer / With the feeling that time is short). There is certainly a degree of stylization, signaled in the formulaic first line, that serves to put readers on their guard. However, the poetry of Brecht's last years provides precisely this kind of stocktaking. One aspect is a preoccupation with death;[18] another is the focus on aging or an awareness of the increasing limitations of the lyric subject.

In his autobiographical notes from around 1954 Brecht reflected: "Das erste untrügliche Zeichen des Alterns geben uns die Augen, denke ich. Es ist nichts weiter als das Gefühl, daß die Augen eben nicht mehr jung sind" (*BFA* 27:362; I think it's the eyes that give you the first inescapable sign of aging. It's nothing more than the sense that the eyes are simply no longer young). It is therefore perhaps unsurprising that failing sight is at the heart of one of the most famous of the late poems:

Schwierige Zeiten

Stehend an meinem Schreibpult
Sehe ich durchs Fenster im Garten den Holunderstrauch
Und erkenne darin etwas Rotes und etwas Schwarzes
Und erinnere mich plötzlich des Holders
Meiner Kindheit in Augsburg.

Mehrere Minuten erwäge ich
Ganz ernsthaft, ob ich zum Tische gehn soll
Meine Brille holen, um wieder
Die schwarzen Beeren an den roten Zweiglein zu sehen.
(*BFA* 15:294)

[Difficult Times

Standing at my desk
Through the window I see the elder tree in the garden
And recognise something red in it, something black
And all at once recall the elder
Of my childhood in Augsburg.
For several minutes I debate
Quite seriously whether to go to the table
And pick up my spectacles, in order to see
Those black berries again on their tiny red stalks.
(*Poems* 449)]

This poem dated to 1955 draws on the same garden imagery as many of the *Buckower Elegien* and associated poems. It has been interpreted many times and has often been understood to characterize late or old-age poetry; Werner Frick even sees in it a kind of apotheosis of *Alterslyrik*, dubbing it "*ein Portrait of the Artist as an Old Man* — und zugleich *eine recherche du temps perdu*."[19] Here a simultaneous (if slightly askew) comparison to the Modernist classics Proust and Joyce underscores the importance of biography but also testifies to memory as an important facet of the work.

An apparently insignificant moment is recorded in which the indistinct sight of an elder bush in the garden (the lyric subject does not have his glasses to hand) prompts a profound moment of memory and reflection. At first it seems to record the losses of old age. The remembered black berries and tiny red stalks (Brecht uses the diminutive "Zweiglein" for the stalks) of the elder bush of youth have blurred in the present to merely "something red" and "something black." It is true that the poem leaves open whether the lyric subject will fetch the glasses to see the greater detail, though the "several minutes" of serious contemplation as to whether he should do this, recorded in the past tense, must surely suggest that he does not. The poem is low key, factual, seemingly inconsequential, but in fact opens out from being a record of limitations into a kind of epiphany. It works with finely balanced oppositions: youth and age, Berlin and Augsburg, East and West, spontaneous emotion (the impulse to fetch the glasses) and controlled reflection (the minutes spent considering whether to do so), nostalgia (note the familiar "Holder") and distance, possibly suggesting a kind of biographical circle or harmonious synthesis as Frick contends.[20] However, the poem does not make explicit what prevents the lyric subject from fetching the glasses, or why it is a matter for serious contemplation. Is the lyric subject wary of the distraction from more important tasks — writing — as signaled by the desk in the first line? Is he wary of the sudden ("plötzlich") and perhaps unwelcome access of emotion? Schuhmann argues that fetching the glasses would mean "ein Wiedersehn [sic], [. . .] eine Selbstbegegung [. . .] unter 'schwierigen' Begleiterscheinungen" (an encounter [literally re-vision], a meeting with himself [. . .] under "difficult" circumstances).[21] It would mean remembering a time of life that, in the most literal sense, cannot be recalled. In deciding not to fetch the glasses, the lyric subject, according to Schuhmann, respects the natural limitations that old age has brought with all the physiological and psychological implications. However, there is surely more to it than this. Acknowledging the difference between the once clear sight of the elder stalks in the town of his birth and the blurred vision of something red and black in the garden in Buckow would actually be to confront all that had intervened between.

A similar thought motivates the poem "Tannen" of 1953 (*BFA* 12:313; Firs, *Poems* 442) from the *Buckower Elegien*, where the lyric subject sees the fir trees glowing copper in the early morning:

So sah ich sie
Vor einem halben Jahrhundert
Vor zwei Weltkriegen
Mit jungen Augen.

[That's how I saw them
Half a century ago
Two world wars ago
With young eyes.]

The alignment of the "jungen Augen" with the phrase "in der Frühe" in the opening line of the poem holds two meanings in suspense. The poem refers both to the early morning and to an early biographical time, youth. The old eyes cannot see in the same way any longer, perhaps because of age. However, the twofold qualification of the phrase "vor einem halben Jahrhundert" underlines the fact that the poem is not only about changes wrought by biological aging. Here the world too has changed, and so has the way it can be looked at. The vast historical and political upheavals of the twentieth century are telescoped into two visions of the natural world that function as a kind of synonym for the lyric subject's life, but also for the epoch. The lyric subject now cannot see the trees in the same way as he did with young eyes: because of the shadow of war that has fallen between these two dates, but also perhaps because of the failure of the revolutionary hope once symbolized by the fir trees but now betrayed by the reality of the GDR.[22]

The difference between the two poems, however, lies in an act of will — the deliberation about whether to fetch the glasses and look — and this points to one final, but significant, aspect. The clue lies in the title "Schwierige Zeiten," which at first seems at odds with the body of the poem itself. A biographical reading in tune with what has been set out here would see the difficulties in the failure of vision (hence Schuhmann's mention of "difficult" circumstances); a political reading, aligned with the interpretation of "Tannen" set out above, might see the title as a discreet allusion to the situation in the GDR. However, the title also inevitably puts one in mind of the "dunkle Zeiten" (dark times) of exile, which — as Brecht claimed looking at the *Svendborger Gedichte* — had put an embargo on a certain kind of lyric diction. Times when "ein Gespräch über Bäume" (*BFA* 12:85; a conversation about trees, *Poems* 318; trans. mod.) could be thought of as a crime because it implied remaining silent about the urgent political realities of the day. The *Buckower Elegien* and other late poems have a far more bucolic bent than the poems of exile: Brecht played up the echo of the word "bucolic" in his first description of the poems to his publishers as "Buckowlichen Elegien" (*BFA* 30:222).[23] But these are not innocent or private poems; and if the times are no longer "dark" for Brecht, they are still difficult. Here "a conversation about trees" implies a beautifully succinct observation on aging, a meditation on twentieth-century history, a covert commentary on the political situation, and a reflection on the possibilities of the lyric.

The axis on which the poem turns is one of memory: the comparison of a time "now" with one "before" that generates the elegiac discrepancy. And many poems of this time function with a similar temporal opposition: implying an alteration for the worse or "Wechsel der Dinge" (*BFA* 15:294; Things Change, *Poems* 449–50), to borrow the title of one of them.[24] Generally this is part of a kind of inventory of loss. Indeed, several commentators see this as one of the key aspects that distinguish old-age poetry, and it is certainly a central feature in more recent studies of late work, including Said's own. In Brecht's poetry it has a number of specific manifestations: from the intimations of decrepitude of "War traurig, wann ich jung war" (*BFA* 15:295; Was Sad When I Was Young) to the stocktaking of past love affairs marked by a "Veränderung, aber zum Schlechten" (*BFA* 15:298–99; Change, But for the Worse) or a kind of thought experiment about the nature of existence and its relationship to change: "Dauerten wir unendlich" (*BFA* 15:294; Were We to Last Forever).

Within the *Buckower Elegien* in particular the temporal opposition also has a quite different and more specifically political aspect. Here the exclamation "Wie in alten Zeiten!" (Just like old times) implies a critical warning that things have not changed enough and that social inequalities continue (*BFA* 12:308; *Poems* 441). The poem "Gewohnheiten, noch immer" (*BFA* 12:307; Still at It, *Poems* 441) situates this continuity within the context of what Knopf calls everyday fascism ("alltäglichen Faschismus").[25] And indeed it is specifically the memory of fascism that acts as a counterpoint to the elegiac memories of childhood. The knowledge that "Vor acht Jahren // Da war eine Zeit. / Da war alles hier anders" (*BFA* 12:314; Eight Years Ago // There was a time / When all was different here, *Poems* 443) acts as a warning against the continuing subterranean influence of fascist attitudes that Brecht highlighted in his outspoken comments on the 17 June uprising.[26] The collection also insists on the failure of the GDR to capitalize on the hopes invested in it in a way that emphasizes a historical opportunity missed: "Große Zeit, vertan" (*BFA* 12:311; Great Times, Wasted, *Poems* 440). But the poetry also looks further back — and indeed further forward — to place the present moment within a larger epochal context.

In several poems from the *Buckower Elegien* and beyond, Brecht references classical sources to draw a comparison between his own time and another historical moment. In "Bei der Lektüre eines spatgriechischen Dichters" (*BFA* 12:312; Reading a Late Greek Poet, *Poems* 445), for example, the isolated, lapidary phrase at the end, "Auch die Troer also…" (The Trojans too, then), acts as hinge between the classical reference and the present day. The poet in question is Constantine P. Cavafy and the poem "Trojans," which Suhrkamp had published in German translation in 1953. The epithet "late Greek" does not therefore apply so much to the late antiquity of classical Greece that forms the backdrop for Homer's account of the fall of Troy, but rather simultaneously to the late-bourgeois capitalist Greece. Yet one can also see in it a reference to the present, another "time after" as it were. In the context of the collection and especially of the events of 17 June, the last line offers a resigned recognition of the need for continued vigilance.

The poem "Beim Lesen des Horaz" (*BFA* 12:315; Reading Horace, *Poems*, 443) functions analogously; this time projecting the present moment into a classical context but insisting on it as a time after a monumental watershed: "Selbst die Sintflut / Dauerte nicht ewig" (Even the flood / Did not last for ever). The "flood" recalls Brecht's use of the term as a symbol of fascism during exile, in "An die Nachgeborenen," for example, but points back beyond that to Biblical models, and also classical sources, including Horace.[27] Its spare diction invokes the survivors, qualified in Brecht's commentary as the "few." Unspoken but nonetheless urgent is the injunction for them to attend to a future where the flood cannot return.

What is striking about these poems is that in both cases the reference to classical times is embedded within the act of reading. This seems to define the poems as "Gelegenheitsgedichte" (occasional poems) for Knopf, for example.[28] But they could also certainly be read as conscious elements in the construction of the image of the contemplative sage: here a mature *poeta doctus*, whose distanced vision sees clearly beyond the vagaries of the different epochs to apprehend fundamental underlying historical patterns. This is part of a project of self-stylization in Brecht's poetry, and it is true that the teacher/pupil motif is a commonplace from much earlier on, as is the implied identification of himself with a tradition of great poets (here Homer, Horace, and Cavafy).

Nevertheless, here the deliberate cultivation of this trope goes hand in hand with a more general application of classical form and diction within the later poems. This has been exhaustively discussed in recent articles and I cannot set out the debates in detail here.[29] But it is worth pointing out one place at least where the classical model is challenged. The placing of the lyric subject in the *Elegien* and other late poems within a garden or enclosed space reminiscent of the "hortus conclusus" has been discussed. However, it is striking that the lyric subject is often liminal, uneasy, not truly at home. In the poem "Ein neues Haus" already mentioned, the lyric subject sits surrounded by his familiar objects in the new state, yet is haunted by a lingering impermanence, as if exile is hard to shake off: "Immer noch / Liegt auf dem Schrank mit den Manuskripten / Mein Koffer" (*BFA* 15:205; Even now / On top of the cupboard containing my manuscripts / My suitcase lies).

In a number of the *Elegien* the lyric subject appears as a marginal, observing presence. In "Der Blumengarten" (*BFA* 12:307; The Flower Garden, *Poems* 438), for example, a poem often read as a metaphorical endorsement of the productivity of socialism, he sits "in der Früh, nicht allzu häufig" (in the morning, not too frequently) and there is a distinct sense of unease about the wisely plotted garden and *dirigiste* "monthly flowers."[30] In what almost seems to be a direct response to the strenuous over-productivity implied here, the lyric subject in "Das Gewächshaus" (*BFA* 15:284; The Abandoned Greenhouse, *Poems* 448), is exhausted ("erschöpft") by the efforts of bygone days ("vergangener Tage Sorgfalt"; the grammar and word order make the phrase stand out in German). He haunts an abandoned greenhouse filled with the remains of rare flowers — "Wie immer, die schönen Empfindlichen / Sind nicht mehr." (As always, the lovely and sensitive / Are no longer.) — in what seems to be a mausoleum for past values. That this poem pinpoints more than botanical neglect is highlighted by the archly rhetorical language and pointed inversions, but also in the comment that the common flowers that flourish outside are those that have no need of art ("Kunst"). Similarly, in the celebrated poem "Der Radwechsel" (*BFA* 12:310; Changing the Wheel, *Poems* 439) the lyric subject sits impatiently ("Mit Ungeduld") precisely at the central axis of the poem between the third and fourth lines but is exiled from the momentum of progress: "Ich bin nicht gern, wo ich herkomme. / Ich bin nicht gern, wo ich hinfahre (I do not like the place I have come from. / I do not like the place I am going to). And there are frequent dreams that suggest if not the all-encompassing "false consciousness" that Philip Thomson detects,[31] then at least a subject existentially not at home. This recalls quite literally Brecht's own journal entry for 7 July 1954: "Das Land ist immer noch unheimlich" (*BFA* 27:349; this country still gives me the creeps, *Journals* 458 — though the translation here misses the nuance). However, what is more important in this context is that the sense of alienation chimes with Said's discussion of exile as a dominant facet of late style and amplifies in a very concrete way the interpretations by Koopmann and Karcher that insist that it is the unshakeable experience of exile that has created an "anachronistic" old-age style in Brecht's late work.

A poem that brings together many of the aspects discussed here but that also offers a new perspective is one of Brecht's last poems, written in May 1956 after he had been in hospital in the Berlin Charité for four weeks:

Als ich in weißem Krankenzimmer der Charité
Aufwachte gegen Morgen zu
Und eine Amsel hörte, wußte ich
Es besser. Schon seit geraumer Zeit
Hatte ich keine Todesfurcht mehr. Da ja nichts

Mir je fehlen kann, vorausgesetzt
Ich selber fehle. Jetzt
Gelang es mir, mich zu freuen
Alles Amselgesanges nach mir auch. (*BFA* 15:300)

[When in my white room at the Charité
I woke towards morning
And heard the blackbird, I understood
Better. Already for some time
I had lost all fear of death. For nothing
Can be wrong with me if I myself
Am nothing. Now
I managed to enjoy
The song of every blackbird after me too.
     (*Poems*, 451–52)]

Set against the inventory of deficit that I have sketched out here, this
poem contemplates a world beyond the lyric subject with equanimity.
Written in a sober, direct style, the lack of rhythm or regular rhyme
creates a sense of immediacy that underscores the biographical aspect of
the poem. Yet for all its apparent simplicity the poem is difficult. At the
very center of the poem is the word "Todesfurcht" (fear of death).[32]
Beyond any sense of personal utterance, however, the poem records
intellectual deliberation on the *idea* of mortality and fear of death. What
Brecht elsewhere calls "die berühmten Verse des Lukrez über die
Todesfurcht" (*BFA* 19:431; the famous lines of Lucretius about the fear
of death) is a reference to third book of *de rerum natura* (On the Nature
of Things). But there is also, as Lausberg has demonstrated, a reference
to Epicurus.[33] The lyric subject has, with some effort of will — "wußte
ich besser" (lines 3–4), "gelang es mir" (lines 7–8) — managed to come
to terms with fear of death through reflection on the classical models. In
this the lines echo the serious contemplation of the old man recalling the
elder tree of his youth discussed above. But this poem captures
something else: a moment of epiphany that transcends materialist
reflection, as the lyric subject discovers joy ("Freude") in contemplating
a life beyond his own existence. The joy finds its objective correlative in
the song of a blackbird, as a representative for the pleasures of life, but
then opens out in the last line of the poem to encompass all blackbird
song. The poem hinges not on the satisfaction of the lyric subject with
lived life; on the contrary: it bears witness as the subject renounces the
last vestiges of his subjectivity that would prevent him taking pleasure in

a world without him, that is, in death.[34] This projection beyond the lyric subject of the moment embraces death and that which comes "after" in a way that is perhaps the most radically "anachronistic" of all Brecht's poems: "*in*, but oddly apart *from* the present."

Late Style

One of the aspects that has troubled commentators on Brecht's late poetry is the lack of a unified tone. Hannah Arendt finds no great poem among the late work and "nichts als Ansätze zu einer Brechtschen Alterslyrik" (only the suggestion of a Brechtian poetry of old-age).[35] Koopmann identifies "Unvereinbarkeiten" (incongruities) and "Gegensätzlichkeiten" (oppositions); Karcher "der Zug des Fragmentarischen" (the sense of fragmentariness) and "Unabgeschlossenheit" (incompleteness). This he sees as central to Brecht's late aesthetic, drawing a parallel with the "Einheit im Widerspruch" (unity in contradiction) of the late work of Gottfried Benn.[36] There is an irony, of course, that in so many ways Brecht's late work and that of his West German contemporary — characterized by Brecht as "den todessüchtigen Benn" (the death-obsessed Benn) in a caustic poetic fragment of 1956 (*BFA* 15:300) — should bear so many similarities. However, what Benn in a letter of 1949 described in his own late work as an "in der Schwebe halten" (keeping in suspense / holding in the balance), he judged to be the only form commensurate with the time ("zeitgemäß").[37] For Benn "the time" here means his own biographical time, but also the historical moment: one he shared with Brecht, despite all their differences. And we see a very similar diversity and openness in Brecht's late work.

Within the microcosm of the *Buckower Elegien* taken as a whole, there are so-called nature or more personal poems that dominated the first wave of reception; but there are also savagely ironic poems that touch on the political reality in allegorical form and have determined another approach to Brecht's late work. If one moves beyond the individual collection, the divergent forms and moods are even more remarkable: ranging from the declamatory agit-prop songs associated with socialist reconstruction, or the aggressive satirical critiques of GDR bureaucracy, to the simplicity of the "Kinderlieder," the sly absurdity of the pornographic sonnets, and the gnomic sententiousness of the poems in the classical vein. In addition, there are Brecht's versions of texts by writers as varied as Ingeborg Bachmann, the Turkish poet Nazim Hikmet, or the critical Polish writer Adam Ważyk, the poems of bare stocktaking, and some remarkable bittersweet miniatures on remembered love. Especially important (and scarcely commented upon in the critical literature) are a number of poems that insist on the "pleasures" of everyday life ("Vergnügungen" is the title of one of them; *BFA* 15:287, *Poems* 448). In this context there is unfortunately no space to set out Brecht's stubborn iteration of basic (often bodily) pleasures in detail. However, poems like "Gegenlied" (*BFA*: 15:296; Counter-Song, *Poems* 450–51), "Orges Wunschliste" (*BFA* 15:297 "Orges List of Wishes, *Poems* 12–13), "1954, Erste Hälfte" (*BFA* 15:281; 1954: First Half, *Poems* 446), "Fröhlich vom Fleische zu essen" (*BFA* 15:285; To Eat of Meat Joyously, *Poems* 448), or "Ach wie solln wir nun die kleine Rose buchen" (*BFA* 15:283; The Little Rose, Oh How Should It Be Listed, *Poems* 447) would provide a starting point in delineating an almost programmatic counterpoint to the overarching sense of loss that runs through Brecht's late work. This "Gegenlied" of sorts is founded on the word joy ("Freude") that appears in almost all of them and recalls the epiphanic joy found in death accepted as part of life in the hospital poem discussed above. Said's comment about "disenchantment and pleasure" remaining within late work in an unresolved state is singularly apt.

Even within a single poem, idyll and irony — lyricism and distance — can rub shoulders; simplicity coincides with misdirection, disappointment at the course reality is taking with a truculent vision of the way things could be. The key point, however, is that they do not cancel one another out but remain suspended within the space of the poem — as demonstrated in "Schwierige Zeiten," "Tannen," or "Als ich im weißen Krankenzimmer" — in a way that permits, even encourages contradictory readings. One of the barriers that have stood in the way of critics thinking of Brecht's late poetry as "late work" is the lack of a dominant mode. Another is the basic undecidability of the late work. But also there is the failure of this diversity of diction and tone to map onto conventional ideas of late style (transcendence, naivety, serenity etc.). However, if one returns once more to Said's understanding of late work as marked by "intransigence, difficulty and unresolved contradiction," the very facet that has for so long perplexed commentators, and indeed forged such rifts in schools of interpretation, can serve to unite the biographical, historical, and aesthetic aspects of Brecht's GDR poetry in a way that makes of them "late work" in the fullest sense of the words.

Notes

[1] Walter Hinck, *Die Dramaturgie des späten Brecht* (1959; Göttingen: Vandenhoeck & Ruprecht, 1997). Compare the discussion in Jan Knopf, ed., *Brecht-Handbuch in fünf Bänden*, vol. 2, *Gedichte* (Stuttgart/Weimar: Metzler, 2001), 415–17 and 439–53.

[2] Alexander Hildebrand, "Bertolt Brechts Alterslyrik," *Merkur* 20, no. 10 (1966): 952–62. See also Peter-Paul Schwarz, *Lyrik und Zeitgeschichte: Brecht; Gedichte über das Exil und späte Lyrik* (Heidelberg: Lothar Stiehm Verlag, 1978).

[3] Jan Knopf, ed., *Bertolt Brechts Buckower Elegien* (Frankfurt a.M.: Suhrkamp, 1986), 125 and 121.

[4] Helmut Koopmann, "Brechts Buckower Elegien — ein Alterswerk des Exils?" in *Hundert Jahre Brecht — Brechts Jahrhundert?*, ed. Hans-Jörg Knobloch and Helmut Koopmann (Tübingen: Stauffenberg, 1998), 113–34, here 134. See also Koopmann, "Brechts späte Lyrik," in *Brechts Lyrik — neue Deutungen*, ed. Koopmann (Würzburg: Königshausen & Neumann, 1999), 143–62.

[5] Compare *Brecht-Handbuch* 2:413. The same biographical point is made by Simon Karcher, *Sachlichkeit und elegischer Ton: Die späte Lyrik von Gottfried Benn und Bertolt Brecht — ein Vergleich* (Würzburg: Königshausen & Neumann, 2006), 308.

[6] *Brecht-Handbuch* 2:439–52.

[7] There is no room to set out the reception history in detail here. See the summary in the *Brecht-Handbuch*, especially 2:440–41.

[8] Karen Painter, "On Creativity and Lateness," in *Late Thoughts: Reflections on Artists and Composers at Work*, ed. Karen Painter and Thomas Crow (Los Angeles: Paul Getty Research Institute, 2006), 1–11.

[9] Compare especially Theodor W. Adorno, "Spätstil Beethovens" (1937), "Zur gesellschaftlichen Lage der Musik" (1932), and "Verfremdetes Hauptwerk: Zur Missa Solemnis" (1959) in Adorno, *Gesammelte Schriften*, 20 vols., ed. Rolf Tiedemann (Frankfurt a.M.: Suhrkamp, 1970–1986), vol. 17, 13–17, vol. 18, 729–77 and vol. 17, 145–61, respectively.

[10] Adorno, "Spätstil Beethovens," 13.

[11] Edward W. Said, *On Late Style* (London: Bloomsbury, 2006).

[12] See Gordon McMullan, *Shakespeare and the Idea of Late Writing: Authorship in the Proximity of Death* (Cambridge: Cambridge UP, 2007).

[13] Brecht published only six of the elegies in *Sinn und Form* in 1953; these appeared again one year later in volume 15 of the *Versuche* under the title "Buckower Elegien." Six further poems appeared in the volume of *Sinn und Form* dedicated to Brecht in 1968 under the title "Aus letzten Gedichten." Since Knopf's 1986 edition there have been various further changes that later editors have made after reading the manuscripts. See the *Brecht-Handbuch* (2:439–53) for a fuller account.

[14] Jan Knopf, *Gelegentlich Poesie: Ein Essay über die Lyrik Bertolt Brechts* (Frankfurt a.M.: Surhrkamp, 1996), 266.

[15] See Werner Hecht, *Brecht Chronik 1898–1956* (Frankfurt a.M.: Suhrkamp, 1997). Subsequent references to this work are cited in the text using the abbreviation *BC* and page number.

[16] Stephen Parker, "What Was the Cause of Brecht's Death? Towards a Medical History," *Brecht Yearbook* 35 (2010): 291–307. See also the essay by Stephen Parker in this volume.

[17] Koopmann, "Brechts späte Lyrik," 144.

[18] See, for example, on death (all from *BFA* 15): "Sie stieg hinauf" (315), "Erst ließ Freude" (315), "Die Chronik" (314), "Der Mord" (312), "Ansichten aus einer sozialistischen Stadt" (312), "Meine Einzige" (296–97), "Der schöne Tag, wenn ich nutzlos geworden bin" (295), "E. P. Auswahl seines Grabsteins" (285), "Wenn du mich lustig machst" (241).

[19] Werner Frick, "'Ich, Bertolt Brecht…': Stationen einer poetischen Selbstinszenierung," in *Brechts Lyrik — neue Deutungen*, ed. Koopmann, 9–47, here 44.

[20] Frick, 44.

[21] Klaus Schuhmann, "Themen und Formenwandel in der späten Lyrik Brechts," *Weimarer Beiträge*, Brecht Sonderheft (1968): 39–60, here 54.

[22] An interpretation offered by Volker Bohn, "Mahnbild vom Schermützlsee," in *Bertolt Brecht: Der Mond über Soho; 66 Gedichte mit Interpretationen*, ed. Marcel Reich-Ranicki (Frankfurt a.M., Leipzig: Insel, 2002), 235–37, here 236; and Karcher, 237.

[23] See Marion Lausberg, "Brechts Lyrik und die Antike," in *Brechts Lyrik — neue Deutungen*, ed. Koopmann, 163–98 for the connection to Vergil's *Bucolica*.

[24] Compare, for example (all from *BFA* 15): "Wie es war" (315) "Erst ließ Freude" (315), "Veränderung, aber zum Schlechten" (298–9), "Wie traurig, wann ich jung war" (295), "Wechsel der Dinge" (294), "Ich, der ich Rosen aber sterben sah" (292), "Und das Lächeln, das mir galt" (286), "Liebeslied aus einer schlechten Zeit" (286), "Einst war ich bereit" (274), "Bitter gedenkst du der Vergangenheit" (273). None apart from "Wechsel der Dinge" appears in *Poems*.

[25] Knopf, *Bertolt Brechts Buckower Elegien*, 61.

[26] See his outspoken comments in the journal entry of 20 August 1953 (*BFA* 27:346 *Journals*, 455), his letter to Peter Suhrkamp of 1 July 1953 (*BFA* 30:182–85; *Letters*, 518), and Patrick Harkin's essay in this volume.

[27] Lausberg discusses this poem in detail, 195–96. Jürgen Link argues that it refers to Stalinism. See Link, "Beim Lesen des Horaz," in *Interpretationen: Gedichte von Bertolt Brecht*, ed. Jan Knopf (Stuttgart: Philipp Reclam jun., 1995), 161–76.

[28] Knopf, *Bertolt Brechts Buckower Elegien*, 95–98 and 113–18 respectively. See also his commentary on "Bei der Lektüre eines sowjetischen Buchs," 105–9.

[29] Compare Lausberg, as above.

[30] Ray Ockenden discusses strategies of misdirection in this poem in his "Empedocles in Buckow: A Sketch Map of Misreading," in *Empedocles' Shoe: Essays on Brecht's Poetry*, ed. Karen Leeder and Tom Kuhn (London: Methuen, 2002), 175–206, here 193–205. Schuhmann reads this poem as a statement of the lyric subject's limitations, 53.

[31] The title of Thomson's chapter on the *Buckower Elegien* is "Poetry, Conscience and False Consciousness." See Philip Thomson, *The Poetry of Brecht: Seven Studies* (Chapel Hill and London: U of North Carolina P, 1989), 120–57.

[32] Compare Erdmut Wizisla's account in the *Brecht-Handbuch* 2:470–72, which also documents the changes and queries on the manuscript. See also "Über die Todesfurcht" (*BFA* 18:80; On the Fear of Death).

[33] Lausberg, 173.

[34] Here I follow the reading by Wizisla. For contrary interpretations see especially Gerlinde Wellmann-Bretzigheimer, "Brechts Gedicht 'Als ich in weißem Krankenzimmer der Charité': Die Hilfe des Sozialismus zur Überwindung der Todesfurcht," *Brecht Yearbook* 7 (1977): 30–51.

[35] Hannah Arendt, *Benjamin, Brecht: Zwei Essays* (Munich: Piper, 1971), 68.

[36] Karcher, 307. Compare also Dorrit Beckmann, *Künstlerische Entwicklungsverläufe im 20. Jahrhundert: Gottfried Benn und Bertolt Brecht* (Berlin: Logos, 1999).

[37] Benn's letter to Friedrich Wilhelm Oelze, 23 March 1949, cited in Karcher, 307.

A Life's Work Curtailed? The Ailing Brecht's Struggle with the SED Leadership over GDR Cultural Policy

Stephen Parker, University of Manchester

S ECURING THE PRESENCE in East Berlin of such an iconic socialist artist as Bertolt Brecht was both a major coup for the leaders of the Socialist Unity Party of Germany (SED) in 1949 and a major headache. Given the same opportunity just two years later, they would probably have declined. Brecht was the most prominent of the German artists who returned to the GDR from exile to participate in the construction of a first German socialist state. However, during the later years of the Weimar Republic and his subsequent exile from Nazi Germany, Brecht already had major differences in his aesthetic theory and practice with artists and cultural politicians who sought to represent an orthodox position for the Communist Party of Germany (KPD) by means of the doctrine of Socialist Realism. In his capacity as editor of the Moscow journal *Das Wort* during the Great Terror, Brecht — himself in Danish exile — clashed in a sectarian struggle with the "Moscow faction," most notably his co-editor Georg Lukács and other influential figures such as Alfred Kurella and Fritz Erpenbeck. When Brecht had to flee Scandinavia in 1941, he pointedly chose to take refuge not in Moscow, where friends such as Carola Neher had been imprisoned, but in California, where he remained as a "western émigré" until his return to Europe in 1947. When Brecht moved from Switzerland to Berlin in 1949, the stage was set for the resumption of the sectarian struggle within the new context of the Cold War. As before, major areas of contention were the treatment of the German cultural heritage and dramatic theory. While Brecht engaged in a critical interrogation of the *deutsche Misere*, the wretched path of German history that had reached its nadir in Hitler's Germany, the SED leadership expected artists to provide exemplary, uplifting narratives from the socialist heritage in support of the new state, contrasting the GDR with an unregenerate West.

Throughout the Cold War, the restricted access to records in the obsessively secretive and security-minded GDR drastically impaired our understanding of Brecht's struggle with the SED's leadership and cultural politicians. There was frequent speculation in the West that Brecht's last seven years in the GDR must surely have contributed to his early death on 14 August 1956, aged just fifty-eight. The official record of his death published in East Berlin stated that Brecht had died of a heart attack. For the GDR authorities, the matter was then closed. Yet almost immediately rumors circulated that the official record was flawed. Fritz Cremer, for example, told the story of his trip to Brecht's flat on Chausseestraße to make the death mask. When he arrived, he found Brecht's corpse sitting in an upright position, with blood running from the mouth.[1] There was, however, no opportunity to test the official pronouncement.

Following the end of the Cold War, documents were extracted from Berlin archives that demonstrated, in much clearer terms than had previously been possible, Brecht's instrumental involvement in the protracted struggle over cultural policy between the SED and the GDR's artistic elite in the East Berlin Academy of Arts.[2] The struggle was at its most intense during two periods. The first was the SED's Formalism Campaign in early 1951. The second followed the SED's proclamation of the Construction of the Foundations of Socialism in 1952. Over a number of months in the first half of 1953, Brecht was subjected to extreme pressure to recant his dramatic theories in favor of a Stanislavskian form of Socialist Realism. However, quite improbably, Brecht and his supporters in the Academy used the profound shock of 17 June 1953 to turn the tables in cultural politics. The outcome in the short term was an uneasy standoff until Brecht's death.

Given the speculation surrounding the possible link between Brecht's health and SED pressure upon him, it is surprising that the official record of the cause of Brecht's death and of the medical treatment preceding it was until recently the subject of only limited re-appraisal. In the absence of firm medical evidence, discussion of the relationship between Brecht's health and his activities has hence largely remained conjecture. The present essay addresses the issue with such evidence, building upon the publication of a first medical history of Brecht and incorporating further details of Brecht's medical condition during his years in the GDR.[3] Those findings are juxtaposed with the record of Brecht's involvement in cultural-political controversies in order to explore four related questions: Can a substantial linkage be established between the two spheres? What was the nature of the authorities' surveillance of Brecht? Did they use their knowledge of his condition in their dealings with him? Finally, were Brecht's life and productivity thereby impaired or even curtailed?

Brecht's Medical Condition on His Return to Germany

Brecht's medical history reveals that when he settled in East Berlin in June 1949 he was more seriously ill than has been suspected hitherto. His markedly failing body was carrying diseases that destined him, come what may, to an early death from chronic heart failure. Those diseases and the complications that might ensue were poorly understood. From childhood onwards, Brecht had known that there were things quite seriously wrong with him medically but had remained frustrated in his attempts to establish what his symptoms actually signified. In particular, Brecht carried with him the abiding effects of his undiagnosed childhood contraction of rheumatic fever, triggered by the streptococcal bacterial infection of pharyngitis or "strep throat," which had attacked his heart and his basal ganglia, triggering carditis and the motorneural condition Sydenham's chorea. Brecht's doctors had simply labeled him a nervous child with an enlarged heart. Only in the 1930s and 1940s did advances take place in medical research that identified strep throat as the trigger for rheumatic fever. It was only from that time, too, that it was possible to supplement diagnosis with antibiotic treatment. In Brecht's adolescence, carditis deteriorated into the lifelong condition of chronic heart failure, the symptoms of which are arrhythmia, or heart palpitations; dyspnea, or shortage of breath; dizziness; and exhaustion. Brecht recorded such symptoms obsessively in his diary as a fifteen-year-old. Then and later, he suffered from frequent bouts of heart failure. His susceptibility increased as his organism deteriorated during the aging process. Meanwhile, Sydenham's chorea, manifested in childhood as a facial tic that the boy held in check with a grimace, recurred at times of stress during his adult years. Again, this condition manifested itself more markedly during the aging process.

Because Brecht's condition was never adequately diagnosed, his doctors were unaware of complications that could ensue from a further disorder, a urological condition that Brecht carried with him throughout his adult life. The condition manifested itself intermittently as kidney stones and pyelonephritis, inflammation of the renal pelvis. The symptoms are fevers, rigors (violent shivering with temperature rises), headaches, and vomiting. The inflammation can easily spread to the heart, particularly, of course, to an already diseased organ, triggering endocarditis, the inflammation of the inner lining of the heart and usually, too, of the valves. Among Brecht's doctors there was no real understanding of how vulnerable he was to the debilitating interaction of urological infection with his underlying cardiac condition. Even without the spread of the inflammation of the heart, when the weak and sickly Brecht contracted urological infections during his adult years he was susceptible to symptoms of chronic heart failure as well as of the urological condition. Records show that he was typically assailed by fever, arrhythmia, dyspnea, and exhaustion. By the time he returned to Berlin, recurrence of the urological condition had become frequent, as had that of the symptoms of chronic heart failure. The threat of the escalation of his condition into endocarditis was always given, with the distinct possibility that death would ensue.

Unpublished correspondence shows that the urological problem plagued Brecht in the period immediately before he moved to Berlin from Switzerland. Brecht wrote to Hans Albers that he was in hospital with pyelonephritis.[4] In a draft of a letter dated 10 August 1948 Berthold Viertel asked Brecht what was wrong with his kidneys.[5] Only days after returning to Berlin, on 22 June 1949 Brecht had an appointment at the Catholic St. Hedwig's Hospital on Große Hamburger Straße in East Berlin with the urologist Ferdinand Hüdepohl. Hüdepohl (1902–1980) was then recognized as Germany's leading specialist in the field. In the Germany of the Third Reich he had been a consultant to the Luftwaffe and, from 1934, a member of the SS.[6] It is an extraordinary thought that, only days after his return to participate in the construction of a socialist Germany, Brecht, later the vigilant voice in such poems as "Der Einarmige im Gehölz" (The One-Armed Man in the Undergrowth), unwittingly entrusted his sickly body to a former SS man. Thanks to his urological expertise, Hüdepohl became Brecht's trusted physician for the next seven years. Until 1956 Brecht played an active part in attempts to secure Hüdepohl's future in East Berlin.[7]

In the report upon his first examination of Brecht, Hüdepohl identified a serious urological condition above and beyond Brecht's susceptibility to pyelonephritis and kidney stones. Brecht was suffering from a urethral stricture with pronounced prostatitis, inflammation of the prostate gland, following a build-up of urine in the prostate. Hüdepohl recommended that Brecht should only be treated in hospital and explained that he had refrained from a further examination out of fear of infection. Hüdepohl admitted Brecht to St. Hedwig's Hospital for three weeks to address the stricture and related issues. The narrowing of the urethra, which causes the stricture, is normally due to scar tissue. The procedure to deal with it is to widen the urethra either by passing a bougie into it or by performing a urethrotomy, a surgical operation. Yet even with surgery, a stricture tends to recur and treatment has to be repeated periodically. As we shall see, Brecht's urological complaint proved to be persistent, his symptoms relating to inflammation of the prostate and of the renal pelvis. Brecht's condition dictated that he regularly consulted Hüdepohl about his urological problems until shortly before his death. There is no evidence that the specialist urologist Hüdepohl was aware of Brecht's cardiac problem.

The SED's Coercive Hostility towards the Ailing Brecht

Against this medical background, Brecht embarked on his postwar career in East Berlin, in which he enjoyed great material support from the state through the Berliner Ensemble. He was driven by his ambition to realize his theatrical vision in a socialist Germany. In 1949 Brecht wrote his famous lines linking the inevitability of the aging process with the arduous struggles to come, the suggestion being that the latter could hasten the former:

> Als ich wiederkehrte
> War mein Haar noch nicht grau
> Da war ich froh.

> Die Mühen der Gebirge liegen hinter uns
> Vor uns liegen die Mühen der Ebenen. (*BFA* 15:205)

> [When I returned
> My hair was not yet grey
> And I was glad.

> The travails of the mountains lie behind us.
> Before us lie the travails of the plains. (*Poems* 415–16)]

Hugely combative yet very protective of his frail constitution, Brecht knowingly accepted the toils that the socialist state would surely have in store for him at a time when he could have chosen a much less arduous path for himself in the West of the German-speaking world. Yet Brecht found the challenge to participate in the establishment of a socialist Germany irresistible. He strongly supported key SED policies for economic and social transformation: land reform through the expropriation of large landowners, nationalization of key industries, and access to further and higher education for the working class. For Brecht, these changes set the GDR on a course quite different from an unregenerate Federal Republic. Yet he was also of the view that progress toward socialism was deeply compromised by the fact that the policies had been promulgated administratively from on high after the Allies' defeat of Nazism, not secured by the German people through revolutionary struggle. Indeed, Brecht himself rapidly came to experience a particular variant upon administrative diktat: SED cultural politicians' coercive hostility toward him personally in the imposition of their agenda.

Brecht's return was heralded in East Berlin with a special issue of the new journal *Sinn und Form*, which was dedicated to the work he had produced in exile, and with the production at the Deutsches Theater of *Mutter Courage und ihre Kinder* (Mother Courage and Her Children, 1939). Both were hailed as great successes. However, even then, before Brecht had actually settled in the city, Fritz Erpenbeck, the influential editor of the journal *Theater der Zeit*, was attacking *Mutter Courage* in terms that would become all too familiar.[8] Erpenbeck criticized the "negativity" of Brecht's work, particularly the absence of uplifting examples with which the audience could identify. Essentially the same charge was leveled in 1950 against Brecht's adaptation of Lenz's *Der Hofmeister* (The Tutor, 1774). Brecht used this adaptation to initiate his exploration of the *deutsche Misere* in the German classics and among German "bourgeois" intellectuals. This approach was quite consistent with Brecht's development but wholly at odds with the SED's self-legitimizing needs. The terms of engagement were set for the coming struggle.

Meanwhile, Brecht remained dogged by symptoms relating to his urological and cardiac conditions. His letters to Ruth Berlau from December 1950 and January 1951, when he was directing rehearsals for *Die Mutter* (The Mother, 1932), chart the recurrence of a bacterial infection, which left him exhausted. Initially, he quite typically emphasized not his own illness but that of the set designer Caspar Neher, claiming that he himself was just a bit tired (*BFA* 30:47). However, Brecht was soon writing that he had contracted a fever and was staying at home, where he had slept the whole day (*BFA* 30:48). On 12 January 1951, which saw the premiere of *Die Mutter*, he was still feeling weak and admitted defeat the following day (*BFA* 30:52). On 15 January Hüdepohl admitted Brecht to St. Hedwig's.

A note in a *BFA* volume edited by Werner Hecht misleadingly claims that Brecht was treated as an outpatient (*BFA* 27:564). Hecht does nothing to dispel this view when he restricts the entry on the matter in the *Brecht Chronik* to 15 January.[9] Brecht was in fact only allowed home on 27 January with a course of penicillin (*BFA* 27:318; *BFA* 30:54, 500). It has hence continued to escape critical attention that Brecht was hospitalized with a serious complaint at the very time when a concerted public attack was being launched upon him in the Formalism Campaign. That Brecht was in hospital cannot have been lost on his opponents in the same way as it has been lost on one of his editors.

Brecht's principal concern in mid-January 1951 was the production of the opera *Das Verhör des Lukullus* (The Trial of Lucullus, 1940). However, he wrote in his journal that the Ministry of Education had once more requested the score (*BFA* 27:317). Brecht was determined to maintain the planned production schedule in the face of the political pressure. However, on 20–21 January the SED launched the Formalism Campaign. First *Die Mutter* was singled out for criticism on account of its supposed formalism, then *Das Verhör des Lukullus*. On behalf of the Ministry for State Security, a request was made on 12 February that a seat should be reserved for one of its officers at the State Opera where *Das Verhör des Lukullus* was to be performed.[10] The Stasi's interest in Brecht can thus be dated from this point at latest. Since all records of that interest preserved in the Ministry appear to have been destroyed, only very limited conclusions can be drawn about the Stasi interest in Brecht. However, the SED leadership itself had a direct interest in the GDR's most prominent artistic personality. On 12 March the Secretariat of the SED Central Committee banned the public performance of *Das Verhör des Lukullus* and instructed that it should be removed from the repertoire of the State Opera. In the face of further attacks, Brecht and Dessau managed to secure a closed performance for an invited audience, which hailed the work a great success. Brecht thanked Walter Ulbricht and others for permitting the performance to take place. However, the ban was re-affirmed on 19 March.

Brecht viewed the SED's approach to cultural policy as wrong but as an understandable product of the time: "Es ist vorauszusehen, daß bei Umwälzungen von solchem Ausmaß die Künste selbst da in Schwierigkeiten kommen, wo sie führend mitwirken" (*BFA* 27:318; It is inevitable that during upheavals of these dimensions the arts will run into trouble even where they help to show the way ahead, *Journals* 433). Brecht's strategy was to seek a dialogue with Party figures in private meetings, demonstrating his preparedness to make alterations to his work, in the hope of persuading them to change direction. Brecht's strategy corresponded reasonably closely to the SED's own, which was to talk to Brecht in private, with a view to prevailing upon him to make corrections in keeping with the Party's position. The conversation about *Das Verhör des Lukullus* involved no less a person than the state President, Wilhelm Pieck, who invited Brecht to his home.[11] Brecht appeared to derive pleasure from the exchanges with Pieck and made alterations to the text. Brecht contrasted Pieck's intervention with the meddling of narrow-minded bureaucrats and took it as proof positive of the SED leadership's appreciation of the contribution that the arts had to make to GDR society.

Yet it became increasingly apparent that, while the respective parties agreed on the ends, they were fundamentally at odds about the means required to achieve those ends. The attacks on Brecht in the Formalism Campaign continued, while the surveillance increased. On 2 May 1951, the Politbüro of the SED Central Committee directed Wilhelm Girnus "mit Bert Brecht eine ständige politische Arbeit durchzuführen und ihm Hilfe zu leisten" (to undertake continuous political work with Bert Brecht and to provide him with help).[12] Girnus, the editor of the arts pages of *Neues Deutschland*, was one of the most forceful, feared, and dogmatic SED cultural politicians of the early 1950s. He reported upon his discussions with Brecht to Walter Ulbricht.[13] Brecht could be in no doubt that Girnus's attentions meant that he was under regular surveillance. The understanding of Brecht's interventions in cultural politics from May 1951 until the summer of 1953 certainly needs to take into account Brecht's "special relationship" with Girnus, particularly when considering Brecht's responses to Girnus's attacks on the Academy's Barlach exhibition and on Hanns Eisler's libretto *Johann Faustus* (Johann Faustus, 1953), which Eisler had produced in consultation with Brecht. Brecht's evident concern to maintain a dialogue with the SED leadership, mediated through his regular dialogue with Girnus, set limits to his criticisms until 17 June 1953. However, as we shall see, Girnus did not always accept Brecht's pieces for publication in *Neues Deutschland*.

Exposed to this continuing cultural-political pressure, Brecht was unable to recuperate. He would never recover. Amid concerns for his well-being, Brecht underwent an examination at the Charité hospital, which included x-rays of his lungs and his heart. The report upon the x-rays, dated 25 May 1951, indicates that Brecht was suffering from chronic heart failure. However, neither Brecht nor the doctors who treated him during the last year of his life showed any awareness of these findings. There is no indication in Brecht's frequent statements about his heart in 1955–56 that they were communicated to him.[14]

Efforts to marginalize Brecht increased. In June 1951, the SED's Cultural Department undertook an analysis of the achievements of the Academy of Arts. Noting that the Brechtian mode of theater was dominant, the Culture Department reported Ilse Rodenberg's view that Brecht was good, but that his methods must not be allowed to catch on. The Department added that the Performing Arts Section needed new Marxist blood.[15] Official complaints continued. On 25 July Erich Honecker requested the removal of Ernst Busch's name from Brecht's *Herrnburger Bericht* (Herrnburg Report, 1951; *BC* 974). In declining this request, Brecht addressed Honecker as Erich Honegger. On 3 August, Brecht wrote in his journal: "Immer noch erschöpft, arbeite ich an der Schreibmaschine doch die frühen Vormittage frisch" (*BFA* 27:324; still exhausted, i [*sic*] nevertheless work at the typewriter freshly in the early morning, *Journals* 439, trans. mod.). Typically, Brecht immediately looked for a way to turn debilitating exhaustion into freshness and strength. However, on 26 August his assistant Käthe Rülicke wrote in her diary that Brecht was really worn out and had not recuperated at all (*BC* 978). He was in a virtually permanent state of exhaustion. On 9 October Rülicke added:

> Brecht klagt über einen allgemeinen Schwächezustand. Er käme sich vor wie ein Nüchterner unter lauter Betrunkenen. Seine Kraft reiche kaum für die Proben aus, er sei mittags völlig erschöpft. — Er habe Depressionen, lebe eingleisig, sehr isoliert — habe andererseits Angst, durch Ablenkungen seinen Rhythmus zu unterbrechen. (*BFA* 27:568)
>
> [Brecht is complaining about a general state of weakness. He says that he feels like the only one who's sober among a lot of drunks; that he scarcely has the strength for rehearsals, by midday he's completely exhausted; that he's depressed and is living on a single track, very isolated; but that he's afraid of disrupting his rhythm through distractions.]

The socialist Germany of the GDR was proving to be a disorienting and dispiriting environment for an innovative artist for whom formulaic Socialist Realism was an unacceptable constraint. Despite his influence on theatrical life, Brecht was a marginalized figure, aware that his approach to dramatic art was anathema in official circles. Brecht was unable to attend the premiere of *Die Verurteilung des Lukullus* (The Condemnation of Lucullus), as the revised version of the opera was now called, because he had a fever (*BC* 984). According to Rülicke, the problem lingered on, leaving him in an exhausted, depressed state throughout that autumn (*BC* 988). In November Horst Bienek, Brecht's "Meister-

schüler" — or scholar — at the Berliner Ensemble, was arrested by the
security services and sentenced a year later to twenty-five years' hard
labor in Siberia. The specter of the Moscow trials loomed large in the
Eastern Bloc.

By January 1952, Rülicke was noting that after conducting two
rehearsals daily Brecht was worn out and needed to take care of himself
(*BC* 996). But there was no question of the driven Brecht being able to
let up. Official measures included a resolution of the Cultural Department of the SED's Central Committee that all Brecht's plays be removed
from the secondary school curriculum (*BC* 997). Shortly after, the
Cultural Department commissioned an "Exposé über die Arbeit des for-
malistischen Brecht-Kreises" (*BC* 1001; Memorandum about the Work
of the Formalist Brecht Circle). Girnus and the art critic Kurt Magritz
led vehement attacks on the exhibition of Ernst Barlach's "formalist"
sculptures at the Academy of Arts. Brecht confided to his journal words
that surely convey his own reduced state, namely that "die wenigen
verbliebenen Künstler in Lethargie geworfen wurden" (*BFA* 27:329; the
few surviving artists were cast into lethargy, *Journals* 441). Brecht responded publicly with a measured defense of Barlach's work, acknowledging its weaknesses as well as praising its strengths.[16] Girnus, however,
rejected Brecht's piece for publication in *Neues Deutschland*. It appeared
instead in *Sinn und Form*.

Despite his abiding exhaustion, Brecht continued to work and, on
occasion, to travel. However, on a visit to Warsaw he had to severely
curtail his program (*BFA* 30:115).[17] In March 1952 Rülicke urged
Brecht to think of himself and go to Hüdepohl.[18] Brecht tended to put
off the distressing clinical procedure to deal with his stricture even
though, as we have seen, the corollary was his near-permanent exhaust-
tion and related symptoms. In addition to treatment by Hüdepohl at St.
Hedwig's, in early May Brecht again had to visit the Charité for a procedure that could not be deferred any longer (*BFA* 30:124). Rülicke
wrote that she had never seen Brecht so nervous, bitter, and unfair
toward others as he was afterwards, when he remained plagued by pains
(*BC* 1014–15). Brecht excused himself from the GDR Writers' Congress
in Berlin and declined an invitation to join the executive, citing his
doctor's advice that he should take it easy for a considerable time (*BFA*
30:124).

Brecht worked with Erwin Strittmatter on the latter's comedy
Katzgraben (1953) in the attempt to produce a dramatic work that dealt
with the early GDR's radical social and economic changes from a
strongly supportive position.[19] For the depiction of individualized

characters contributing to these historic upheavals, Brecht needed a different approach from the familiar Brechtian caricature adopted in the interrogation of the *deutsche Misere*. Brecht looked to Stanislavsky's writings for stimulus.[20] In the 1930s Brecht had opposed Stanislavsky's dramatic theories. Now, however, his needs were different, both dramatically and also in terms of cultural-political strategy, since Stanislavsky was being actively promoted in official quarters as a model for GDR drama in opposition to Brecht.

At Buckow, Brecht initially mustered fresh energy for *Katzgraben*, rising at 6:00 a.m. and working with Rülicke from 8:00 a.m. to 2:00 p.m., then again in the evening for two to three hours (*BC* 1021–22). However, four years to the day before Brecht died, Rülicke noted: "Manchmal erschrecke ich, wie grau und zusammengefallen Brecht morgens aussieht [. . .]. Mir ist erst hier klargeworden, daß Brecht alt wird — vorzeitig eigentlich." (*BC* 1025; Sometimes I am frightened how gray and broken-down Brecht looks in the morning. It has only become clear to me here that Brecht is growing old — prematurely in fact.) It was not only that Brecht's hair had turned gray. The SED's pressure upon him since his hospitalization in January 1951 had undoubtedly accelerated the aging process. Around this time, Brecht began to reflect on impending death: "Ich, Bertolt Brecht, Sohn bürgerlicher Eltern / Hab diesen Sommer im Gefühl, die Zeit sei knapp / Durchblättert mein Gewissen" (*BFA* 15:263; I, Bertolt Brecht, the son of bourgeois parents / Have leafed through my conscience this summer / With the feeling that time is short).[21] Brecht further curtailed his activities, writing to the organizers of the Peoples' Congress for the Protection of Peace in Vienna that he could not attend because his doctor forbade it (*BFA* 30:153). Meanwhile, Hüdepohl admitted Brecht for a clinical procedure from 29 January to 9 February 1953 (*BC* 1044).

17 June 1953: An Improbable, Short-Lived Victory

A fresh phase of hostilities against Brecht began, which culminated in the momentous events around 17 June 1953. In this extreme situation, despite his straitened circumstances, Brecht for the last time demonstrated his great mental energy and agility. The SED's Construction of the Foundations of Socialism was intended to signal an end to the "compromises" in the arts.[22] Brecht and the Academy of Arts were twin targets that were brought into a single focus in a campaign orchestrated by Alexander Abusch. As a Jewish "western émigré," Abusch had been stripped of all his Party responsibilities and had then been recruited by the Stasi to combat the influence of "western émigrés" and Trotskyism, though not directly Brecht and the Academy.[23] However, Abusch ensured that Brecht was confronted in a concerted fashion on those very issues where the SED's need for self-legitimation clashed with Brecht's artistic theory and practice. In an act that undermined the Academy's authority, the State Commission for Artistic Affairs announced that on 17–19 April the Academy would be the venue for the First German Stanislavsky Conference. It was an open secret that the event was designed as an attack on Brechtian theater through which Brecht would be forced to recant his theoretical position. Some people believed the liquidation of the Berliner Ensemble to be on the agenda.[24]

It counted for nothing that Brecht himself was looking for common ground with Stanislavsky in rehearsals for *Katzgraben*. Intimidation of Brecht included the Stasi's arrest of another of Brecht's "Meister-schüler," Martin Pohl, who was subjected to sleep deprivation and forced to sign a dictated confession, which he later retracted.[25] Brecht intervened on Pohl's behalf until he was released in 1955. In its resigned, weary tone Brecht's journal entry of 4 March 1953 echoes the entry after the attack on Barlach:

> Unsere Aufführungen in Berlin haben fast kein Echo mehr. In der Presse erscheinen Kritiken Monate nach der Erstaufführung, und es steht nichts drin, außer ein paar kümmerlichen soziologischen Analysen. Das Publikum ist das Kleinbürgerpublikum der Volksbühne, Arbeiter machen da kaum sieben Prozent aus. Die Bemühungen sind nur dann nicht ganz sinnlos, wenn die Spielweise späterhin aufgenommen werden kann, d.h. wenn ihr Lehrwert einmal realisiert wird. (Das gilt, obwohl wir alles tun, für jetzt, für die Theaterabende, für das Publikum von jetzt unser Bestes zu liefern.) (*BFA* 27:346)

> [our performances in berlin have almost no resonance any more. the press notices appear months after the first night, and there is never anything in them anyway apart from a few pathetic bits of sociological analysis. the public is the petty bourgeois public of the volksbühne, workers make up scarcely 7% of it. the effort will only be worthwhile if the manner of acting can be taken up later, i.e. when its didactic value has been realized. (this is true, although we, here and now, put all we can into our theatre evenings and do the best we can for the public we have at the moment.) (*Journals* 454; lower case in original)]

Brecht, for whom intervention in the pressing matters of the day was a matter of artistic principle, found himself in the German socialist state working once more for posterity.

Helene Weigel protected Brecht, as she often did, by representing the Berliner Ensemble against the weight of official voices at the Stanislavsky Conference. Brecht was subjected to pressure on a second front when Abusch orchestrated a new regular discussion forum in the Academy, the Mittwoch-Gesellschaften. The first item for debate was Eisler's *Johann Faustus*. Girnus joined Abusch and others in the deeply coercive atmosphere for a concerted assault on the "Brecht faction." But wholly improbably, Brecht and his supporters turned the tables when the strikes and demonstrations of 16–17 June shattered the SED's fragile authority.

There was no question of Brecht placing himself at the head of a popular movement for reform. Indeed, Brecht re-affirmed his support for the SED leadership's achievements. Brecht was, however, instrumentally involved in the formulation of the Academy's recommendations to reform cultural policy.[26] The principal target was the cultural bureaucracy, the baleful effects of which Brecht and others like Eisler and Arnold Zweig had experienced.[27] When publication of the recommendations was blocked, Brecht threatened to resign from the Academy. Publication followed in *Neues Deutschland*.[28] The *Berliner Zeitung* then published Brecht's scathingly satirical poems "Nicht feststellbare Fehler der Kunstkommission" (Unidentifiable Errors of the Arts Commission) and "Das Amt für Literatur" (The Office for Literature). Brecht discussed his piece "Kulturpolitik und Akademie der Künste" (Cultural Policy and the Academy of Arts) with Girnus at Buckow. It contained outspoken criticism of the cultural bureaucracy. Girnus, now on the defensive, published it without delay in *Neues Deutschland*.

Girnus's record of the conversation for Ulbricht reveals the depth of Brecht's concerns.[29] Brecht had dismissed the SED's entire cultural policy as wrong. He had insisted that the Shdanovite measures deployed in Stalin's Soviet Union were wholly inappropriate for the GDR and that the Formalism Campaign was a Nazi phenomenon, as was the SED's use of the term "Volk." Brecht was plagued by the deep fear that the SED was contributing to a resurgence of Nazism by pandering to an unreconstructed institutional and popular racism. This fear informs Brecht's famous journal entry, "Der 17. Juni hat die ganze Existenz verfremdet" (*BFA* 27:346; 17th june has alienated the whole of existence, *Journals* 454). Immediately preceding that entry are references to Brecht's most important poetic and dramatic responses to 17 June, the *Buckower Elegien* (Buckow Elegies, 1953) and *Turandot oder Der Kongreß der Weißwäscher* (Turandot or The Whitewashers' Congress, 1953). Brecht enlarged upon his fears in the "Vorwort zu *Turandot*"

(Foreword to Turandot, 1953), which concludes: "Unter neuen Befehlshabern setzte sich also der Naziapparat wieder in Bewegung. [. . .] Unüberzeugt, aber feige, feindlich, aber sich duckend, begannen verknöcherte Beamte wieder gegen die Bevölkerung zu regieren" (*BFA* 24:410; So, under the new commanders, the Nazi apparatus once more set itself in motion. [. . .] Unconvinced but cowardly, hostile but cowering, ossified officials began again to govern against the population, *BAP* 336).

Brecht's critique of the continuity of such a pernicious mentality informs Brecht's reworking of the *Turandot* material, his exploration during the Weimar Republic and exile of the false consciousness of intellectuals, whom he labeled "Tuis." The Tui Ka Mü remarks: "Und dies hier ist neue Musik. Die wird verfolgt, weil sie nicht volkstümlich ist" (*BFA* 9:183; And this is new music. It's in trouble because it's not "true to the spirit of the people," *Plays* 8:184). Brecht's earlier confident, satirical treatment of the theme is superseded in the burlesque of *Turandot* by the sobering experience of Stalinist power politics and of the fledgling German socialist state. Henceforth, Brecht's hopes for world revolution rested not with the Soviet Union and the Eastern Bloc but with China.

After the momentous events of the summer, in November 1953 Brecht's thoughts turned once more to the prospect of impending death. In a document that he placed in an envelope for Helene Weigel to open after the event, he stipulated what was to be done after his death.[30] In 1954, Brecht acknowledged for the first time that his creative powers and intellectual resilience were failing him (*BFA* 27:362). His slight frame had become bloated, as had his face. This can be readily attributed to his deteriorating medical state.[31] *Turandot* and other dramatic projects like *Büsching*, which dealt with the economic and social development of the GDR, remained unfinished. After struggling with *Büsching*, Brecht was forced to concede to his "Meisterschüler" Claus Küchenmeister and his wife Wera: "Ich kann nicht mehr, das müßt ihr Jungen weitermachen." (*BC* 1117; I can't do it anymore. You younger people have got to take things forward.) He noted wistfully: "Natürlich war ich auch begabt, vor vierzig Jahren besonders." (*BFA* 1:573; Of course I was gifted too, particularly forty years ago.) Brecht's extraordinary intellectual energy was nearly spent. The irony is that this occurred just as he achieved the international acclaim that he craved: in 1954, the Berliner Ensemble's performance of *Mutter Courage* was hailed for its transformative impact on world theater, when the company was awarded first prize at the Théâtre des Nations festival in Paris. At a time when the

GDR had few friends abroad, the SED leadership could bask in the reflected glory of Brecht's renown. However, Brecht's success in the West, not to mention his award of the Stalin Prize the following year, changed nothing in the GDR. In 1955, as the attacks gained fresh momentum, he saw his life as threatened by the forces ranged against him: "Daß du untergehst, wenn du dich nicht wehrst / Das wirst du doch einsehen" (*BFA* 15:295; That you'll go down if you don't stand up for yourself / Surely you see that, *Poems* 452).[32] The summer of 1955 saw the onset of Brecht's final, protracted illness. After contracting a bacterial infection that affected his kidneys, then spread to his heart, triggering endocarditis and septicemia, he died of chronic heart failure.[33]

As we have seen, Brecht was destined for an early death, come what may. However, the concerted campaign of public attacks, surveillance, and intrigue that the SED leadership conducted against him undoubtedly accelerated the aging process. As a result, Brecht's life and work were certainly impaired. If further material comes to light, it is likely that it will confirm the strong impression that the actions of the SED leadership served to curtail Brecht's life's work.[34]

Notes

This essay was written during the tenure of a Major Research Fellowship awarded by the Leverhulme Trust.

[1] Fritz Cremer's story, told to the journalist Rudy Hassing, is included in John Fuegi, *The Life and Lies of Bertolt Brecht* (London: Harper Collins, 1994), 606.

[2] See Peter Davies and Stephen Parker, "Brecht, SED Cultural Policy and the Issue of Authority in the Arts: The Struggle for Control of the German Academy of Arts," in *Bertolt Brecht: Centenary Essays*, ed. Steve Giles and Rodney Livingstone (Amsterdam and Atlanta: Rodopi, 1998), 181–95; Peter Davies, *Divided Loyalties: East German Writers and the Politics of German Division 1945–1953* (Leeds: Maney, 2000).

[3] Stephen Parker, "What was the Cause of Brecht's Death? Towards a Medical History," *Brecht Yearbook* 35 (2010): 291–307. Subsequent discussion of Brecht's medical history draws upon this article unless otherwise indicated.

[4] Brecht's undated letter to Hans Albers is in BBA 507/81. It is estimated that the letter was written in 1947. Subsequent references to files from the BBA are given in the main body of the text.

[5] In a further draft Viertel thought better of asking such a personal question and omitted it. The drafts of Viertel's letter to Brecht of 10 August 1948 are in Deutsches Literaturarchiv Marbach in A: Viertel, 69.2031/1–3.

[6] For details of Hüdepohl's career, see Slatomir Joachim Wenske, *Die Herausbildung urologischer Kliniken in Berlin. Ein Beitrag zur Berliner Medizingeschichte* (PhD diss., Charité — Universitätsmedizin Berlin, 2008), 132.

[7] In August 1953 Brecht supported Hüdepohl's nomination for the award of "Verdienter Arzt des Volkes" (*BFA* 30:190 and 555; Doctor of the People of Merit). In February 1955 Brecht wrote to Otto Grotewohl about Hüdepohl, pleading that Hüdepohl should be awarded an individual contract, for which he would not normally be eligible because he worked in a private hospital (*BFA* 30:308). Brecht explained that at St. Hedwig's Hüdepohl only earned the salary of an actor, as a result of which, despite being greatly overworked, he had to perform operations in the West, where he lived. In fact, Hüdepohl had no intention of leaving West Berlin for the Eastern part of the city, where he had severely restricted his activity, and in 1956 he accepted an appointment in West Berlin (*BFA* 30:638).

[8] The following section draws upon Davies/Parker, 183.

[9] Werner Hecht, *Brecht Chronik 1898–1956* (Frankfurt a.M.: Suhrkamp, 1997), 945. Subsequent references to this work are cited in the text using the abbreviation *BC* and page number.

[10] *Das Verhör in der Oper: Die Debatte um Brecht/Dessaus "Lukullus" 1951*, ed. Joachim Lucchesi (Berlin: BasisDruck: 1993), 66–67.

[11] Lucchesi, 185. Pieck also invited his comrades Grotewohl, Wandel, Ackermann, and Lauter.

[12] Lucchesi, 220–21.

[13] On occasion, Brecht worked together with Girnus, the latter wearing his hat as editor of *Neues Deutschland*. See *BC* 1021.

[14] Given Girnus's role and Mielke's boast (see note 34 below), it is conceivable — though it must be stressed that no evidence has as yet come to light — that the findings about this prominent figure were passed on to the authorities and that they were aware of Brecht's condition. In that case, they would have known more than Brecht and the doctors treating him during the final year of his life, particularly that Brecht's urological and cardiac conditions meant that he would most likely die quite soon. The SED's ongoing campaign against Brecht would, of course, take on a more sinister character still if seen in such a light.

[15] *"Die Regierung ruft die Künstler": Dokumente zur Gründung der "Deutschen Akademie der Künste" (DDR) 1945–1953*, ed. Petra Uhlmann and Sabine Wolf (Berlin: Henschel, 1993), 171.

[16] For a balanced appreciation of Brecht's defense of Barlach, see Matthew Philpotts, *The Margins of Dictatorship: Assent and Dissent in the Work of Günter Eich and Bertolt Brecht* (Oxford: Peter Lang, 2003), 299–305.

[17] Marcel Reich-Ranicki, who met Brecht in his hotel room, could see no evidence of any illness. See Marcel Reich-Ranicki, *Ungeheuer oben: Über Bertolt Brecht* (Berlin: Aufbau, 1996), 103.

[18] Rülicke's unpublished letter to Brecht of 21 March 1952 is in BBA 972/113.

[19] Strittmatter's wartime service in the "Ordnungspolizei," which was assigned to the SS, was recently discovered. See Werner Liersch, "Erwin Strittmatters unbekannter Krieg," *Frankfurter Allgemeine Sonntagszeitung*, 8 June 2008.

[20] Philpotts, 278–81.

[21] This and later statements show the untenability of Werner Mittenzwei's contention that Brecht did not begin to countenance death until shortly before the event. See Werner Mittenzwei, *Das Leben des Bertolt Brecht oder: Der Umgang mit den Welträtseln*, 3rd edn (East Berlin and Weimar: Aufbau, 1988), 2:655–56.

[22] The present section follows Davies/Parker, 185.

[23] *Wer war wer in der DDR*, ed. Bernd-Rainer Barth et al. (Frankfurt a.M.: Fischer, 1995), 13.

[24] Werner Hecht, "Das Vergnügen an einer ernsten Sache: Ein Leben im Dienste Brecht — Erinnerungen von und an Käthe Rülicke," *Der Tagesspiegel* (Berlin), 3 November 1992, cited by Philpotts, 280.

[25] *Denken heißt verändern: Erinnerungen an Brecht*, ed. Joachim Lang and Jürgen Hillesheim (Augsburg: Maro, 1998), 131. The Pohl case provides a plausible background for Mielke's comments about Brecht's alleged accusations of Stasi malpractice.

[26] The present section follows Davies/Parker, 191–92. The recommendations were first discussed at an Academy plenary on 26 June 1953. In *BFA* 23:549–50 the meeting is dated 16 June and the discussion placed in the context of the New Course without reference to 17 June. In Werner Hecht, *Brecht Chronik: Ergänzungen* (Frankfurt a.M.: Suhrkamp, 2007), 111, Hecht dates the meeting 26 June 1952. This is not an isolated dating error on Hecht's part in that work concerning the events in the Academy around 17 June. For example, Hecht (121) dates the meeting of the Academy commission concerning the future of *Sinn und Form* as 2 June, a month before the meeting actually took place. See Parker, "*Sinn und Form*, Peter Huchel und der 17. Juni: Bertolt Brechts Rettungsaktion," *Sinn und Form* 46, no. 5 (1994): 738–51, here 747.

[27] Although Abusch was not required to report upon the Academy to the Stasi, he reported upon the positions energetically taken up by Brecht and his supporters against the cultural bureaucracy and against Abusch himself after 17 June. See Matthias Braun, *Kulturinsel und Machtinstrument: Die Akademie der Künste, die Partei und die Staatssicherheit* (Göttingen: Vandenhoeck & Ruprecht, 2007), 76–77.

[28] Hecht, *Brecht Chronik: Ergänzungen*, 123–24.

[29] Girnus's letter to Ulbricht of 27 July 1953 is summarized in *BC* 1070–71.

[30] The document bearing the date November 1953 in Brecht's hand is in the collection of papers recently acquired by Augsburg city library from Barbara Brecht-Schall. Hitherto this document has been attributed to the same period of time as Brecht's letter of 15 May 1955 to Rudolf Engel, the administrative director of the East Berlin Academy, in which Brecht sets out arrangements for his funeral. This dating is no longer tenable.

[31] When Bernhard Reich saw Brecht in Moscow in May 1955 for the first time in fourteen years, Brecht had changed a lot in appearance. His face was broad and his body stocky. See *BC* 1166.

[32] In similar fashion to Brecht's attack on the cultural bureaucracy after 17 June 1953, members of the Berliner Ensemble took the fight to the enemy with pieces in *Theater der Zeit*. Hans Bunge countered Erpenbeck's negative review of *Der kaukasische Kreidekreis* (The Caucasian Chalk Circle, 1944) and Erpenbeck's critique of epic theater in general. Manfred Wekwerth and Peter Palitzsch similarly countered Günter Kaltofen's critical review of the production of Becher's *Winterschlacht* (Battle in Winter, 1942). See *BC* 1154.

[33] See Parker, "What was the Cause of Brecht's Death?" for details of Brecht's treatment from the summer of 1955 until his death.

[34] The recent discovery of a sound recording of an in-house address by Deputy Minister for State Security Erich Mielke to senior Stasi officers shortly after Brecht's death can only add to that impression. Mielke departed from his prepared text to boast: "Ich möchte eins der krassesten Beispiele bringen, Genossen, weil es wichtig ist, dass man als Staatssicherheitsmann, nich' wahr, genau weiß, wie diese Brüder gedacht haben. . . : dass also in der Staatssicherheit die Verhafteten geschlagen und misshandelt worden sind, auch hier in der DDR. (Pause) Und dass deshalb also der bekannte Schriftsteller (Pause) und, äh, Dramaturg Brecht Strafantrag stellen wollte gegen also einen leitenden Funktionär der Staatssicherheit. Und dann ist der Brecht erlegen einen [*sic*] Herzschlag." (I'd like to give you one of the crassest examples, comrades, because it's important, isn't it, that we state security men know what these fellows have been thinking . . .: that the state security has been beating and abusing prisoners, here in the GDR too [pause]. And that for this reason the well-known writer [pause] and, erm, dramaturge Brecht wanted to bring criminal charges against a leading functionary of the state security. And then Brecht succumbed to a heart attack.) In the final sentence Mielke, seemingly knowingly, placed the emphasis on "dann" (then). See Peter von Becker, "Erich Mielke und des Dichters Herzschlag," *Der Tagesspiegel* (Berlin), 15 August 2006. No documents have emerged hitherto that directly substantiate Mielke's boast.

Brecht and 17 June 1953: A Reassessment

Patrick Harkin, University of Edinburgh

THE UPRISING OF 17 June in the German Democratic Republic was inevitably instrumentalized on different fronts in the Cold War. In the GDR, it was portrayed as a Western plot to undermine the first Workers' and Peasants' State on German soil. In the West, it was commonly held that the people of the GDR had risen up against a repressive communist regime, only to be bloodily crushed by Soviet tanks. Each side in this ideological standoff flatly rejected the other's interpretation, or indeed any interpretation that did not concur with its own.

Bertolt Brecht's views did not fit neatly into either narrative. In the GDR, he was regarded with hostility and suspicion in official circles: his views were inimical to the GDR's ruling Socialist Unity Party (SED), because they focused on the failure of its disastrous policies and the need for widespread reform. In the West, his robust defense of the GDR system of beliefs rankled, and accounts of his actions on 17 June attracted venomous comment and retaliation in sociopolitical and cultural circles. Yet these accounts were constructed from a hotchpotch of facts, rumors, and legends. They are incomplete and inaccurate. In this essay, I will establish what we know of Brecht's actions on 17 June and consider subsequent criticisms of his conduct. The main body of the essay will then explore Brecht's views concerning 17 June and his analysis of its causes and consequences, as evidenced in diary entries, letters, and other texts that he wrote in the summer of 1953. Contrary to the common view that Brecht was complicit in the SED's suppression of its own people,[1] these texts demonstrate that he adopted a far more oppositional stance toward the regime, and that a reassessment of this stance is overdue.

Brecht on 17 June: Establishing the Facts

Brecht left no personal record of how he spent the day of 17 June, so we have to rely on the memoirs of his friends and colleagues and the available archive material. Since he is forever marked by his actions on 17 June, it is imperative to sift the material carefully to construct a credible account of his day. This task is not made easier by inconsistencies between statements by different eyewitnesses and critics. For example, Brecht's colleague Manfred Wekwerth claims that Brecht spoke to the Berliner Ensemble (BE) staff for an hour around 1:00 p.m. on 17 June, whereas the critic Meredith Heiser-Duron notes that the meeting lasted for a mere ten minutes (although she does not indicate the source of her information).[2] The actor Erwin Geschonneck recalls chairing a meeting of the BE's staff on 17 June at which Brecht's wife Helene Weigel spoke, but she was at a conference in Budapest on that day.[3] Confusion also surrounds Brecht's words and actions as the Soviet tanks rolled onto the streets of East Berlin. Wekwerth wrote a letter in the late 1960s in which he stated that Brecht had waved to the tanks when he was on the streets.[4] However, he seems to be vaguer about this in his memoirs. There is no mention of Brecht waving to the tanks; indeed, he expresses skepticism concerning reports that Brecht said or did anything of an exhortatory nature.[5] Werner Mittenzwei also writes, in his account of Brecht's life, that the latter had waved to the Soviet tank crews, but makes no further comment.[6] There are further puzzling instances of omission and commission. For example, on the afternoon of 17 June, Brecht attended an impromptu meeting of the Academy of the Arts. The meeting and Brecht's presence are noted by a number of critics and clearly minuted in the Academy's records.[7] Yet Mittenzwei, Fuegi, Wekwerth, and Geschonneck fail to mention the meeting. In fact, according to Mittenzwei, Brecht returned home at around 2:00 p.m. with some colleagues to discuss and review the day's events (*LBB* 499). It is strange that Mittenzwei and Fuegi, Brecht's major biographers, should have ignored this crucial event in his itinerary.

These inconsistencies, whether due to authorial partiality or the receding memory of eyewitnesses, reinforce the impression that Brecht's conduct on 17 June was at times shrouded in uncertainty and that its interpretation requires more care than has often been exercised. The inconsistencies are not, however, so irreconcilable that we cannot construct a reasonably accurate account of his movements on 17 June.

Brecht returned from Buckow to his Berlin home in Weißensee on the evening of 16 June. Throughout the day, Peter Palitzsch, a director at the BE, had kept him informed by telephone of developments in the city.[8] Brecht invited his colleagues Käthe Rülicke, Wekwerth, and Palitzsch to Weißensee to discuss the day's events. Wekwerth was astonished to hear Brecht say he would arm the workers to protect them not only from resurgent fascists but also from the government (*EL* 110). If Brecht did volunteer this suggestion, it indicates just how far he underestimated the seriousness of the situation. It is inconceivable that he would have proposed arming the workers after he had seen the numbers and events on the streets the following day.

Early on 17 June, Brecht drove with his overnight guests to the venue on Reinhardtstraße used for the BE's rehearsals. He seems to have spoken to the theater's staff, urging them to demonstrate support for the government (*LBB* 492–93). Like everyone else in the GDR, Brecht would have heard the running commentary of events being transmitted by the US-controlled Radio in the American Sector (RIAS). In the first of several attempts on 17 June to galvanize GDR radio to counter these transmissions, Brecht sent Wekwerth and Elisabeth Hauptmann to offer the BE's services to the radio authorities: according to Wekwerth, they met with derisive laughter (*EL* 111).

Around this time, Brecht decided to rush off letters to Walter Ulbricht, General Secretary of the SED; his deputy, Otto Grotewohl; Vladimir Semyonov, head of the Soviet forces in the GDR; and Gustav Just, then responsible for art and culture in the Central Committee of the SED.

The four letters incorporated three ideas: solidarity with the SED and the Soviet Union in the letters to Ulbricht, Grotewohl, and Semyonov; the need for dialogue between the Party and the people in the letter to Ulbricht; and, in the letters to Grotewohl and Just, constructive deployment of the media, and radio in particular, as a communication tool.

Brecht's letter to Ulbricht was his most significant action of the day in terms of its consequences. The letter read:

> Die Geschichte wird der revolutionären Ungeduld der Sozialistischen Einheitspartei Deutschlands ihren Respekt zollen.
>
> Die große Aussprache mit den Massen über das Tempo des sozialistischen Aufbaus wird zu einer Sichtung und zu einer Sicherung der sozialistischen Errungenschaften führen.
>
> Es ist mir ein Bedürfnis, Ihnen in diesem Augenblick meine Verbundenheit mit der Sozialistischen Einheitspartei Deutschlands auszudrücken. (*BFA* 30:178)

[History will pay its respects to the revolutionary impatience of the Socialist Unity Party of Germany.

The great debate with the masses about the tempo of socialist construction will have the effect of testing and safeguarding the achievements of socialism.

At this moment I feel I must assure you of my allegiance to the Socialist Unity Party of Germany. (*Letters* 515–16, trans. mod.)]

The first paragraph, couched in ideological vocabulary, was little more than a formulaic expression of optimism that the Party would prevail. The call for a great debate, reflected in the second paragraph, was to become a familiar mantra over the next few months, but at this stage, no criticism of the Party was implied. Brecht was simply writing what the Party leadership itself was saying. It was the final sentence that was to whip up a storm of antipathy toward Brecht in the West from which he would never fully recover. When Ulbricht had an edited version of the letter published on 21 June in the Central Committee's official newspaper *Neues Deutschland*, only this final sentence, pledging solidarity with the SED, was printed. Clearly, Ulbricht sought to gain maximum benefit from a public expression of support by such a cultural luminary. No doubt he felt that the inclusion of the first two sentences would have added little, indeed, might even have detracted from the overall effect he, Ulbricht, wished to achieve.

It is generally maintained that Brecht walked around the streets at midday, arriving back in time for the pre-arranged 1:00 p.m. meeting with the BE's staff.[9] There are no reliable accounts of what he said at this meeting, but we do have the minutes of an impromptu meeting that he attended later that afternoon at the Academy of Arts. They show that he blocked a proposal to send a declaration of confidence to the government, indicating that his attitude had shifted away from his earlier inclination to demonstrate support for the regime.[10] I will return to this meeting later: suffice it to say at this point that Brecht's action was hardly in keeping with the sentiments in the edited letter that appeared in *Neues Deutschland*.

The Academy minutes mark the last impartial information we have on Brecht's 17 June. Wekwerth maintains that he and Brecht listened to an evening radio transmission in which the truncated version of Brecht's letter to Ulbricht was read out (*EL* 114). In light of other evidence, this seems most unlikely. According to other historical sources, Rülicke returned with Brecht to his house in Weißensee; she subsequently recalled that he did not think the Party leadership would survive the day.[11] Whether he said this in a mood of despair or hope is not recorded.

We have a reasonably clear picture, then, of how Brecht conducted himself on 17 June. It seems strange that he, who rarely did anything rash, should have sent off letters before he had actually seen and assessed the events on the streets. His precipitous action does appear to be that of someone caught unawares. Instinctively, he judged from the reports coming in from RIAS and his own colleagues that the GDR was in danger and the Party needed unconditional loyalty during this hour of need. As a natural communicator, he was convinced of the necessity to confront and expose RIAS propaganda. Beyond this, the letters did not actually say a great deal. It was only later, after he had been on the streets and discussed matters with the BE staff, that reason took over from instinct. It seems perverse, therefore, to judge Brecht's conduct on 17 June on the basis of these letters rather than on his more deliberate reflections.

It was, however, the letter to Ulbricht, or more accurately, the version of the letter that appeared in *Neues Deutschland*, that excited vehement reaction. In the West, there was a widely held view that Brecht had been complicit in state repression, propping up an undemocratic regime. In the immediate aftermath of 17 June, his plays were routinely withdrawn from Western theaters.[12] Peter Suhrkamp, his West German publisher, wrote to him on 30 June, warning him that the Western boycott of his plays had already begun (BBA 0787/058–59). Mittenzwei writes of wild speculation and a poisonous hate campaign waged against Brecht (*LBB* 495 and 506). Nor was the antipathy short-term. Following the Hungarian Uprising of 1956 and the erection of the Berlin Wall in 1961, renewed efforts were made in West Germany to enforce boycotts of Brecht's work.[13] In the Bundestag in 1957, the year after Brecht's death, the West German Foreign Minister, Heinrich von Brentano, likened Brecht's poems to the Nazi Horst Wessel Song (a charge he repeated in 1973). Carola Stern links antipathy toward Brecht directly with the Cold War: every time the East-West conflict flared up, a Brecht boycott was recommended in West Germany.[14]

Most of the vitriol directed at Brecht in the years after 1953 emanated from politicians and the press, but Western intellectuals also contributed. A notable example was Günter Grass's play *Die Plebejer proben den Aufstand* (The Plebeians Rehearse the Uprising), first performed in West Berlin in January 1966.[15] The play is set in the BE's rehearsal rooms on 17 June 1953. The Boss is directing a rehearsal of his adaptation of Shakespeare's *Coriolanus*, an adaptation that reflects his own ideological views. In Shakespeare's play, Coriolanus is a tragic but noble figure and the plebeians are coarse and mean, but the Boss's version reverses the characterizations: the workers are noble and their ultimate victory over the exploitative Coriolanus is assured. However, when the Boss is confronted by real-life workers demanding real-life justice, he is unable to translate his fine principles into practice. When striking workers force their way into the theater and urge him to apply his literary and political skills to help them get their message across to the Party and public, he prevaricates. Subsequently, at the behest of a functionary, he writes a note of solidarity with the government, in order to preserve his theater. The Boss seems to grow to regret not having supported the workers and, with an air of resignation, goes off to his country retreat to write poetry.

Grass has always maintained that the play was not an attack on Brecht per se, but on the failure of GDR intellectuals in 1953, or indeed on the failure of all German intellectuals to oppose the GDR and the Third Reich.[16] While this may be a valid reading of the play, it is hardly the most obvious one. The Boss in Grass's play seems clearly modeled on Brecht, in which case the play is a direct and personal attack on him. He caves in to Party demands rather than supporting the workers in their search for justice, preferring to exploit them as dramatic fodder, all in the cause of his own cynical self-interest. This was how the play was widely interpreted, in both East and West, when it first appeared.[17] Marcel Reich-Ranicki, for example, argued that it was impossible to watch Grass's Boss and not conclude that the character was the incarnation of Brecht.[18] And two years before publishing the play, Grass had actually given a lecture to the West Berlin Academy of Arts and Letters in which he referred to Brecht's thoughts and actions on 17 June in such a way as to make it quite explicit that the Boss was Brecht and the Boss's actions were Brecht's.[19] Whatever Grass's subsequent claims regarding his intentions, the play was widely seen as a disparaging and damaging commentary by a Western intellectual on Brecht's behavior on 17 June.

In the East, reaction to Brecht's actions and comments in the wake of 17 June was more muted. In the weeks following the uprising, Brecht engaged in a public battle with the cultural bureaucracy, and he and his colleagues won a few concessions from the authorities. In the ensuing general thaw in relationships between the Party leadership and intellectuals that lasted until the end of 1956 and therefore until after Brecht's death, the relentless persecution of Brecht eased off. It was, however, an uneasy truce: the old complex love-hate relationship endured. Brecht won the Stalin Peace Prize in 1954 but his plays were hardly ever staged outside the Berliner Ensemble.[20] As Stephen Parker has explained earlier in this volume, Brecht's health worsened markedly toward the end of

1953. Clearly, this would have weakened his appetite for further resistance to the authorities, and their need for further preoccupation with him.

The Eastern and Western views were not, then, so very far apart, although they were grounded in the opposing certainties of the Cold War. Underlying the Western view was the belief that Brecht was not driven by his socialist convictions, but rather by narrow personal interests. The Eastern view was also that the strength of Brecht's socialist ardor was suspect. Both views were informed by the thoughts and words of cultural and political elites on either side of the Cold War divide. Neither view is supported by Brecht's own thoughts and actions.

Brecht in His Own Words

In one respect, an examination of Brecht's own thoughts on the subject of 17 June is reasonably straightforward, because the body of texts in which he engages with it is restricted to no more than a score of individual texts. The earliest of these is a statement that was dated 21 June and that appeared two days later in *Neues Deutschland*; it is known by the title "Dringlichkeit einer großen Aussprache" (The Urgent Need for a Major Discussion). The statement demonstrates Brecht's fury at the fact that his letter to Ulbricht had been so blatantly exploited, and it represents an attempt to set the public record straight. While Brecht confirmed that he had indeed declared his solidarity with the SED on the morning of 17 June, the turgid aphorisms of the original letter were replaced with a sharper and altogether more direct language. Brecht conceded that provocateurs had been present on the streets, but it was now his view that the workers' unhappiness was entirely understandable, and that it was imperative to start a public dialogue about the many mistakes that had been made on all sides (*BFA* 23:250). Whether Brecht knew it or not, this was directly at odds with the narrative Ulbricht was already constructing, and it seems surprising that *Neues Deutschland* allowed its publication. One possible explanation is that at the time a deadly power struggle was unfolding in the Politbüro between Ulbricht and Rudolf Herrnstadt. Herrnstadt was not only a member of the Politbüro; he was also the editor of *Neues Deutschland*.[21]

This statement marked Brecht's first considered analysis of the causes of 17 June and the measures now required to restore order and advance socialism. Here he clearly identified government errors as a key cause of the disturbances, and communication between the government and the people as the urgent remedy. At a series of meetings with BE staff on

24–26 June, he further explored this failure in communication, identifying it as one of the Party's gravest mistakes. Because the Party had prohibited any discussion of the Nazi era, he maintained, the germ of fascism remained in the hearts and minds of the people.[22] The failure openly to confront past and present fascism was compounded by a lack of discussion on the merits and achievements of socialism. In his short essay, "Zum 17. Juni 1953" (Concerning 17 June 1953), he reiterates this analysis: the government had failed the people and opened the door to exploitative fascism; it was now imperative that the government turn away from its mistaken policies onto a proper socialist path (*BFA* 23:249–50).

Brecht's letter to his publisher Peter Suhrkamp dated 1 July 1953 is a key text (*BFA* 30:182–85). It was, of course, a letter to a Westerner in response to Western charges that Brecht had conspired to suppress democratic calls for freedom. Brecht hoped that the letter would find its way into the public domain, thereby helping to set the record straight. Ernst Schumacher recalls discussing the possible publication of the letter with Brecht. Brecht had said that any decision to publish the letter must be Suhrkamp's, but that he, Brecht, would be more than happy if Suhrkamp decided to make it public.[23]

The letter was in four parts. After a brief introduction summarizing the questions Suhrkamp had put to him, Brecht submitted his analysis of the events. Firstly, the workers had had legitimate grounds for going onto the streets to protest. The government, through a combination of ruinous measures and bad luck, had so exacerbated the workers' grim conditions that the real achievements of socialism in the GDR had been obscured. By far the greatest cause of the public chaos on 17 June, however, were the provocative and rabble-rousing activities of fascists, some of whom had crossed over into East Berlin from the West to join forces with local fascist elements, which had not been seen assembled in such numbers for years, *but which were still there*. The emphasis was Brecht's and highlighted his dread that Germany's fascist legacy had not yet been eliminated and that, as long as this residual fascism remained, the danger of another world war was ever present. He went on to describe the day's events in terms that were evocative of past fascist terror: the sight of smoke rising from the Columbushaus recalling those unhappy days of smoke rising from the Reichstag, attacks on innocent bystanders, and the burning of stacks of books on the streets. In the fourth and final part of the letter, he admitted that the Party had made mistakes, but stated that he nevertheless respected the socialist progress it had achieved. In the light of the dangers to society that had manifested themselves on 17

June, only one course of action was open to him: in the struggle to avert war and eliminate fascism, he stood shoulder to shoulder with the Party.

It is noticeable that this letter dealt with the causes of 17 June but not the lessons to be learned. There was no mention here of the great dialogue that must be initiated between the Party and the people. The reason, of course, is that Brecht was addressing the West here and not his own Party and people. He said nothing that conflicted with his other texts, and indeed repeated the charge that the SED had made mistakes, but it was a defiant and unapologetic response to his Western detractors. As in other texts primarily addressed to a Western readership, Brecht was fiercely loyal to the Party and government.

This same loyalty to his own state manifested itself in a poem titled "Nicht so gemeint" (*BFA* 15:270–71; Not What Was Meant), written in the summer of 1953 but not published until after Brecht's death. The poem reminded Westerners that Brecht's criticisms were calls for reform within his own society and must never be mistaken for or equated with approval of Western society. Brecht wrote the poem following very vocal approval in the West for the Academy's resolution demanding cultural reform in the GDR. But it warned that Western approval was tainted with fascism and imperialist motives. Just as the West had betrayed the working class, it was now attempting to betray artists, but neither Brecht nor the Academy were to be fooled. We can only speculate as to why Brecht did not publish this text. His letter to Suhrkamp demonstrates that he was quite prepared to confront the West, and the poem would surely have earned him plaudits in the GDR. But at this juncture, Brecht's battle with the Party's cultural functionaries was fully engaged and he may have felt that the publication of a rebuke to the West would serve only to muddy cultural waters he was determined to keep crystal clear.

The battle with the cultural functionaries had in fact begun on 17 June itself. If Brecht's action in sending off a letter to Ulbricht during the morning was uncharacteristically rash, then, by the time he arrived at the impromptu Academy meeting in the afternoon, he seems to have recovered his usual equilibrium in time to block the attempt to send the government a statement of support. The minutes of the meeting show that Brecht objected on two grounds. First, the meeting lacked a quorum. More importantly, it was not the Academy's job to rush off public statements before the government had itself assessed the situation. Individuals could of course offer their own personal services (again, Brecht suggested that radio work would be particularly useful), but the

Academy's main focus should be a renewal of cultural life and an urgent public debate on misguided cultural policies.[24]

This was a remarkable turnaround from Brecht's dispatch earlier in the day of personal messages of loyalty and support to Ulbricht and Grotewohl. We can only speculate on the reasons behind his change of attitude. He had sent off the letters before actually witnessing any of the events, and his midday walk around the streets may have altered his opinions. It may also be that he felt more comfortable and less exposed working within the framework of the Academy. Moreover, while Brecht had previously declared his loyalty to the *Party*, an ideological concept, the proposed Academy resolution was addressed to the *government*, a collection of failed individuals. In any event, with this move, Brecht launched his post-17 June bid to secure cultural reform, a bid that occupied a great deal of his time over the ensuing months.

The second day of the series of BE meetings on 24–26 June was devoted largely to a discussion of cultural issues and the need for reform. Brecht reaffirmed his conviction that artists must be allowed to practice their art free from intervention. However, there was still a role for the Party: it was unthinkable that every artist could do as he pleased, particularly in a state with such a tragic Nazi history as Germany.[25] Here Brecht acknowledged the historic role of the Party: it must lead, and artists must, like everyone else, bow to the Party's will. In a Germany still, in 1953, riddled with fascism, the Party's leadership role was all the more crucial. There was, of course, a problem here. Brecht's insistence on artistic freedom ran directly counter to recognition of the Party as arbiter in all matters cultural. It was a conundrum he never really solved.

While Brecht was conducting his own personal feud with the cultural authorities, the Academy was itself engaged in a struggle to wrest control of cultural policy away from the Party. At the end of June, it published a list of proposals amounting in effect to a demand that responsibility for art be returned to artists. As Stephen Parker notes earlier in this volume, the proposals were published in *Neues Deutschland* on 12 July, after Brecht had threatened to resign from the Academy if publication continued to be blocked. The minutes of the Academy meetings in which the proposals were launched, reviewed, and endorsed show that Brecht took a very active and indeed leading role in this initiative.[26]

The proposals met with vigorous resistance from leading cultural functionaries such as Walter Besenbruch, who held that the Academy had not proved itself sufficiently sound ideologically to warrant its self-appointment as arbiter of cultural matters (*LBB* 514–15). To counter this and other opposition from functionaries in the Arts Commission and the Office for Literature, Brecht published two poems, "Nicht feststell-bare Fehler der Kunstkommission" (*BFA* 15:268; Unidentifiable Errors of the Arts Commission) and "Das Amt für Literatur" (*BFA* 15:267–68; The Office for Literature) in the *Berliner Zeitung* on 11 and 15 July respectively. Complementing the poems was an article by Wolfgang Harich that appeared in the same paper on 14 July. In inflammatory terms, Harich named high-ranking officials in GDR cultural circles, acc-using them of a multitude of failings, including arrogance, ignorance, stupidity, and stifling bureaucracy.[27] It was a dangerous move. Brecht shared Harich's views, but not his rash language. He replaced Harich's strident hostility with biting sarcasm and delicious irony in his account of the conduct of cultural functionaries, avoiding names and accusations. According to "Nicht feststellbare Fehler," a fine old custom (at that point at least three weeks old) was being observed at the Arts Comm-ission: functionaries were murmuring confessions of mistakes made. Not specific mistakes, Brecht hastened to add (for that would necessitate corrective action), but mistakes in the abstract, as the custom demanded.

Brecht maintained the momentum with an article entitled "Kulturpolitik und Akademie der Künste" (*BFA* 23:256–60; Cultural Policy and the Academy of Arts), which was published in *Neues Deutsch-land* on 13 August 1953. The article, a response to Besenbruch's reject-ion of the Academy proposals,[28] defended the Academy's right and competence to influence cultural policy, while it attacked the practices employed at the Arts Commission and Office for Literature. Although Brecht was once again sharply critical of these cultural institutions, his article was very measured, calling for an inclusive cultural policy. It was Brecht's last public contribution to the cultural debate in 1953. He would, of course, have been encouraged by Ulbricht's public acknowledgment of the merit of the Academy's proposals in a speech at the Fifteenth Plenary Session of the Central Committee in July 1953, and would have been delighted about the demise of the Arts Commission at the end of 1953.

In private, from late summer onwards, Brecht spent time reflecting more maturely on the sociopolitical meaning of 17 June. His previous thoughts had been dominated by shock and pessimism, but all traces of shock had now disappeared. It was in this spirit that Brecht made his journal entry on 20 August 1953, "der 17 juni hat die ganze existenz verfremdet" (*BFA* 27:346; 17 june has alienated the whole of existence, *Journals* 454–55; lower case in the published translation).

Brecht's use of the word "verfremdet" here has sometimes been interpreted in the negative sense of alienation or "Entfremdung," a sign that the events of 17 June had left him a resigned and disillusioned man. Earlier in this volume, for example, Stephen Parker relates the comment to Brecht's fear that the SED was inadvertently contributing to a resurgence of fascism. Klaus Völker writes of Brecht finding 17 June a source of massive disillusionment, leaving him feeling that his whole existence had been "alienated."[29] And certainly a number of Brecht's friends detected a weariness in him after 17 June. More generally, however, critics have sought to interpret Brecht's use of the word in line with his deployment of the concept within his theatrical work. John Willett writes that for Brecht, *Verfremdung* was a matter not of alienation in the negative sense, but rather of gaining new insights into the world by glimpsing it in a different and unfamiliar light.[30] According to Mittenzwei, when Brecht felt his whole existence "verfremdet," he felt obliged to reflect in a new way about many things (*LBB* 508).[31]

We may therefore read "verfremdet" as distanced, not in a negative sense, but rather in the sense of being detached, able to view the world from a fresh angle. For Brecht, 17 June cast everything ("die ganze existenz") in a different light. In this more reflective light, he proceeded to weigh the negative aspects of 17 June against the positive ones. In his journal entry, he noted that the working class had demonstrated a total lack of purpose, direction, and organization, and had been thoroughly infected by fascism. The Party had been shaken to its very core by its reception from the masses, a bloody nose rather than the embrace it might have hoped for, but had shown a firm resolve and leadership in taking the measures necessary to protect the GDR and its socialist project, even if it meant doing so in the face of dissent from its own workers. Out of this very unpromising concatenation of factors, Brecht saw an opportunity for socialism to advance: the working class had shown itself capable of revolutionary fervor (even if misdirected and exploited on 17 June) and the Party had shown true leadership. Together, the Party and the working class could ensure victory for socialism over fascism and capitalism (*BFA* 27:346). Read thus in its entirety, the journal entry is undoubtedly Brecht's most optimistic and positive interpretation of 17 June.

At around the same time, in late summer 1953, Brecht wrote his "Vorwort zu Turandot" (*BFA* 24:409–10; Preface to Turandot). The mood was similarly reflective, but on the whole more pessimistic. Here, he returned to the theme of residual fascism in the GDR and the Party's fundamental failure to address this issue. He argued that great socialist advances had been made, but they had not been accompanied by similar changes in society's attitudes. He conceded that social and economic conditions resulting from the cataclysmic defeat and reparations burden made it very difficult to create an environment in which to eradicate fascism. The politicians were inexperienced and the people who might have been leaders were either dead or demoralized. In effect, a social and political vacuum had been created in which the spirit of Nazism was stirring again. It was a bleak message, quite different in tone from his reflection of 20 August 1953, with all optimism dissipated, and it indicates that, in Brecht's opinion, the ice between a socialist GDR and the dark waters of fascism was very thin indeed.

At the time of writing his journal entry of 20 August and the "Vorwort zu Turandot," Brecht was also busy composing his *Buckower Elegien* (Buckow Elegies, 1953). There is a strong case to be made for the view that the *Elegien* were inspired and informed by 17 June, but the only poem in the cycle that mentions 17 June specifically is "Die Lösung" (The Solution). The poem is in two parts. The first part describes an actual event. The Secretary of the GDR Writers' Union, Kurt Barthel, commonly known as Kuba, had published an article in *Neues Deutschland* on 20 June entitled "Wie ich mich schäme" (I Am So Ashamed). The article castigated the workers for their disloyalty to the government on 17 June, and warned them that they would have to work very hard indeed to regain the Party's trust. The second part of Brecht's poem is in the form of a question prompted by Kuba's reprimands:

> Wäre es da
> Nicht doch einfacher, die Regierung
> Löste das Volk auf und
> Wählte ein anderes? (*BFA* 12:310)

> [Would it not be easier
> In that case for the government
> To dissolve the people
> And elect another? (*Poems* 440)]

The proposition is, of course, absurd. How can a people be dissolved and where would a whole new population be found? Here Brecht is ridiculing Kuba and, by extension, the bureaucratic pomposity of all the GDR's cultural functionaries; the poem does not, however, as is frequently asserted, attack the Party or government as such. In this respect, the poem is very similar to "Nicht feststellbare Fehler der Kunstkommission" and "Das Amt für Literatur." Unlike these two poems, however, Brecht chose not to publish "Die Lösung." Whether that was because it targeted an important individual or because he had by now become disengaged from public discourse on cultural politics is not clear.

Brecht therefore seems to have settled, once the initial shock and reverberations passed, into a frame of mind at times optimistic — that the Party and the people would combine forces to ensure victory for socialism — and at times pessimistic — that the people would never be weaned off their fascist tendencies, indeed that Germany's unhappy past would endure. In this duel between optimism and pessimism, pessimism may not have been the outright victor, but it was clearly the dominant force.

Conclusion

What, then, are we to make of Brecht's actions and demeanor during those turbulent summer days of 1953? Much of the existing criticism lacks balance: Grass and Fuegi, for example, find no redeeming features, while Mittenzwei avoids awkward questions. Another strand of criticism, exemplified in the work of Heiser-Duron, Clark, and others, uses a range of documents to conduct a more rigorous examination of Brecht's engagement with politics in the summer of 1953. Much of this analysis focuses on his cultural activities and highlights his concerns regarding artistic production in the GDR. However, other texts, less assiduously examined, show that Brecht was deeply dismayed by the conduct and direction of social politics under the SED, in particular, by the Party's failure to eradicate fascism.

Brecht was a committed socialist, with a visceral loathing of fascism, unwavering since the 1930s. He subscribed to the concept of Party hegemony and the Party's mission to lead the people to the promised land of socialism, but rejected the Stalinist mode of governance espoused by the SED. He believed, rather, in a German path to socialism, drawing on traditional German cultural values and confronting the specifically German fascist inheritance. This belief incorporated the notion that a liberated cultural community would work in harmony with the Party to create a new society.

The events of 17 June had demonstrated to Brecht how dangerously the Party under Ulbricht had been behaving. It had failed dismally to enlighten the people about the achievements of socialism and the dormant fascism in the GDR that threatened those achievements. Furthermore, in seeking to impose a Soviet Socialist Realist aesthetic, the Party had stifled cultural creativity, thereby denying artists their proper participation in the creation of a new German socialist society.

It was on these interlinked failings that Brecht's texts in 1953 focused. Only some of these texts, however, were published in Brecht's lifetime, and there is no evidence indicating that he sought to publish the others. Publication of each of his letters sent to GDR politicians and his Western publisher was of course at least as much under the recipients' control as under Brecht's: the truth of this observation was graphically borne out when Ulbricht had the distorted version of Brecht's letter of 17 June published in *Neues Deutschland*. It seems unlikely that fear of punishment by the authorities led Brecht to withhold texts; the unpublished "Zum 17. Juni 1953" offered an analysis that was kinder to the Party than some of the texts that were published, such as his scathing indictment of functionaries in "Nicht feststellbare Fehler der Kunst-kommission." Nor can the nonpublication be explained by a desire to avoid further Western opprobrium: Brecht's letter to Suhrkamp (in effect a response to his Western critics) is a robust defense of his socialist stance. Yet one pattern does emerge. Those texts that Brecht chose to publish attacked the Party's cultural policies and demanded reform. Those that he withheld addressed wider sociopolitical problems in the GDR, in particular, residual fascism and the Party's failure to deal with this issue. It may be that cultural reform was, in his opinion, of more pressing importance and accordingly required priority. It may also be that he felt on safer ground here.

Brecht's opposition to the GDR's cultural prescriptions had been present since he arrived in the GDR in 1949, and it intensified in 1953, before and after 17 June. His persistent and courageous opposition can be traced through his texts, which show that — contrary to the view expressed by some Western critics — his actions in the GDR were not driven purely by the desire to protect his own privileged status or to win a permanent home for the Berliner Ensemble. His opposition to the regime's social shortcomings, however, was less open. This was Brecht's dilemma of opposition, a source of inner conflict for him. He knew where the Party had gone wrong, but there was simply no alternative. To have directed open criticism at Ulbricht and his circle might have been, in Brecht's view, warranted, but it would have been used by the GDR's enemies to subject the Party and the socialist state to censure. We may not be able to establish definitively the extent to which such considerations influenced his decision to leave some texts unpublished, but we do know his loyalty to the Party was unconditional. As he declared in his letter to Peter Suhrkamp, he had always supported the Party in the struggle against war and fascism, and always would (*BFA* 30:182–85).

Notes

[1] John Fuegi says, for example, that Brecht was regarded in the West as "the loyal henchman of the executioners" after 17 June. See John Fuegi, *The Life and Lies of Bertolt Brecht* (London: Flamingo HarperCollins, 1994), 547.

[2] Compare Manfred Wekwerth, interview in *"Denken heißt verändern . . .": Erinnerungen an Brecht*, ed. Joachim Lang and Jürgen Hillesheim (Augsburg: Maro, 1998), 159–83, here 179, with Meredith A. Heiser-Duron, "Brecht's Political and Cultural Dilemma in the Summer of 1953," in *Communications from the International Brecht Society* 30 (2001): 47–56, here 49.

[3] Erwin Geschonneck, interview in *"Denken heißt verändern. . .,"* ed. Lang and Hillesheim, 41–56, here 52.

[4] See Paul Gerhard Klussmann, "Volksaufstand und Literatur: Bert Brecht und der 17. Juni 1953," in *Der Volksaufstand am 17. Juni 1953 — ein gesamtdeutsches Ereignis?*, ed. Silke Flegel et al., 36–56 (Bochum: Institut für Deutschlandforschung der Ruhr-Universität Bochum, 2004), 40.

[5] Manfred Wekwerth, *Erinnern ist Leben: Eine dramatische Autobiographie* (Leipzig: Faber & Faber, 2000), 113. Subsequent references to this work are cited in the text using the abbreviation *EL* and page number.

[6] Werner Mittenzwei, *Das Leben des Bertolt Brecht oder der Umgang mit den Welträtseln*, 2 vols. (Berlin and Weimar: Aufbau, 1988), vol. 2, 497. Subsequent references to this work are cited in the text using the abbreviation *LBB* and page number.

[7] The meeting is referred to by Heiser-Duron, "Brecht's Dilemma," 49 and Mark W. Clark, "Hero or Villain? Bertolt Brecht and the Crisis Surrounding June 1953," *Journal of Contemporary History* 41, no. 3 (2006): 451–75, here 466. For the Academy minutes, see Ulrich Dietzel and Gudrun Geißler, eds., *Zwischen Diskussion und Disziplin: Dokumente zur Geschichte der Akademie der Künste (Ost) 1945/1950 bis 1993* (Berlin: Stiftung Archiv der Akademie der Künste, 1997), 78–79.

[8] Peter Palitzsch, interview in *"Denken heißt verändern. . .,"* ed. Lang and Hillesheim, 113–32, here 118.

[9] Mittenzwei, *Das Leben des Bertolt Brecht*, 496–97 and Fuegi, *The Life and Lies of Bertolt Brecht*, 544 agree on this point. Wekwerth, *Erinnern ist Leben*, 113, maintains (improbably) that the meeting preceded Brecht's walk.

[10] Dietzel and Geißler, *Zwischen Diskussion und Disziplin*, 78–79.

[11] Usschi Otten, "Die Krippen sind dieselben, nur die Ochsen haben gewechselt: Bertolt Brecht, Buckow und der 17. Juni," in *Der Bär von Berlin: Jahrbuch des Vereins für die Geschichte Berlins*, ed. Sibylle Einholz and Jürgen Wetzel (Berlin and Bonn: Westkreuz, 2003), 115–34, here 127.

[12] See Arno Paul and Martha Humphreys, "The West German Theatre Miracle: A Structural Analysis," *The Drama Review* 24, no.1 (1980): 3–24, here 3.

[13] Carl Weber, "Brecht in Eclipse?" *The Drama Review* 24, no.1 (1980): 115–24, here 116.

[14] Carola Stern, *Männer lieben anders: Helene Weigel und Bertolt Brecht* (Berlin: Rowohlt-Berlin, 2000), 180.

[15] Günter Grass, *Die Plebejer proben den Aufstand: Ein deutsches Trauerspiel* (Göttingen: Steidl, 2003). First published by Hermann Luchterhand in 1966.

[16] See Thomas K. Brown, "Die Plebejer und Brecht: an Interview with Günter Grass," *Monatshefte für deutschen Unterricht* 65, no.1 (1973): 5–13, and Martin Esslin, "Grass versus Brecht: The Plebians Rehearse the Uprising," *Theatre Australia* 11, no. 3 (1979): 18–19.

[17] For example, Alexander Abusch referred dismissively to the "Stück gegen Brecht von Günter Grass" at an Academy meeting of 30 November 1965. See Dietzel and Geißler, *Zwischen Diskussion und Disziplin*, 280.

[18] Marcel Reich-Ranicki, *Literatur der kleinen Schritte: Deutsche Schriftsteller heute* (Munich: Piper & Co., 1967), 175.

[19] Günter Grass, "Vor- und Nachgeschichte der Tragödie des Coriolanus von Livius und Plutarch über Shakespeare bis zu Brecht und mir," in *Essays und Reden 1: 1955–1969* (Göttingen: Steidl, 1993), 58–84, here 82–83.

[20] Martin Esslin, *Brecht: A Choice of Evils: A Critical Study of the Man, His Work and His Opinions* (London: Eyre & Spottiswoode, 1971), 170.

[21] Heinrich Mohr, "Der 17. Juni als Thema der Literatur in der DDR," in *17. Juni 1953: Arbeiteraufstand in der DDR*, ed. Ilse Spittmann and Karl Wilhelm Fricke (Cologne: Wissenschaft und Politik, 1982), 87–111, here 109.

[22] "Diskussionen des BERLINER ENSEMBLES über die Lage am 24. Juni 1953," BBA 1447/001–015.

[23] Ernst Schumacher, "In der 'Eisernen Villa,'" *Berliner Zeitung*, 15/16 September 2001.

[24] Dietzel and Geißler, *Zwischen Diskussion und Disziplin*, 78–79.

[25] "Diskussionen des BERLINER ENSEMBLES über die Lage am 25. Juni 1953," BBA 1447/016–29.

[26] See Dietzel and Geißler, *Zwischen Diskussion und Disziplin*, 80–93 for a list of the proposals as well as the minutes of the meetings convened to advance them.

[27] Wolfgang Harich, "Es geht um den Realismus," *Berliner Zeitung*, 14 July 1953.

[28] Walter Besenbruch, "Über berechtigte Kritik und über Erscheinungen des Opportunismus in Fragen der Kunst," *Neues Deutschland* (East Berlin), 19 July 1953.

[29] Klaus Völker, *Bertolt Brecht: Eine Biographie* (Munich and Vienna: Hauser, 1976), 396.

[30] John Willett, *Brecht in Context* (London: Methuen, 1984), 220.

[31] In the academic literature, the term "Verfremdung" is now usually translated as "defamiliarization" or "estrangement." See note 27 in Loren Kruger's essay in this volume.

II. The Management of Brecht's Legacy

Private or Public? The Bertolt Brecht Archive as an Object of Desire

Erdmut Wizisla, Bertolt Brecht Archive, Berlin

I N THE STORY "Die Freiherren von Gemperlein" (The Barons of Gemperlein, 1879), one of Marie von Ebner-Eschenbach's characters asks "Wo sind die Schlüssel des Archivs?" (Where are the keys to the archive?).[1] Figuratively, these keys stand for *access* to the archive, which is determined by archivists, heirs, rights-holders, owners, administrative institutions, and also by states. The relations between the parties involved are usually regulated by contracts, and infringements of these contracts and differences over their interpretation are by no means the exception. For a start, there is the question as to who is actually to be granted access to an archive. Is only a particular clientele allowed in? Do users have to meet certain conditions by proving their scholarly competence or interests, supplying a letter from their supervisor confirming their research topic, paying fees, or belonging to a particular state or family? Once a user has gained entry to an archive, the accessibility of archive materials depends on whether they can be found, and this depends in turn on the quality of the catalogues and the commitment and expertise of the staff. Details that were not recorded during the cataloguing process are only disclosed when a user of the archive orders the documents and is presented with them. And even here, users encounter restrictions in every archive: there are some documents that have to remain in the stacks for reasons of conservation. There are sources to which access is limited due to copyright, property, or privacy laws. And there are items or entire archives to which political authorities deny users access, if they do not destroy them entirely.

This essay is concerned first and foremost with problems of accessibility that are rooted in sociopolitical matters. On 1 December 1956, a good quarter of a year after Brecht's death, Helene Weigel founded the Bertolt Brecht Archive with the agreement of their children

Barbara and Stefan as well as Brecht's daughter Hanne. From the very moment of its inception it was a political issue, and at times, particularly after the death of Helene Weigel, it was even a site of real struggle. The GDR authorities' approach to the question of access to the Brecht Archive repeated and reflected their treatment of Brecht himself: he was an author whose political desires largely corresponded to the state's proclaimed goals, but who put up a growing resistance to each and every form of cultural assimilation, both during his life and posthumously. Helene Weigel put it best: "Brecht war ein großer Name" (Brecht was a big name), she said in 1969 when Werner Hecht asked her about the relationship of Soviet cultural officials to the Berliner Ensemble. Her answer holds equally true for the relationship of GDR officials to Brecht. "Sie haben's im großen und ganzen gelitten. Wir waren doch nicht ganz das, was sie wollten, aber sie wollten nicht verlieren, was sie mit uns hatten" (They put up with it on the whole. We were not entirely what they wanted, but they did not want to lose what they had in us).[2] An uncomfortable author and therefore an uncomfortable archive.

The story of the Brecht Archive oscillates between two poles: on the one hand, the courageous way in which it was established and managed, and, on the other, the continuous attempts made by state bodies to control access to Brecht's estate with a view to appropriating his legacy. In this respect, the Brecht Archive, like the author whose name it bears, remained a bone of contention. Using documents that have hitherto barely been consulted, if at all, this essay will consider critical junctures in the conflict between *private* and *public*. The discussion covers key moments in the history of the Brecht Archive, a history that has yet to be written.[3]

Weigel's Cunning

It was with admirable energy that Weigel sought to fulfill Brecht's dying wishes. Her guiding principle for the theater was a sentence that Brecht is reputed to have said to her on the last day of his life: "Halte das Ensemble so lange Du meinst, dass es das Berliner Ensemble ist" (Keep the Ensemble going as long as you believe it to be the Berliner Ensemble).[4] There was no comparable instruction regarding the papers that he left behind, and yet by establishing his archive the poet's widow honored a commitment that arose from Brecht's desire to continue having an impact even after his death. Helene Weigel ensured that everything that Brecht had left behind remained together: "Ich kümmere mich darum, damit nichts verschwindet" (I am seeing to it that nothing goes missing).[5] She did not stop there either, but added an impressive collection to the archive by asking colleagues and friends for originals, or at least copies, of all material produced in collaboration with Brecht. Few could resist the charm and authority of the wife and theater manager. Weigel invested considerable sums into buying back Brecht's letters and manuscripts from private ownership, or, when the first manuscripts became available on the open market, acquiring them at auctions. Textual scholars have emphatically praised this approach. Bernhard Zeller singles out the dedication of Brecht's heirs as exemplary, saying that to his knowledge no literary estate in the twentieth century has been preserved and secured in this way.[6]

The overriding imperative governing all of Helene Weigel's efforts was that the archive should be open, as she wrote unequivocally to Brecht's publisher Siegfried Unseld on 12 October 1966: "Das Archiv ist, wie Sie wissen, für jeden zugänglich" (The archive is, as you know, open to everyone).[7] In 1968, she announced on the radio that the archive had become what she had envisaged, that is, "eine Arbeitsstätte" (a place of work).[8] And when Werner Hecht commented that she had opened the archive to users quite quickly, Weigel reacted with disarming frankness, saying: "Warum sollte es sonst geschaffen werden? Ich weiß nicht, wie es mit anderen Archiven steht. Ich meine, sie müßten alle benutzt werden können!" (Why else should it have been created? I don't know how things stand with other archives. I think they all ought to be open for use!).[9]

The archive's initial status as a private establishment was inevitably seen as anachronistic in the "workers' and peasants' state." Although this kind of arrangement was unheard of, it turned out to be an advantage because it provided a means of keeping Brecht's estate out of the authorities' reach. After all, being open to everyone did not mean forfeiting copyright. Helene Weigel was suspicious from the outset of any hint of censorship in the editing of Brecht's texts, as Siegfried Unseld has explained.[10] In such matters, she was quite capable of taking an uncompromising stance. By the mid-1960s, the GDR authorities' demands for censorship had reached absurd proportions. Debates went on for months, years even, above all about *Me-Ti: Buch der Wendungen* (Mozi: Book of Changes, 1934–55), the seventh volume of the *Gedichte* (Poems), which was published in 1964 and contained "Die Lösung" (The Solution), and about the *Journal*, extracts of which Weigel had sent as early as 1964 to Wilhelm Girnus for publication in the periodical *Sinn und Form*. In a letter to the Central Committee of the SED dated 30 August 1965, Klaus Gysi, the head of the Aufbau publishing house, complained that the situation in the archive, the collaboration between Weigel, Elisabeth Hauptmann, and the publishing house Suhrkamp, as well as the existing contractual obligations meant that the authorities were never safe from surprises.[11]

It was particularly awkward that Helene Weigel even had to defend herself against accusations from her immediate colleagues. Manfred Wekwerth, who at this time did not even know Brecht's *Me-Ti*, issued a diatribe against the announcement that, of all people, Uwe Johnson, who had left the GDR in 1959, was to edit these fragments. Wekwerth did not mince his words when dealing with Helene Weigel. On 25 May 1964, he wrote to her:

> Vor allem erscheint mir Johnson als Brecht-Herausgeber problematisch. Mir gefällt schon nicht die Umgebung, in die Brecht durch den Verlag gesetzt wird, wo sich Mittelmäßigkeit an Brecht emporrankt. Aber die Verbindung eines anarcho-trotzkistisch — avantgardistisch — pluralistisch — existentialistischen, genialischen (was weiß ich) Wirrkopfes mit dem Namen Brecht kann schwer der Sache dienen, der politischen Haltung nur schaden. Es wäre eine Legitimation dieser merkwürdigen Leute, die Brecht wegen politischer Schludrigkeit und genialischem Unwissen so hasste. Selbst wenn seine Arbeit am *Buch der Wendungen* (ich würde es furchtbar gern einmal lesen) erstklassig wäre, ist die Verbindung Brecht-Johnson unheimlich.[12]

> [Above all, Johnson seems to me to be problematic as an editor of Brecht. For a start, I do not approve of the context in which the publisher is placing Brecht, allowing a mediocre figure to use Brecht to elevate his own status. But the association of an anarcho-Trotskyist — avantgardist — pluralist — existentialist, brilliantly eccentric (what do I know) scatterbrain with Brecht's name is hardly going to serve our cause, and it can only damage our political position. It would serve to legitimize those strange people whom Brecht so hated on account of their political sloppiness and brilliant ignorance. Even if his work on the *Book of Changes* were first class (I would really like to read it some day), the association of Brecht with Johnson is problematic.]

As a result of objections like this, the GDR publication of the *Buch der Wendungen* came ten years after the Suhrkamp edition, and the *Journal* appeared in the GDR five years later than in the Federal Republic. Wekwerth had helped to see to that too by opposing its publication in a letter to the Central Committee of the SED dated 13 July 1971, that is, after Weigel's death: "Ich halte diese Herausgabe für einen Schaden, der durch die politisch falsche Herausgabe erfolgt, noch dazu von einem

Bürger der DDR" (I see this publication as harmful because of the politically erroneous editing, carried out — what is more — by a citizen of the GDR).[13] The final phrase was a reference to Werner Hecht.

In a fit of weakness or loyalty to the Party line, even Elisabeth Hauptmann, who had been the Berliner Ensemble's Party Secretary from 1957 to 1960, suggested that, in view of the flood of Brecht publications in the West and the ebb in the East, the GDR editions could be published without texts that seemed offensive in the Suhrkamp editions, such as the poem "Die Lösung" or parts of the *Tui-Roman* (Tui-Novel, 1933–43).[14] Helene Weigel decisively rejected this suggestion on 14 January 1967:

> Du kennst meine Gründe, warum ich meine Meinung aufrechterhalten muss, dass diese zwei Ausgaben wortgetreu sein müssen. Ich bin gern bereit, nicht darüber zu sprechen, dass und warum hier nicht weitergedruckt wird. Aber ändern kann ich an dem Zustand nichts.[15]

> [You know my reasons for insisting that the two editions must correspond to each other word for word. I am quite willing not to speak about the fact that we are not proceeding with publication here, and why. But I cannot change a thing about this situation.]

As Weigel subsequently explained, she had done everything possible to ensure that the texts published by Suhrkamp and Aufbau were identical, and she added that it would have been dreadful ("schrecklich") if she had not succeeded.[16] These were victories that could only be achieved through Brechtian cleverness. Weigel turned a deaf ear to the publisher Aufbau's demands for cuts. She invented the title *Arbeitsjournal* (Work Journal) in order to direct the censors' attention away from aspects that were politically and personally controversial, and toward the factual character of the notes and their relevance to Brecht's works. As the editions would not have been possible without the archive and were, for the most part, put together in the GDR, there was never any danger of Weigel losing control over the process. She also managed to persuade Suhrkamp to be patient, so that the difference between the dates of publication in East and West would not become too obvious. It is true that Weigel did not live to see the publication of the *Arbeitsjournal* by Suhrkamp in 1973 and by Aufbau in 1978. But it would not be going too far to assume that her invention of the title made the publication of this book in the GDR possible in the first place.

The interminable debates in the East went hand-in-hand with allegations in the West, which Weigel also sometimes countered with reference to the Brecht Archive — as she did in a letter of 7 February

1970 to Fredrik Martner, the friend from her days in exile in Denmark, nicknamed Crassus:

> Was die Äußerung betrifft, die von mir gemacht worden sein soll: "Ich bin Staatsbürger von Österreich, und falls ihr nicht mit mir zufrieden seid, kann ich meinen Koffer packen und morgen reisen!" so ist das natürlich ein absoluter Idiotismus. Brecht und ich haben uns dieses Land ausgesucht, um darin zu leben. Meine Kinder sind hier. Das große Brechtarchiv, das Du kennst, habe ich hier aufgebaut. Welch ein niederträchtiger bösartiger Kopf sich so etwas ausgedacht hat, möchte ich wissen. Man müsste ihn finden.[17]

> [As for the statement I am supposed to have made — "I am a citizen of Austria, and if you're not happy with me, I can just pack my suitcase and be off tomorrow!" — that is of course sheer idiocy. Brecht and I chose to live in this country. My children are here. I have established the great Brecht Archive, which you know of, here. I only wish I knew which vile, malicious crook came up with such an idea. He ought to be caught.]

It would be fair to say that Weigel and her daughter Barbara managed to fend off these assaults successfully. While there were delays and one or two victories for the censorship authorities, Brecht went virtually uncensored in the GDR. Instead, it was on the level of interpretation and historical contextualization, that is, in the field of education, that the violation took place. It was there that Brecht was appropriated, cropped, and misinterpreted. The Brecht Archive was not directly at the mercy of cultural dogmatism. Weigel kept its doors open even for politically controversial figures from the West such as Uwe Johnson or Peter Weiss, or for figures under attack in the East, such as Wolf Biermann or Thomas Brasch. And she was able to keep it independent as an institution for many years. A corollary of this was her desire, set out in her will, to establish an independent foundation and to run the archive as the Bertolt Bertolt Archive of Bertolt Brecht's heirs. This idea also features in one of her last letters. On 27 April 1971, nine days before her death, Helene Weigel conveyed her thoughts regarding the future of the Brecht Archive in a letter to Werner Hecht. She made sure that the key positions were held by people who could be trusted to act in accordance with her wishes. She recommended her close associate Gisela Knauf as a future director of the archive, and expressed the hope that her daughter Barbara would be able to answer the crucial questions with good sense ("mit Verstand") and in conjunction with Hecht and Knauf.[18] A legacy indeed.

Hans Bunge, the Customs Official

Where Brecht's estate was concerned, the tension between *private* and *public* had a prehistory that was bound up with the name Hans Bunge. Bunge enjoyed Helene Weigel's confidence for a long time, having helped to establish the archive and having managed it since 1956. But on 16 October 1959, Bunge resigned; after serious differences of opinion, he and Weigel had parted company.[19] The reasons for his resignation are to be found in a letter that Bunge wrote to Weigel on 31 March 1960:

> Sehr verehrte Frau Weigel, heute ist mein letzter Arbeitstag im Archiv. Ich brauche nicht zu verschweigen, daß mir das Ausscheiden aus meiner Arbeit — die ich vor nicht langer Zeit noch als meine Lebensaufgabe betrachtet habe — sehr schwer fällt. Aber eine produktive Weiterführung der Arbeit Brechts scheint mir nur gewährleistet, wenn ein Kollektiv unter staatlicher Aufsicht gebildet wird, welches sämtliche Maßnahmen im Zusammenhang mit der Weiterführung der Arbeit Brechts gemeinsam plant, berät, koordiniert und in der Durchführung kontrolliert.[20]

> [Dear Frau Weigel, today is my last day working at the archive. I do not need to hide the fact that leaving my work — which, until only recently, I still regarded as my life's work — is very hard for me to take. But it seems to me that a productive continuation of Brecht's work will only be guaranteed if a collective is formed under state supervision, whose members will jointly plan, advise, and coordinate all measures connected to the continuation of Brecht's work, and manage their execution.]

On the same day, Bunge turned to Bode Uhse, who at this time was secretary of the Division for Literature and Language at the Academy of Arts. Entirely in the spirit of his suggestion that a supervisory body should be established, Bunge issued a warning that showed just how bizarre the situation really was. The director of the archive was trying to protect the manuscripts from being taken without authorization. In so doing, he was not afraid to treat even Brecht's widow with suspicion. Bunge regarded the Brecht Archive as the institution that was currently entitled to exercise control, and this meant in practice that Brecht's entire works and the Brecht Archive would be placed under state supervision. In exercising its duty, the Archive could even withhold material from Helene Weigel. In Bunge's letter to Uhse, it is particularly worth noting the distinction he makes between "strittigem Material" (contentious material) and "ganz 'harmlosen' Mappen" (completely "harmless" files):

Sehr geehrter Herr Uhse,

in meiner Sorge um den Nachlaß Brechts sehe ich mich veranlaßt, Ihnen heute noch folgendes zur Kenntnis zu bringen:

Wie ich Ihnen bereits mündlich berichtet habe, hat Frau Weigel vor einiger Zeit begonnen, sich ein eigenes Archiv von Fotokopien der Manuskripte Brechts anzulegen. Diese Fotokopien, die in der Wohnung Frau Weigels und nicht im Archiv gelagert werden, werden auch nicht von uns selbst hergestellt, sondern von einer Privatfirma. [. . .] Ich stehe dieser Angelegenheit sehr skeptisch gegenüber. Zu den bis vor einiger Zeit streng eingehaltenen Grundprinzipien unserer Archivarbeit gehörte, daß kein unveröffentlichtes Material außer Haus gegeben wird. Die Gefahr, daß das Material in unberechtigte Hände gerät, wäre zu groß, weil seitens des Archivs keinerlei Kontrolle möglich ist. [. . .] Frau Weigel [hat] von sich aus nicht die geringste Einschränkung über den Umfang des auszuliefernden Materials gemacht, so dass beispielsweise die Sammlung von politischen Meinungen Brechts ebenfalls an Herrn Krüger [den Mitarbeiter der o. g. Privatfirma] gegeben worden wäre — wenn nicht die Mitarbeiter des Archivs von sich aus bestimmtes Material vorher ausgesondert hätten. Aber dabei konnten keinesfalls sämtliche Dokumente erfaßt werden, deren unberechtigte Veröffentlichung — beispielsweise in Westdeutschland — uns nicht gleichgültig sein könnte, denn bei dem von uns angewandten Archivierungssystem befinden sich Einzelblätter von derartigem strittigem [!] Material auch in sonst ganz "harmlosen" Mappen.[21]

[Dear Herr Uhse,

Out of concern for Brecht's literary estate, I feel obliged to bring the following matter to your immediate attention:

As I have already reported to you verbally, Frau Weigel began some time ago to assemble her own archive of photocopies of Brecht's manuscripts. These photocopies, which are stored in Frau Weigel's apartment and not in the archive, are not even produced by us, but by a private company. [. . .]

I am very skeptical about this. One of the fundamental principles of our archive work, which has been strictly observed until only recently, is that no unpublished material should be removed from the archive. The danger of the material ending up in the wrong hands would be too great, because the archive would be unable to exercise any control. In this case too, Frau Weigel has not seen fit to place even the slightest restriction on the amount of material being taken out, so that, for example, the collection of Brecht's political statements would also have been given to Herr Krüger [employee of the aforementioned private company], if the staff at the archive had not taken it upon themselves to remove certain material already. But they were unable to catch all the documents whose unauthorized publication — for example in West Germany — would not be a matter of indifference to us, as our archiving system means that there are single sheets of this kind of con tentious [!] material even in what are otherwise completely "harmless" files.]

An insane situation. Bunge's services to the Brecht Archive are undisputed. He devoted himself to his work with a passion that was free from bureaucratic routine, but that was based on sources and contact with Brecht's collaborators. Besides, Bunge was regarded as politically openminded. He was in close contact with Wolf Biermann, Robert Havemann, Wolfgang Neuss, Uwe Johnson, Klaus Baumgärtner, Heiner Müller, Peter Weiss, Hans Magnus Enzensberger, and many others. His later activities for the state security services as an informer codenamed "Hans," which cannot be elaborated on here, do not simply speak against him.[22] The fact that a man with this mindset argued that a state-led collective should supervise and coordinate the treatment of Brecht, must, at the very least, give us pause for thought.

At the opening of the Hans Bunge Archive on 3 December 2009 in the Academy of Arts, Manfred Bierwisch, who was also a friend of Bunge's, recalled Brecht's "Legende von der Entstehung des Buches Taoteking auf dem Weg des Laotse in die Emigration" (Legend of the Origin of the Book Tao-Tê-Ching on Lao-Tsû's Road into Exile):

Das, wofür dem Zöllner Dank gebührt, ist ein Leitmotiv in Bunges Leben. Niemand hat mehr Verstand und Spürsinn, Ausdauer und Geschick an den Tag gelegt, die Weisheit der Weisen zu erkennen, abzufragen und zu dokumentieren, als er. Natürlich hat Brecht gewußt und geschätzt, was Fragen und Dokumentieren bedeutet, und der geistig interessierte Zöllner ist alles andere als ein Statist. Aber Bunge hat, weit über die üblichen Praktiken hinaus, daraus eine Wissenschaft und Kunst — oder eigentlich mehrere Künste gemacht.[23]

[The services for which the customs official deserves thanks are a leitmotif of Bunge's life. No one displayed more understanding and intuition, perseverance and skill, in recognizing the wisdom of the wise, gleaning it through asking questions, and documenting it, as he did. Of course, Brecht knew and appreciated what it is to ask questions and to document, and the intellectually curious customs official is anything but a bit-player. But Bunge went above and beyond the usual practices, and turned them into a science and an art — or, more accurately, into numerous arts.]

Bunge wanted to de-privatize Brecht's estate, to curb the influence of private interests, perhaps assuming that it might be harmful for Brecht's

literary estate and his reception if those who had been close to Brecht —
in particular, his widow — were to have sole control over everything. But
in 2009, Bierwisch declared:

> Diese aufrichtig und ohne Rückhalt geführte Auseinandersetzung, in
> der Bunge das öffentliche Interesse wahrzunehmen glaubte, während
> die Weigel den Zugriff staatlicher Instanzen abwehren wollte, hat
> Bunge verloren. Und es war nicht erst das berüchtigte Plenum des ZK
> der SED, das ihn dazu gebracht hat, diese Niederlage richtig zu finden.
> Der Bruch mit der Weigel und der darauf folgende Bruch mit der
> eigenen Position — das sind zwei Aspekte der gleichen Geradlinigkeit
> unter schwierigen Bedingungen. Denn es war richtig, daß der Staat, in
> dem wir lebten, die Vormundschaft über das Werk Brechts nicht haben
> durfte. Bunge war nüchtern genug, um zuzugestehen: Die Weigel
> hatte die größere Weisheit besessen.[24]

[This was a debate that was waged sincerely and with no holds barred, a
debate in which Bunge believed that he was representing the public
interest, while Weigel was seeking to fend off the encroachment of the
state authorities, and Bunge lost. And it did not take the notorious
Eleventh Plenary Session of the Central Committee of the SED to
make him to see this defeat as right. The split with Weigel and the
ensuing break with his own position: these are two aspects of the same
principled behavior in difficult circumstances. For it was right that the
state in which we lived could not be permitted to be the custodian of
Brecht's works. Bunge was sufficiently levelheaded to admit that Weigel
had been wiser.]

Bunge initially clung to the idea of state supervision of the Brecht
Archive for quite some time. On 25 July 1962 he wrote in a letter to
Willi Bredel, the President of the Academy of Arts:

> Der eigentliche Grund für die Misere scheint mir in der Tatsache zu
> bestehen, daß wir auch beim Aufbau des Sozialismus noch dem bürger-
> lichen Erbrecht verhaftet sind. Bertolt Brecht hatte in seinem letzten
> Testament u.a. verfügt, daß seine "Manuskripte und Modellbücher der
> Akademie der Künste zu übergeben" seien. Das Testament ist formal-
> juristisch ungültig, die Erben sind demzufolge nicht verpflichtet, die
> Wünsche Brechts zu erfüllen. Aus dieser Sachlage ist die Einrichtung
> eines Privatarchivs der Erben zu erklären. Wären die Erben — Brechts
> Wünschen entsprechend — nur Inhaber der Urheberrechte und nicht
> auch der Manuskripte, hätte der Abschluß eines Vertrags zwischen
> Erben und Akademie vermutlich weniger Schwierigkeiten gemacht und
> wäre zustandegekommen.
>   Ich sah mich zur Kündigung meiner Tätigkeit als Leiter des
> "Bertolt-Brecht-Archivs" und der "Arbeitsgruppe historisch-kritische

Ausgabe der Schriften Bertolt Brechts" veranlaßt, weil zwei Grund-
bedingungen nicht erfüllt wurden, deren Durchsetzung ich auch heute
noch für die Voraussetzung einer staatlichen Beteiligung an der wissen-
schaftlichen Ausgabe halte:

a) Vereinigung von Archiv und Arbeitsgruppe zu einer Institution,
die staatlicher Aufsicht untersteht,

b) Bildung eines Gremiums, das alle Maßnahmen, die mit der
Weiterführung der Arbeit Brechts in Zusammenhang stehen, gemein-
sam plant, berät, durchführt und kontrolliert.[25]

[The actual reason for this wretched state of affairs seems to me to lie in
the fact that we are still held captive by bourgeois inheritance laws, even
though we are establishing socialism. In his will, Bertolt Brecht
decreed, among other things, that his "manuscripts and model books"
were "to be presented to the Academy of Arts." In formal legal terms,
the will is void, so the heirs are not obliged to fulfill Brecht's wishes.
This situation explains why the heirs established a private archive. If the
heirs — in accordance with Brecht's wishes — were in possession only
of copyright and not of the manuscripts as well, it would probably have
been far less difficult to agree a contract between the heirs and the
Academy, and a contract would have been concluded.

I saw myself with no option but to resign from my post as director
of the "Bertolt Brecht Archive" and of the "Working group on the
historical-critical edition of the works of Bertolt Brecht" because two
fundamental conditions, which I still regard today as a prerequisite for
state involvement in the scholarly edition, had not been met:

a) the merger of archive and working group to form an institution
that is under state supervision,

b) the formation of a committee whose members will act together
to plan, advise, execute, and control all measures related to the
continuation of Brecht's work.]

The extensively documented conflict is fascinating. Bunge wanted to
fight for Brecht's interests and did not notice how, in attempting to ward
off the danger that he perceived, he conjured up a new one: the danger
that the archive and the edition might be placed under state supervision.
Bunge ought to have been aware of the significance and consequences of
any such arrangement.

Heiner Müller offers a version of the disagreements between Bunge
and Helene Weigel, which corresponds to the truth only insofar as it too
essentially concerns access to the Brecht Archive. In his autobiography,
Krieg ohne Schlacht (War without Battle, 1992), Müller tells us:

Bunge arbeitete bei "Sinn und Form," nachdem die Weigel ihn aus
dem Brecht-Archiv hinausgeworfen hatte, weil er Photomaterial,

Brecht-Dokumente nach Moskau habe bringen lassen, damit das Material zugänglich bleibt. Moskau war lange Zeit der einzige Platz in der Welt, wo man Zugang zu dem ganzen Brecht hatte.[26]

[Bunge worked for *Sinn und Form* after Weigel had thrown him out of the Brecht Archive because he had photos and documents relating to Brecht brought to Moscow, so that the material would remain accessible. For a long time, Moscow was the only place in the world where people had access to the complete works of Brecht.]

The microfilms from the Brecht Archive were not presented to the Lenin Library in Moscow behind Weigel's back. In fact, she had ordered the gift herself, and Bunge spoke publicly on her behalf at the official ceremony in Moscow.[27] This measure was part of a plan by Brecht's heirs to secure his works. The plan corresponded to a precaution that Brecht had himself envisaged; he had considered a systematic dispersal of his archive advisable in the face of the growing global potential for destruction. It might not be a bad thing, Brecht had written to his childhood friend Hanns Otto Münsterer on 29 August 1953, "an verschiedenen Punkten der Erdoberfläche das eine oder andere, was Mühe gekostet hat, zu haben" (*BFA* 30:197; to have one thing or another that has taken effort at various points on the globe). Additional copies of the archive were sent to the Academy of Arts, to Stefan Brecht in New York, who made them available in the Houghton Library at Harvard, as well as to a law firm in Zurich and also, for a while, to Ireland. Apart from the fact that Bunge had actually resigned, Müller's anecdote is inaccurate in that the disagreement between Bunge and the heirs over whether the Brecht films should be used in Moscow or just left in storage there was indeed a contributing factor to but not the cause of the split.[28] Moreover, no publication has ever come to light citing documents that were withheld in Berlin but were accessible in the Lenin Library. Such documents were accessed instead in the holdings of the Houghton Library, when John Fuegi used them for his controversial biography.

Be that as it may: the constellation of *private* versus *public* could hardly have been more contradictory. Of course, every thinking person must prefer public access to private. But in circumstances in which "public" had the same meaning as "state-controlled," a private set-up may well have been the more democratic principle.

The Brecht Archive as Bargaining Chip

The question of who holds the keys to an archive can be meant literally, as we can see from an attack perpetrated by the security services, or Stasi, the day after Helene Weigel's death. It suddenly became clear just how necessary her plans for the archive's future had been. For 7 May 1971 marked the start of attempts to curb the influence of Brecht's heirs. At around ten o'clock in the morning, the director of the headquarters of the Sparkasse savings bank on Alexanderplatz was ordered to search the vault that the Brecht heirs had rented since 1957, and to secure it so that no one could gain entry. This course of action was illegal. In the lease agreement, the heirs had been guaranteed that the bank would not examine the contents of the safes in the vault, and that no one would be allowed entry apart from those people that they themselves had authorized. In the bank, the story that a key had gone missing had to serve as an explanation for the illegal action taken by its director. The vault was sealed.

These events are documented in detail in the records that the Stasi collected on Helene Weigel. According to a State Security memorandum dated 7 May 1971, the State Security Administration ordered the arrangement or execution of "Maßnahmen zur Sicherung von Deposita der am 06.05.71 verstorbenen Prof. Helene *Weigel* bei der Sparkasse der Stadt Berlin" (measures to secure deposits of Prof. Helene *Weigel*, deceased 5/6/71, at the savings bank of the city of Berlin).[29] In fact, the Stasi's activities concerning Weigel seem to have centered on the originals from the archive: 115 pages of her file consist of documents regarding the vault's legal status, and another 105 pages are reports about the vault's security and those authorized to enter it.[30]

The attempt to deny the heirs access to their property was successfully blocked. Until the start of the 1990s, the originals were stored three or four stories beneath Alexanderplatz. It had a conspiratorial feel to it when originals were fetched from the bank safe so that they could be used for editorial work or for research. The Academy of Arts and Brecht's heirs had agreed that they would only access Brecht's literary estate and the collection of the archive jointly. Staff from both institutions were always present when materials were taken out and returned, and the whole process was meticulously recorded. Helene Weigel, and later her daughter Barbara Brecht-Schall, had the key in their possession and had to grant individuals the power to use it. This went on for over three decades, and it was probably so successful partly because it allowed both the heirs and the Academy to believe that they could keep each other in check.

Even so, this cooperation lacked any form of contractual basis until after the death of Helene Weigel. The negotiations had begun in 1957 and were eventually blocked by Weigel's veto. At the same time, Helene Weigel knew that she would not be able to continue to resist the offers of support from the Academy of Arts, which masked the state's massive interest in taking control. She saw through the offers of support but could not refuse to enter negotiations because Brecht's heirs were not in a position to pay the considerable costs required to secure the Brecht Archive and make it accessible to users.[31]

The unlawful penetration of the vault on 7 May 1971 represented a bizarre escalation of attempts to confiscate Brecht's estate from his heirs. Using a resolution passed by the Council of Ministers, the GDR government tried on 11 May 1971 to turn the apparent legal uncertainty following Helene Weigel's death to its advantage. Right from the start, the resolution made no secret of its intentions. The preamble states that after his return from exile in 1948, Brecht had found his true home in the GDR, adding — with embarrassing tautology — that he had been "bis zu seinem Tode der größte lebende sozialistische Dramatiker deutscher Sprache" (the greatest living socialist German-language dramatist until his death). It went on to declare that the protection, cultivation, and dissemination of Brecht's works, as well as of the literary estates of Brecht and Weigel, were the responsibility of the GDR. The harshest measure is formulated in the second point of this document. In a striking breach of international law, the Council of Ministers set out to rob Brecht's and Weigel's heirs of copyright:

> Die Wahrnehmung der Urheberrechte an dem Werk und an den beiden literarischen Nachlässen in der Deutschen Demokratischen Republik sowie deren wissenschaftliche Betreuung werden der Deutschen Akademie der Künste zu Berlin übertragen.[32]

> [The task of enforcing copyright for the works and the two literary estates in the German Democratic Republic, along with the scholarly supervision of these, is transferred to the German Academy of Arts in Berlin.]

As a generous concession, the heirs were allowed to retain their legal claims to a financial stake in the use of Brecht's work for the duration of the copyright, although this was restricted to fifty years in the GDR, as opposed to the seventy years internationally agreed in Geneva in 1952.

The far-reaching consequences of this resolution were clear to those responsible. While the wording of the law still seemed to allow some room for interpretation, internal communications reveal that it was an attempt to strip Brecht's heirs of any power. This is clear from a letter sent on 5 July 1976 by the Minister of Culture Hans-Joachim Hoffmann to the SED's chief ideologue, Kurt Hager. In this letter, the Minister explained that he wanted to transfer the responsibility for enforcing copyright to the Academy of Arts, to Brecht's publishers in the GDR (Aufbau and Henschel), and to an advisory body. He stated:

Bekanntlich wurde durch Beschluß des Ministerrates von 1971 entsprechend dem § 35 des Gesetzes über das Urheberrecht, die Wahrung der Urheberrechte an den Werken Brechts zur Aufgabe des Staates erklärt und die künftige Wahrung der Rechte der Akademie der Künste der DDR übertragen. [. . .]

Dieser Beschluß ist in den vergangenen fünf Jahren nicht konsequent praktiziert worden. [. . .]

Damit die Zuständigkeiten nicht nur auf den Verlag verlegt werden, beabsichtige ich weiter, die Akademie der Künste und den Verlag anzuweisen, daß von seiten der Akademie ein von mir bestimmtes Beratungsgremium unter Leitung des Genossen Schnabel, Generaldirektor der Akademie der Künste, gebildet wird. Der Verlag wird außerdem verpflichtet, Rechte an Werken Brechts nicht ohne Beratung und Zustimmung durch dieses Gremium zu vergeben. [. . .] Es muß Frau Schall aber nunmehr eindeutig klar gemacht werden, daß sie nicht weiter persönlich berechtigt ist, Aufführungsrechte innerhalb der DDR zu vergeben und entsprechende Verträge zu unterzeichnen.[33]

[As you know, a resolution passed by the Council of Ministers in 1971, in accordance with § 35 of the law on copyright, declared the protection of copyright on Brecht's works to be the duty of the state, and the future protection of rights has been transferred to the Academy of Arts of the GDR. [. . .]

This resolution has not been enforced rigorously over the past five years. [. . .]

So that jurisdiction is not simply transferred to the publishing house, I further intend to instruct the Academy of Arts and the publishing house that the Academy will set up an advisory body under the leadership of Comrade Schnabel, General Director of the Academy of Arts, and I shall appoint its members. Furthermore, the publishing house will be instructed not to grant the rights to Brecht's works without consulting this body and securing its approval. [. . .] It must however be made plain to Frau Schall now that she is no longer personally entitled to grant performance rights within the GDR, or to sign contracts to this effect.]

The GDR authorities piled on the pressure. In a major heated exchange on 29 September 1976, Culture Minister Hoffmann urged Brecht's daughter, Barbara Brecht-Schall, to join the planned working group, arguing that this might prevent "die marxistisch-leninistische Sicherung des Brecht-Bildes" (efforts to secure the Marxist-Leninist image of Brecht) from being misinterpreted as her subjective quest.[34] The Minister's arguments demonstrate beyond doubt that the attempts to seize control of Brecht's assets were ideologically motivated. It was imperative at present, Hoffmann wrote to Barbara Brecht-Schall, to do everything possible to avoid any suspicion that decisions regarding the treatment of Brecht's works were being made subjectively. Above all, he explained, theatre practitioners needed to be given secure backing for their efforts to interpret the plays along Socialist Realist lines. Behind closed doors, the argument was expressed even more clearly. Hoffmann asked Hager to inform Erich Honecker that his chosen approach was right, both for the present and for the future. He explained:

> Angesichts der weltweiten Klassenauseinandersetzungen, in die auch das Erbe Brechts einbezogen ist, sollte eine Sache zu Ende geführt werden, die wir schon viele Jahre vor uns herschieben.[35]

> [In view of the worldwide class conflict, in which Brecht's legacy is also involved, a matter that we have been putting off for many years needs to be seen through to its conclusion.]

The cultural officials had some last-minute qualms because they knew that the resolution of the Council of Ministers only applied within the borders of the GDR state.[36]

But Brecht's heirs had no illusions either. They were well aware of the dangers. Barbara Brecht-Schall once explained that if she really had wanted to emigrate, then the authorities would have stripped her of her father's estate. She told the journalist Jacques Schuster that in 1971, six days after her mother's death, she had been summoned to appear before the Party authorities. The officials present had demanded that she hand them the keys to the bank safe on Berlin's Alexanderplatz, in which the family had stored Brecht's manuscripts. In addition to this, she was to relinquish all her rights. After all, they explained, her father was a communist poet and as such he belonged to the people. Brecht-Schall added: "Kurt Hager, diese fiese Typse, murmelte, dass man schließlich auch andere Methoden kenne. Ich wusste, dass er blufft. An einer Brecht hätte er sich nicht zu vergreifen getraut." (Kurt Hager, that nasty piece of work, muttered that they did have other methods at their disposal too. I knew that he was bluffing. He wouldn't have dared to touch a relative of Brecht's.) Thanks to her persistence, Barbara Brecht-Schall eventually succeeded in fending off this confiscation, a task in which she was supported by her siblings, Stefan S. Brecht and Hanne Hiob, and by her lawyers. One stroke of tactical genius was the offer to hand over the Brecht Archive to the Academy of Sciences, on the grounds that the Academy of Arts was not showing any particular interest and the negotiations had reached an impasse. This is what Werner Mittenzwei, the director of the Academy's Institute for Literary History who subsequently went on to edit Brecht's works, recorded on 20 April 1972 in the minutes of a conversation with Barbara Brecht-Schall. He reported that she said that:

> Das Archiv gehöre noch rechtlich den Erben Brechts. Entsprechend dem Wunsch ihrer Mutter wolle sie es jedoch dem Staat übergeben. Sie fände es nur vernünftig, daß Schriftsteller-Archive in die Obhut des Staats übergehen.[37]

> [The archive still legally belongs to Brecht's heirs. But, in accordance with the wishes of her mother, she wants to give it to the state. She thinks that it is only reasonable for writers' archives to pass into the state's care.]

The situation only calmed in the run-up to Brecht's eightieth birthday: under the direction of Werner Hecht, the Brecht Center of the GDR was to assume responsibility for coordinating the cultivation of Brecht's works, a coordination that had previously been lacking. Ruth Berghaus was removed from her position as manager of the Berliner Ensemble. Manfred Wekwerth succeeded her, and Ekkehard Schall, Barbara Brecht-Schall's husband, was appointed as deputy manager. This created a situation that was not free from conflict, but that was acceptable to both sides.

But Brecht's heirs did not relinquish their trump card. They shrewdly retained their ownership of the originals for as long as the GDR continued to exist. It was not until December 1992 that Brecht's literary estate and his heirs' collection were acquired by the federal state of Berlin.

BBA 7: The Stalin File

When it came to Brecht, the GDR censorship authorities were only able to chalk up a few victories. One of these was the suppression of the four poems that Brecht had written after the Twentieth Party Conference of the Communist Party of the Soviet Union (CPSU) in 1956. In these poems, Brecht had called Stalin the "verdiente[n] Mörder des Volkes" (*BFA* 15:300; outstanding murderer of the people), among other things. Alfred Kantorowicz had already made this phrase public in 1959 in his *Deutsches Tagebuch* (German Diary). Twenty years later, at the International Brecht Society Congress in College Park, Maryland, John Fuegi informed Brecht scholars about the poems.[38] They were first published with permission in 1982 in the edition *Gedichte aus dem Nachlaß* (Previously Unpublished Poems), edited by Herta Ramthun.[39] They too exemplify the dialectic of *private* versus *public*.

In October 1959, shortly before his resignation, Hans Bunge had refused to give Stefan Brecht copies of all of Brecht's statements regarding 17 June 1953 and the Twentieth Party Conference of the CPSU. Initially, he gave the excuse that he had no time at present to search for the material. Brecht's son demanded the material more insistently, expressing the view that its publication in West Germany would be useful, as the views that Brecht expressed in these texts were positive about the GDR. Even when Helene Weigel declared that she supported Stefan Brecht's desire and ordered that the material should be given to him, Bunge did not comply with the demand.[40]

Bunge's fear that Brecht's unpublished works — "teilweise ausge-sprochen politischen Inhalts" (the contents of some of which were decidedly political) — might be published without authorization played into the hands of the GDR cultural bureaucracy. Twenty years later, on 9 November 1979, Culture Minister Hoffmann suggested in a letter to Kurt Hager that Barbara Brecht-Schall should be advised not to grant permission for the publication of the so-called Stalin file. He gave the reasons for his recommendation:

> Die vorliegenden Texte Brechts befassen sich ja offensichtlich mit den negativen Aspekten der Persönlichkeit Stalins. Sie lassen aber seine Verdienste, z. B. im Großen Vaterländischen Krieg, außeracht [*sic*] und geben dadurch kein ausgewogenes Bild.[41]

> [The Brecht texts in question are clearly concerned with the negative aspects of Stalin's personality. Yet they take no account of his achievements, e.g. in the Great War for the Fatherland [as the Second World War was known in the Soviet Union], and so they do not paint a balanced picture.]

Here, the precautions concerning the vault in the bank on Alexander-platz once again proved their worth. Until 1980, two files of originals were indeed missing from the archive's collection of working copies: the file BBA 7, with letters and texts pertaining to 17 June, and the Stalin file, BBA 95. Helene Weigel had reclaimed them from the archive's collection of copies.[42] In the catalogue of Brecht's letters, the entries for the letters written on 17 June remained blank. While the catalogue numbers did appear under the recipients' names, there was no indication of the date or, what is more, the customary keywords indicating the letters' contents. This state of affairs did not lack a certain absurdity, as the contents of the files BBA 7 and 95 had already been published almost in their entirety by the end of the 1980s — at least in the West. In 1988, under the influence of glasnost and perestroika, Gerhard Seidel made the contents of the incriminating Stalin file known. Just in the nick of time, he published Brecht's wonderful satirical attack on the real-socialist cultural and political bureaucracy, "In den neunziger Jahren" (In the Nineties).[43]

Archives are a fundamental part of reception history. They resist attempts to appropriate them. Unless they are destroyed or plundered, they have the last word, regardless of whether they are meant to be private or public. Sources are, like facts, a lasting way of setting things straight. This experience also corresponds entirely to Brecht's conception of the archive. It has great staying power, and it puts its faith in posterity and in the wisdom of patience.

Translated by Michael Wood and Laura Bradley.

Notes

I would like to thank Manfred Bierwisch, Asja Braune (Bertolt Brecht Archive), Gisela Knauf (Secretariat of the Bertolt Brecht Estate), and Sabine Wolf (Literature Archive of the Academy of Arts) for discussing the subject matter of this essay and for recommending documents.

[1] Marie von Ebner-Eschenbach, "Die Freiherren von Gemperlein," in *Gesammelte Schriften*, vol. 4, *Erzählungen* (Berlin: Gebrüder Paetel, 1893), 1–77, here 24.

[2] Werner Hecht, *Helene Weigel: Eine große Frau des 20. Jahrhunderts* (Frankfurt a.M.: Suhrkamp, 2000), 41.

[3] On the history of the Brecht Archive, see e.g. Hans-Joachim Bunge, "Über das Bertolt-Brecht-Archiv," *Sinn und Form* 11, no. 1 (1959): 140–45; Gerhard Seidel, *Bertolt Brecht: Arbeitsweise und Edition; Das literarische Werk als Prozeß* (Berlin: Akademie-Verlag, 1977); Seidel, "An den Quellen der Brecht-Forschung," *Sinn und Form* 31, no. 1 (1979): 178–85; Seidel, "Das Bertolt-Brecht-Archiv der Akademie der Künste der DDR: Ein kollektives Gedächtnis der Forschung," *Zeitschrift für Germanistik* 2, no.1 (1981): 121–25; Erdmut Wizisla, "'Seid ihr immer noch nicht fertig mit dem Ramsch?' Das Bertolt-Brecht-Archiv im Jahre 1994," *Der*

122 ◆ Erdmut Wizisla

Deutschunterricht 46, no. 6 (1994): 75–80; Wizisla, "50 Jahre Brechtarchiv," *Dreigroschenheft* 2 (2007): 24–25.

[4] *"Wir sind zu berühmt, um überall hinzugehen": Helene Weigel; Briefwechsel 1935–1971*, ed. Stefan Mahlke (Berlin: Theater der Zeit / Literaturforum im Brecht-Haus Berlin, 2000), 133.

[5] Hecht, *Helene Weigel*, 56.

[6] Bernhard Zeller, *Autor, Nachlaß, Erben: Probleme der Überlieferung von Literatur* (Mainz: Akademie der Wissenschaften und der Literatur, 1981), 18.

[7] Weigel, *"Wir sind zu berühmt, um überall hinzugehen,"* 181.

[8] Hecht, *Helene Weigel*, 57.

[9] Hecht, *Helene Weigel*, 57.

[10] Hecht, *Helene Weigel*, 7.

[11] Bundesarchiv (henceforth BArch) DY 30/IV A 2/2.024/71 (also in Hecht, *Helene Weigel*, 92).

[12] Weigel, *"Wir sind zu berühmt, um überall hinzugehen,"* 139. See also Manfred Wekwerth's commentary from the year 2002, in *Johnson-Jahre: Zeugnisse aus sechs Jahrzehnten*, ed. Uwe Neumann (Frankfurt a.M.: Suhrkamp, 2007), 1092–93.

[13] Hecht, *Helene Weigel*, 94.

[14] Letter to Helene Weigel, 11 January 1967, in Weigel, *"Wir sind zu berühmt, um überall hinzugehen,"* 184–85.

[15] Weigel, *"Wir sind zu berühmt, um überall hinzugehen,"* 185.

[16] Hecht, *Helene Weigel*, 56.

[17] Weigel, *"Wir sind zu berühmt, um überall hinzugehen,"* 231–32.

[18] Hecht, *Helene Weigel*, 133.

[19] Manfred Bierwisch, "Erinnerungen an Hans Bunge," *Sinn und Form* 62, no. 6 (2010): 784.

[20] Bierwisch, "Erinnerungen an Hans Bunge," 784.

[21] Akademie der Künste (henceforth AdK), Historisches Archiv, file 338 (Das Verhältnis des Brecht-Archivs zu der Akademie und den Brecht-Erben).

[22] Since 1959, the Ministry for State Security (MfS) had been collecting intelligence on Dr. Bunge. In 1966, when Bunge was working for the periodical *Sinn und Form*, he was dismissed from the German Academy of Arts without notice. This dismissal and his marginalization, which went on for years, were instigated by the MfS. In January 1971, he agreed in writing to cooperate with the MfS. Manfred Bierwisch describes this as "Erpressung, Ausnutzung einer verzweifelten Ohnmacht, die in niederträchtiger Berechnung herbeigeführt worden war" (blackmail, the exploitation of a despairing helplessness that had been brought about through malicious calculation). In 1979, the State Security Service ended its attempts to force Bunge to act as an informer and decided not to continue working with him "wegen unkontrollierter Kontakte zu gegnerischen Kräften und Dekonspiration" (due to his unregulated contact with oppositional forces and his loss of cover). See Bierwisch, "Erinnerungen an Hans Bunge," 789–90.

[23] Bierwisch, "Erinnerungen an Hans Bunge," 783.

[24] Bierwisch, "Erinnerungen an Hans Bunge," 784. Bierwisch bases this on numerous conversations in which Bunge admitted that he had been wrong. Bierwisch did not look for written evidence of this position, as his friend had informed him of everything exactly (information from a conversation on 25 January 2011 in the Academy of Arts).

[25] Hans Bunge to Willi Bredel, 25 July 1962, AdK, Historisches Archiv, file 338.

[26] Heiner Müller, *Werke*, vol. 9, *Eine Autobiographie*, ed. Frank Hörnigk (Frankfurt a.M.: Suhrkamp, 2005), 153–54.

[27] The handover took place on 28 May 1959. In a note, Bunge recorded that he handed over the film to the director of the Lenin Library "im Auftrage Frau Helene Weigels" (on behalf of Frau Helene Weigel). See also letter from Hans Bunge to the executive committee of the German Academy of Arts, 2 June 1959, AdK, Historisches Archiv, file 338.

[28] Under the date 4 November 1959, Bunge recorded: "Die Erben erheben Einwände gegen eine nach ihrer Meinung allzu großzügige Verwendung der Mikrofilme in der Lenin-Bibliothek. Sie verlangen von Bunge Unterlagen über dessen Verhandlungen mit der Leninbibliothek. Bunge hatte nicht den Wunsch der Erben nach bloßer Einlagerung vorgetragen." (The heirs are raising objections to what they see as a far too generous use of the microfilms in the Lenin Library. They are demanding records from Bunge regarding his negotiations with the Lenin Library. Bunge did not state the heirs' wish for everything just to be put into storage.) See Hans Bunge, "Zur Geschichte des BERTOLT-BRECHT-ARCHIVS und der Arbeitsgruppe HISTORISCH-KRITISCHE AUSGABE DER SCHRIFTEN BERTOLT BRECHTS" [Fassung A], AdK, Historisches Archiv, file 338, 22.

[29] BStU 8661/76, 4–6. See also Helene-Weigel-Archiv (henceforth HWA), file 189.

[30] BStU 8661/76. See also HWA, file 189.

[31] Information from Gisela Knauf in conversations on 13 October 2010 and 6 December 2010.

[32] Legal gazette of the German Democratic Republic, 24 November 1971, part 2, no. 75, 637.

[33] Hans-Joachim, Minister of Culture, to Kurt Hager, Central Committee of the SED, 5 July 1976, BArch DY 30/IV B 2/2.024/102.

[34] Jochen Genzel, "Gedächtnis-Protokoll eines Gespräches zwischen dem Minister für Kultur und Frau Barbara Schall am 29.9.1976," BArch DY 30/IV B 2/2.024/102, 3.

[35] Hans-Joachim Hoffmann to Kurt Hager, 2 December 1976, BArch DY 30/IV B 2/2.024/102.

[36] Hans-Joachim Hoffmann to Kurt Hager, 5 July 1976, BArch DY 30/IV B 2/2.024/102.

[37] Werner Mittenzwei to H. Hörnig, Central Committee of the SED, Science Division, BArch DY 30/IV B 2/2.024/102.

[38] James K. Lyon, "Brecht und Stalin — des Dichters 'letztes Wort,'" in *Exilforschung*, vol. 1, ed. Thomas Koebner et al. (Munich: edition text und kritik, 1983), 120–29.

[39] Bertolt Brecht, *Gesammelte Werke*, supplementary vol. 4, *Gedichte aus dem Nachlaß 2* (Frankfurt a.M.: Suhrkamp, 1982), 436–38.

[40] Bunge, "Zur Geschichte des BERTOLT-BRECHT-ARCHIVS und der Arbeitsgruppe HISTORISCH-KRITISCHE AUSGABE DER SCHRIFTEN BERTOLT BRECHTS" [Fassung A], 18.

[41] Hans-Joachim Hoffmann to Kurt Hager, 9 November 1979, BArch DY 30/IV B 2/2.024/102.

[42] Written communication from Gisela Knauf, 2 February 2011. Knauf's comments here include:

"Helene Weigel hatte Frau Ramthun in meinem Beisein darauf hingewiesen, daß sie vertrauensvoll davon ausgeht, daß es keinerlei Kopien mehr von diesen Mappen im Archiv gibt. Das wurde von Frau Ramthun bestätigt.

Wie sich Jahre später herausstellte, hatte Frau Ramthun aber ja Kopien davon angefertigt und im Archiv verwahrt."

(Helene Weigel had indicated to Frau Ramthun, in my presence, that she trusted that there were no more copies whatsoever of these files in the archive. This was confirmed by Frau Ramthun.

As it emerged years later, Frau Ramthun had actually made copies and stored them in the archive.)

[43] Bertolt Brecht, "In den neunziger Jahren," *Sinn und Form* 40, no. 1 (1988): 16. See also Gerhard Seidel, *Saiäns-Fiktschen bei Brecht*, ibid., 17–20. For years, Brecht scholars had speculated about these poems.

Remembering Brecht: Anniversaries at the Berliner Ensemble

Laura Bradley, University of Edinburgh

IN THE GDR, a dense network of anniversaries was central to the construction of a German socialist culture rooted in the humanist heritage of Goethe and Schiller and connected to socialist commemorations across the Eastern bloc. Anniversaries provided an opportunity for the young state and its institutions to remember their origins, review their achievements, and set out their goals for the future. But as Geoffrey Cubitt argues, anniversaries also allow the different constituencies within a community to stake their claims to a share in the past, and in its present and future uses.[1] This fact was evident each year from the rival commemorations held to mark shared anniversaries in the two German states, and also from the way in which anniversaries came to function as particularly sensitive occasions in the GDR. In the case of Brecht's anniversaries at the Berliner Ensemble (BE), we are not dealing with a clear-cut conflict between state-sanctioned memory and private, oppositional memory, but rather with the interaction of a variety of interested parties, including Brecht's heirs, his collaborators, and a new generation of East German scholars and artists. These groups subscribed to the official line that the GDR was Brecht's cultural home, but their members held different views on how his legacy should be developed for the future.

The BE played a key role in commemorations of Brecht in the GDR. The theater drew its raison d'être from performing Brecht's plays and applying his staging methods to works by other writers; in his last will and testament, Brecht had asked Weigel to continue the company as long as she believed that she could maintain its style ("so lange sie glaubt, den Stil halten zu können").[2] And initially, at least, that was relatively straightforward: Brecht's former assistants directed productions of plays such as *Arturo Ui* (1941) and *Die Tage der Kommune* (Days of the Commune, 1948–49) to considerable acclaim. The problems came when this role was nearing completion. Weigel acknowledged in 1969 that the theater was running out of new Brecht plays,[3] and by this time Brecht's ideas were no longer the specialist preserve of the BE. In this context, some of the company's directors saw Weigel's insistence on Brechtian "style" as outdated. Manfred Wekwerth had argued as early as 1965 that devices such as the half-curtain had become so ubiquitous that they had lost their critical force. In his view, Brecht's own practice needed to be subjected to a process of *Verfremdung*.[4] Wekwerth's comments were symptomatic of a broader and growing dissatisfaction with conservative approaches toward the GDR's cultural heritage, and in 1971 Erich Honecker seemed to give encouragement to reformers by announcing that there would be no taboos on artistic experimentation.[5] This statement opened the way for bold reworkings of canonical texts, yet Brecht's heirs continued to argue that the BE should adhere to his staging practices. The seventieth, seventy-fifth, and eightieth anniversaries of Brecht's birth in 1968, 1973, and 1978 offer an opportunity to examine how the BE negotiated this period of transition, which hinged on a contest for the legitimate ownership of the legacy and the forms that commemoration might take. They reveal how the BE staged itself publicly under its three GDR managers, Helene Weigel, Ruth Berghaus, and Manfred Wekwerth.

Critics reporting on the BE's commemorations, whether for the GDR press or the Western media, were well aware that the celebrations served present-day needs. In fact, critics read the commemorations exclusively as a designed performance, even though some aspects were contingent and some plans had not come to fruition. This habitual emphasis on agency and manipulation risks obscuring the way in which anniversaries started to affect the development of the BE, and the rapidity with which this process set in. In 1968, Weigel was staging the theater's first large-scale commemoration of Brecht, and the BE was judged on the results, not on how they compared to previous commemorations. But the 1968 "Brecht Dialogue" set the standard, and the memory of it was part of the context in which subsequent commemorations had to be devised.[6] In the two years leading up to the 1973 anniversary, members of the theater's management team already seemed afraid of failure. Even though the BE was not marking a decennial anniversary, the director Peter Kupke reportedly argued that the celebrations would have to be an international occasion, as anything else would undermine the BE's international status; he added that a "small" event would be disastrous.[7] The GDR's broader anniversary culture meant that the weeklong activities in 1968 could not be treated as a one-off, and they were repeated in 1973, 1978, and 1988. As the examination of new archival evidence in this essay will reveal, this inexorable cycle of commemoration came to generate substantial pressures for the BE and its managers.

An International Family Reunion (1968)

In the 1960s, Brecht was still part of the lived experience of many of the BE's members. The theater's annual commemorations of his birth were relatively small scale, and they carried a personal touch. Weigel and her colleagues ensured that flowers were put next to Brecht's bust in the theater, that a minute's silence was held before the day's rehearsal, and that theater practitioners placed a wreath on Brecht's grave.[8] In 1963, the square outside the theater was renamed in Brecht's honor, and the BE held a ceremony inside afterwards.[9] But by 1968, the seventieth anniversary of Brecht's birth, the participants from his own generation were aging; this was the last major anniversary that Weigel could expect to shape. We can sense this valedictory element in a letter that she wrote to Joe Losey, who had directed the Californian premiere of *Galileo* with Brecht in 1947. Referring to the anniversary celebrations, Weigel told Losey that she was glad that major projects such as the Brecht edition and Brecht Archive catalogue were about to reach a form of conclusion.[10]

In 1968, Weigel and her colleagues were searching for a form of commemoration that would fit Brecht's own ideas. As Wolfgang Jeske has commented, Brecht made a repeated show of being uninterested in birthdays or commemoration.[11] His alter ego, Herr Keuner, states that he is not in favor of anniversaries or celebrations (*BFA* 18:37), while a poem that Brecht wrote in 1933 opens with the words "Ich benötige keinen Grabstein" (*BFA* 14:191; I need no gravestone, *Poems* 218). But as the 1933 poem goes on to demonstrate, Brecht was rejecting a certain form of commemoration, one that does not serve a useful function for those remembering. This notion is epitomized in the poem "Die Teppichweber von Kujan-Bulak" (*BFA* 12:37–39; The Carpet-Weavers of Kujan-Bulak) of 1929–30; the poem describes carpetweavers who decide not to build a statue to Lenin but to honor his memory by draining the swamp outside their factory instead. In 1968, the BE decided to enact this idea of "Ehrung durch Arbeit" (honoring through work) by holding a working conference and series of performances, with politics in theater as the lead theme. The dramaturge and critic Werner Hecht compared this move to the actions of the carpetweavers in

Brecht's poem, arguing that the BE would avoid giving the impression that it was staging a show simply out of a sense of obligation.[12]

It was important to Weigel to retain the *Gestus* of modesty ("Bescheidenheit") at the conference, and she planned to limit the guests to Brecht experts and friends of the BE. On 24 February 1967, she wrote that she wanted the event to be very small, modest, but first-class — a practice that had served the theater well throughout its eighteen-year history.[13] Weigel extended the principle of "modesty" to the look of the conference pack: "graue Mappen, die man am besten sofort in Arbeit gehen lässt" (gray folders, which are best put to immediate use for work).[14] The centerpiece of the commemorations was to be the GDR premiere of *Die heilige Johanna der Schlachthöfe* (Saint Joan of the Stockyards, 1932), directed by the BE's chief director Manfred Wekwerth, the only one of Brecht's assistants still working at the company. Weigel insisted that Brecht's daughter Hanne Hiob should play the title role as a guest, and the production also featured Weigel in the role of Frau Luckerniddle, her daughter Barbara as Martha — one of the "Black Straw Hats" — and her son-in-law Ekkehard Schall as the stockbroker Slift. Together with the emphasis on modesty, this explains why the GDR's International Theater Institute (ITI) saw Weigel's initial plans as amounting to "ein 'familiäres' Gespräch"[15] — an informal or even "family" conversation involving people who had worked with Brecht in the past or helped to bring his works to the attention of audiences in other nations. They included Bernard Dort from France, Giorgio Strehler from Italy, and John Willett from the UK [Fig. 1].

Fig. 1: Helene Weigel (far left) and John Willett (far right) at the "Brecht Dialogue," 1968. Photo: Vera Tenschert. BBA FA 30/100.

Others, however, were concerned to use the anniversary to showcase Brecht to the world as an example of GDR culture, and to achieve more international recognition for the GDR. When the management of the ITI came to examine the design for the conference pack, those present objected that the title page did not show that the event was taking place in the GDR.[16] One theater manager reportedly rejected the suggestion that the GDR's name could be printed in the program inside, arguing that there was no need to relegate the most important national task — achieving international recognition for the GDR — "shamefully" to page two.[17] Walter Felsenstein, the manager of the Komische Oper, is said to have questioned subsequently whether it was right to limit events to the BE, warning that this might lead to false modesty ("Bescheidenheits-koketterie").[18] The fact that the Komische Oper also had Brecht productions in its repertoire may well have influenced Felsenstein's criticisms. The BE lost official charge of the event to the ITI on 10 March 1967, just two weeks after Weigel had insisted that the BE should remain in control.[19]

The East German press coverage connected the commemorations at the BE to the SED's master narrative about the GDR's national culture and identity.[20] It stressed Brecht's ties to the GDR, argued that the BE owed its international success to its position in the GDR, and linked the commemorations to the debate about the new constitution.[21] The press coverage also emphasized the cosmopolitan nature of the event; the status and reputations of the BE's international guests confirmed the theater's prestige and proved that GDR culture had already achieved international recognition, compensating for the limited diplomatic recognition that the state had secured. While the idea of a working conference struck commentators as more Brechtian than the rival gala celebrations in Frankfurt am Main, some did express reservations about the scale of the BE's commemorations, which far exceeded Weigel's initial plans. The journalist Michael Stone, for example, wrote that it was the sort of event usually seen only after the death of a monarch or a royal wedding.[22]

Some Western critics used the anniversary as an opportunity to revive accusations that the BE had turned into a museum, and Klaus Völker interpreted the absence of guest productions as a sign that the BE was afraid of competition.[23] This was unfair: the BE had actually planned to invite the Piccolo-Teatro from Milan and a theater from Moscow, ideally with a production by the controversial and innovative director Yuri Lyubimov. When Giorgio Strehler was unable to bring a production from Milan, the BE decided against inviting a Soviet theater.[24] But

Völker's accusation did highlight the weakness of the BE's own contribution. It had failed to deliver the planned centerpiece of the "Brecht Dialogue," the GDR premiere of *Die heilige Johanna*. The BE also had to cancel a planned public rehearsal of Peter Weiss's play *VietNam Diskurs* (Discourse on Vietnam, 1968), partly due to objections from Hans Anselm Perten — who was due to stage the premiere in Rostock — and partly because the production was not ready, as rehearsals for *Johanna* had taken priority.[25] It is worth bearing in mind that the BE had originally planned to stage both *Johanna* and Helmut Baierl's GDR adaptation of the play, *Johanna von Döbeln* (1968).[26] So instead of staging new productions in honor of Brecht's anniversary, the BE's contribution to contemporary political awareness came through the activity surrounding its existing productions. It showed a film about Vietnam, appealed to spectators to donate blood for the Vietcong, and sold records and books to raise money.[27] Future perspectives for Brecht's legacy were provided not by the BE but by an exhibition of six hundred drawings by GDR children [Fig. 2], the attendance of delegates from developing countries, and a production of *Die Ausnahme und die Regel* (The Exception and the Rule, 1932) in Arabic.

Fig. 2: Helene Weigel and Politbüro member Kurt Hager in front of drawings inspired by Brecht's works, 1968. Photo: Vera Tenschert. BBA FA 30/125.

It is entirely normal for a theater's plans to change, and it was not the BE's fault that the Piccolo-Teatro was unable to perform at the "Brecht Dialogue." But it is significant that the BE failed to deliver any new productions of its own. Even though the "Brecht Dialogue" was a success, the gulf between the theater's initial plans and the actual commemorations indicates the weak points in the BE: its lack of a clear strategy for the future and its difficulty in delivering new stagings on time. The problem was not — as some Western observers assumed — that the BE's management had run out of ideas, but rather that its members had different views about how the theater should look. Weigel was determined to stage all of Brecht's plays, and she resisted experimentation with new staging methods, no doubt mindful of Brecht's instruction to maintain the BE's "style." In contrast, Wekwerth says that he — together with the dramaturgical department and Party management — made the radical suggestion of not staging Brecht's plays at all for the anniversary, but plays by authors such as Georg Büchner, Volker Braun, and Heiner Müller instead.[28] While Wekwerth produced a detailed critical analysis of the BE's development during this period, he never found out whether Weigel had even read it.[29]

The different interest groups put the question of the BE's future on hold until after the anniversary. Hecht, who had played a leading role in organizing the "Brecht Dialogue," was relieved that the theater had negotiated the anniversary successfully. He commented that the theater had risen to the challenge, as it often did during international tours.[30] But less than a month later, the crisis broke: six directors and assistant directors threatened to resign. They explained that they were finding it increasingly difficult to see a long-term perspective for themselves in the company, especially given the slow turnover of productions.[31] This complaint demonstrates just how much the BE's working culture had changed since the 1950s, when — as David Barnett has shown earlier in this volume — Brecht had been quick to promote his protégés to positions of responsibility. Yet it was not only the younger directors who were dissatisfied: in May 1968, Wekwerth announced he would not extend his contract beyond the following season, and that he would be prepared to leave immediately.[32] The focus on the extended Brecht family — so important in the 1968 celebrations — had alienated other members of the company. One director is said to have commented in 1969: "die Schauspieler sind jetzt so weit, dass sie sagen: Lass doch die vier, die zur Familie gehören, und die zwei grossen Schauspieler ein Programm machen, wir wollen damit nichts zu tun haben."[33] (The actors have now reached the point of saying: just let the four members of the family and the two star actors put a program together; we don't want anything to do with it.) By this time, tensions within the BE had been exacerbated by its members' contrasting reactions to the suppression of the Prague Spring.[34] Yet even though Brecht's anniversary was over, the authorities were scared to confront Weigel lest she close the BE and leave for the West; Alexander Abusch, Deputy Chair of the Council of Ministers, warned against the risks of associating Weigel's own forth-coming seventieth birthday with a political row.[35] The situation was only resolved when Weigel agreed to appoint Berghaus as her deputy, and Berghaus subsequently took over as manager on Weigel's death in May 1971. The rift between Wekwerth and Brecht's heirs seemed irreparable: he writes in his autobiography that he and his wife were turned away from Weigel's funeral.[36]

Experimentation and Uncertainty (1973)

Just five days after Weigel's death, the Council of Ministers published a decree stating that the GDR was responsible for protecting and cultivating the legacy of Brecht and Weigel.[37] The decree placed the Academy of Arts in charge of the copyright and academic management of their archives, giving it the right to decide on the performance and publication of Brecht's works. As Erdmut Wizisla has shown earlier in this volume, this was nothing short of an attempt to expropriate Brecht's heirs. However, the Academy was slow to use its new powers: Barbara Brecht-Schall continued to decide which theaters could perform Brecht's plays, and Berghaus and the BE took the initiative in preparing for Brecht's seventy-fifth birthday in 1973. Berghaus wrote to the Politbüro member Kurt Hager toward the end of 1971, saying that it was essential to start planning for the anniversary, and she met him in January 1972 to discuss her ideas.[38] In November 1972, Berghaus complained of a lack of support from other GDR institutions, arguing that it was not enough for the BE to press ahead on its own, when the event was supposed to be being organized in conjunction with the Academy of Arts, Academy of Sciences, Ministry of Culture, Union of Theater Practitioners, and ITI.[39] Although representatives of these institutions did eventually form a working group for the anniversary, the BE regarded it as a "Notgemein-schaft," a community born of exigency.[40] Berghaus was appointed chair only on 18 December 1972, less than two months before the anni-versary.[41]

The question is whether Berghaus had the authority to perform this role effectively. Her appointment as Weigel's deputy and then as the

BE's manager had come as a surprise, as most observers had regarded Wekwerth as Weigel's natural heir. The loss of both Weigel and Wekwerth, along with other longstanding members of the BE, meant that it was no longer able to function as a commemorative community in the same way as it had done in 1968. While it was inevitable that personal memories of Brecht would recede over time and that knowledge would become concentrated in a few experts, the most prominent experts were now outside the BE: Wekwerth and the dramaturge Joachim Tenschert had left, and the directors Benno Besson, Manfred Karge, and Matthias Langhoff were at the Volksbühne. Berghaus was reliant on new appointments such as Karl Mickel and Heiner Müller, and Brecht's legacy was not their key concern. While Hecht provided valuable continuity, the loss of expertise limited the kind of event that the BE could offer. Hecht himself argued that the BE could not enter into a major theoretical debate about Brecht when it no longer had an internationally renowned Brecht expert.[42] His comments were borne out when Wekwerth — rather than a current member of the BE — published the lead article in the Party newspaper *Neues Deutschland* on Brecht's birthday and addressed Brecht's significance for GDR theater in front of the Union of Theater Practitioners.[43] The BE was no longer able to speak for Brecht as it had done in 1968.

Berghaus's solution was to place the responsibility for Brecht's legacy on broader shoulders. Where the discussions at the "Brecht Dialogue" had showcased the BE's expertise and invited international input, Berghaus aimed to show that Brecht's work had been integrated into socialist culture in the GDR. This strategy was related to her view that the BE had achieved its international success at the price of neglecting its domestic function.[44] So instead of prioritizing the international aspect of the commemorations, Berghaus turned to amateur theater in the GDR. The Dorfstheater Ebersdorf — a village theater from Brandenburg — performed *Mutter Courage* (Mother Courage, 1939), while members of secondary schools presented songs, poems, and sketches by Brecht. But the attempt to involve other GDR theaters — and thus to take stock of Brecht reception outside the BE — failed. As a result, the only other productions in Berlin were a staged reading of interviews with Hanns Eisler at the Deutsches Theater and Benno Besson's 1970–71 production of *Der gute Mensch von Sezuan* (The Good Person of Szechwan, 1941) at the Volksbühne. The BE did host a guest production by an amateur theater from Denmark, the Fiolteatret Kopenhagen, but plans for the Piccolo-Teatro to stage *Die Dreigroschenoper* (The Threepenny

Opera, 1928) fell through. This was certainly a return to "modesty," but not as Weigel had understood it.

While the GDR critic Werner Mittenzwei argued that the weeklong celebrations had been a success, he added that they demonstrated one striking weakness: they offered no orientation for Brecht reception in the GDR.[45] Yet Berghaus's own speech for the anniversary, made to the Union of Theater Practitioners, did signal her intention to break with the past. She told the Union that the balance between tradition and innovation had been disturbed at the BE, probably an allusion to Weigel's preference for revivals of Brecht's model productions.[46] In a management meeting at the BE, Berghaus toyed with the radical suggestion that Wekwerth claims to have proposed in 1968: of not staging a Brecht production, but performing a play by a GDR author instead — in this case, Heiner Müller's *Zement* (Cement, 1972).[47] But Berghaus eventually fixed on *Turandot* (1953), and she conceded that the results were mediocre.[48] The 1973 anniversary represented a missed opportunity for Berghaus to put her own distinctive stamp on Brecht's reception by exploiting the increased space for experimentation with the cultural heritage. Her speech received little coverage in the GDR press, perhaps partly because it was not yet supported by the BE's repertoire.

The failure to attract other GDR theaters suggests that stagnation ran further than the BE, or that its lack of leadership was affecting Brecht's reception in theater more generally. The Union of Theater Practitioners argued that many of its members were indifferent in the run-up to the anniversary, and that their attitude verged on resignation.[49] The BE's responsibility for Brecht seemed to absolve other theaters, while its near-monopoly on Brecht stagings in Berlin prevented former BE directors now working at the Deutsches Theater and Volksbühne from mounting new productions. The BE's internal analysis reported that some members of these theaters had attacked the BE in discussions and publications during the week of the anniversary.[50] For the first time, the BE's role — to perform Brecht's plays in Berlin and to develop his staging methods — had become the subject of open debate. The public unity of 1968 was over, and different interest groups were using the anniversary to lodge their claims regarding the management of Brecht's legacy, motivated by the lack of clear direction from the BE. But at this point, Brecht's heirs had not yet joined the fray, as they still belonged to the BE. This was to change in the run-up to the 1978 anniversary.

The Restoration of the Old New Order (1978)

The BE had only a brief breathing space between the 1973 anniversary and the start of preparations for Brecht's eightieth birthday in 1978. 1973 and 1974 saw an upturn in the theater's productivity, with high-profile premieres including *Zement* and *Die Mutter* (The Mother, 1932). But the BE ran into difficulty in 1975, when the authorities orchestrated a press campaign against its production of August Strindberg's *Fräulein Julie* (Miss Julie, 1888), directed by Einar Schleef and B. K. Tragelehn. Berghaus responded to this pressure by removing *Fräulein Julie* from the repertoire after just ten performances.[51] This was a sign that the space for experimentation had begun to narrow, and the BE's innovative set designer Andreas Reinhardt defected to the West in the summer of 1975. These developments, and the rise in Stasi surveillance of the GDR theater community, predated Wolf Biermann's expatriation in November 1976.[52]

Records of management meetings point to a sense of helplessness and a lack of ideas about the BE's contribution to the 1978 anniversary. The dramaturge Hans-Jochen Irmer reportedly told his colleagues: "Bei mir liegen Anfragen von staatl. Stellen vor, die Auskünfte über den 80. Geburtstag Brechts haben möchten. Wir haben nichts."[53] (I have received enquiries from state institutions asking for information about Brecht's eightieth birthday. We've got nothing.) The Academy of Arts had already questioned the wisdom of staging major commemorations of Brecht at five-year intervals,[54] and in 1978 the BE's members were feeling the pressure. They sensed that the BE could not hope to match the events that Weigel had staged in 1968. Kupke explained that the "Brecht Dialogue" in 1968 had been a mammoth event ("eine Mammutveranstaltung"), and that the sheer volume of publications on Brecht meant that the BE was no longer in a position to place itself at the head of a debate. In his view, other institutions needed to take on that task.[55]

Discussions at the BE show that anniversaries themselves were starting to contribute to stagnation in the repertoire. As the theater did not have enough new productions of Brecht's plays, it had to keep performing the old ones until the 1978 anniversary. The management team acknowledged in 1976 that this was far from ideal: there were visible signs of wear and tear in *Turandot* and *Schweyk*, a production that had been premiered as long ago as 1962. Irmer argued that the amount of effort involved in "regeneration" rehearsals was disproportionate to the use, adding: "Wenn nicht der 80. Geburtstag Brechts bevorstehen würde, würde die Entscheidung sicher leichter fallen, Stücke abzusetzen."

Ich halte es für bedenklich, die Stücke aus diesem Anlaß am Leben zu erhalten."[56] (If Brecht's 80th birthday weren't just around the corner, it would certainly be easier to decide to remove plays from the repertoire. I think it is questionable to keep plays alive for this reason.) Mickel agreed that the BE needed to make a clean sweep, but only after the anniversary.[57] As in 1968, the pressures of a forthcoming anniversary were leading the company to postpone necessary decisions.

The main problem, however, was the rising tension between Berghaus and Brecht's heirs. Berghaus's iconoclastic production of *Die Mutter* had convinced Barbara Brecht-Schall that the director could not be trusted with Brecht's plays, even if she was the BE's manager.[58] In January 1976, Berghaus complained to Erich Honecker: "Die ständige Obstruktion der Brecht-Erben behindert nun fast vollständig die Erfüllung meines Auftrages, d.h. die Durchsetzung der sozialistischen Kulturpolitik im Berliner Ensemble."[59] (The constant obstruction of Brecht's heirs is now almost completely preventing me from carrying out my tasks, i.e. from implementing socialist cultural policy at the Berliner Ensemble.) Brecht-Schall was not blocking all Brecht productions at the BE, but she did make permission for productions conditional on the involvement of particular directors — such as Peter Kupke — and on their production concepts.[60] This approach was never going to satisfy the new directors and dramaturges in Berghaus's team; at a meeting on 3 June 1976, B. K. Tragelehn reportedly argued that the BE had to allow new interpretations of Brecht's plays, a view supported by Heiner Müller.[61] As a result of the conflict, Ekkehard Schall resigned from the company.

On 22 June 1976, representatives of the Ministry of Culture, Central Committee, and East Berlin's SED authorities discussed the steps that Minister of Culture Hans-Joachim Hoffmann wanted to take to stabilize the situation at the BE. According to the minutes of the meeting, the overriding goal was to ensure that the BE would make a worthy contribution to Brecht's eightieth birthday in 1978. Hoffmann announced that a committee would be created at the Academy of Arts; its members would include Barbara Brecht-Schall, but she would have only an advisory function.[62] Brecht-Schall was understandably reluctant to relinquish her control over performance rights, particularly at a time when she believed — with some justification — that the BE was in crisis. According to the Ministry's reports of a meeting in September, she told Hoffmann that Berghaus had done everything she could to ruin the BE, whereas Brecht-Schall had fought persistently to ensure that the BE would remain Brecht's theater. The exchange continued:

Minister: Keine Prioritäten in der Arbeitsgruppe.
Barbara Schall: Warum nicht? _Ich_ bin die Brecht-Erbin.
Minister: Das sind wir alle in der DDR.
Barbara Schall: Rechtlich bin _ich_ es.[63]

[Minister: No priorities in the working group.
Barbara Schall: Why not? _I_ am Brecht's heir.
Minister: We are all Brecht's heirs in the GDR.
Barbara Schall: But _I_ am legally.]

This extract encapsulates the conflicting claims on Brecht's legacy in the
GDR: the public demands of the state and the private legal rights of
Brecht's heirs. The dispute was not resolved until April 1977, when
Hoffmann agreed to change the clause stating that the President of the
Academy of Arts had the final say over performance rights.[64] This
represented a significant concession to Brecht's heirs, and Brecht-Schall
became the head of the committee at the Academy of Arts.

In the summer of 1976, the Ministry of Culture wanted to keep
Berghaus in post, at least for the time being. While Hoffmann warned
Hager on 5 July that the day might come when the Ministry would no
longer be able to support Berghaus's work in public, it hoped that this
could be staved off until after Brecht's eightieth birthday.[65] But Berghaus
was away from work due to illness from December 1976, leaving the
theater in limbo. Her colleagues did not know whether her production
of Büchner's _Dantons Tod_ (Danton's Death, 1835) would be able to go
ahead, and the uncertainty made it difficult to plan for alternatives. As
the theater's trade union representative pointed out, "[e]s wäre alles
nicht so schwierig, wenn ein klares Programm zum Brecht-Geburtstag
vorliegen würde."[66] (It would not all be so difficult if we had a clear
program for Brecht's birthday.) At this point, the BE was relying on its
former members to come to the rescue: Karge and Langhoff were due to
direct _Baal_ (1918/1919), and the company was considering a suggestion that Besson should direct _Johanna_.[67] The theater's plans were
changing month by month: plans for the Karge/Langhoff production
were dropped when the directors reportedly insisted on permission to
stage _Mutter Courage_ at the Volksbühne in return, and the BE suggested
that Wekwerth might premiere _Galileo_ later in 1978.[68]

On 29 March 1977, a meeting of Hager, Hoffmann, and Brecht's
heirs agreed that Wekwerth would replace Berghaus, with Schall as his
deputy. Hager emphasized that Berghaus was leaving at her own request,
for health reasons, and he insisted that no one should criticize her: "Sie
ist eine gute Kommunistin und soll für ihre neue Tätigkeit an der

Staatsoper (Regisseur) keine Schwierigkeiten haben."[69] (She is a good communist and should not have any difficulties in her new work at the State Opera House [director.]) As Berghaus left the BE just months after Biermann's expatriation, it is important to note that there was no question either about her political loyalty or about the fact that she should continue to direct productions in Berlin. It was her inability to sustain the confidence of Brecht's heirs that made her position at the BE untenable, particularly when a decennial anniversary was imminent.

Given the BE's uncharacteristic initial lack of leadership in the run-up to the 1978 anniversary, it was appropriate that the "Brecht Dialogue" had been broadened to include the other arts, rather than focusing on theater as it had done in 1968. The number of institutions involved in the preparations reflects the growing professionalization of commemorative activity for Brecht; the plans in the Central Committee's files mention fourteen GDR institutions, from the Central Council of the Free German Youth to the Union of Artists.[70] Yet in the ten months since his return to the BE, Wekwerth and his team had put together a program of over seventy events at the theater, including an opening ceremony, the premiere of *Galileo Galilei* (the Danish version of Brecht's play), a series of seminars and colloquia, and a "Directors' Dialogue" featuring texts by Piscator, Stanislavsky, Reinhardt, Meyerhold, and Brecht. Wekwerth succeeded in delivering plans that had not come to fruition in 1968 or 1973: for example, the Taganka Theater staged a production directed by Lyubimov, while GDR theaters from Schwerin, Gera, and Radebeul staged further productions of Brecht's plays.

Despite the BE's eventual success in 1978, the primary focus of media attention shifted from the theater to the new Brecht Center in Brecht's house on Chausseestraße. The Center took over as the main public site of memory in the media on 10 February 1978, when it was depicted on the front page of *Neues Deutschland*. In some ways, the creation of the Center represented a positive outcome for the BE, relieving it of the responsibility that had become such a burden since Weigel's death. Hecht was appointed director of the Center, and its creation completed the professionalization of *Brechtpflege* (the conservation or "cultivation" of Brecht) in the GDR. It would be wrong, however, to see the BE as competing with the Brecht Center for control of Brecht's legacy. Wekwerth and Hecht were keen to ensure that the two institutions would work together, and a memorandum of understanding set out the details of their working partnership. One clause even harked back to an earlier informal style of working relationship: members of the BE would be allowed to use the Brecht Center's restaurant, in return for members of the Brecht Center being allowed to use the theater's sauna.[71]

Conclusion

There are clear resemblances between GDR celebrations of Brecht's anniversaries at the BE, from the opening ceremony and the laying of a wreath on Brecht's grave to the *Gestus* of "Ehrung durch Arbeit." But the commemorations devised for successive anniversaries each presented a distinctive face to the public. In 1968, the emphasis was on an international celebration, a reunion of Brecht's extended family of like-minded collaborators, with a fresh generation of directors from the developing world. In 1973, Berghaus's choice of themes and performances put the spotlight back on Brecht and the GDR, particularly his legacy in amateur theater and schools. In 1978, the new Brecht Center and restaurant on Chausseestraße served as the official face of the celebrations; while the BE remained a key player, it did not tower above other institutions as it had done in 1968 and 1973. In each case, those responsible for the commemorations tried to show that Brecht's practice was embedded in socialist culture, whether by staging an exhibition of children's drawings at the BE in 1968, by hosting amateur performances in 1973, or by inviting the builders responsible for renovating Brecht's house to a performance at the BE in 1978.

Brecht's surviving relatives were central to the BE's commemorations in the period up to 1971; Weigel combined her institutional authority as the BE's manager with her personal and legal authority as Brecht's heir. But for Berghaus and Wekwerth, Brecht's anniversaries were first and foremost state occasions, linked to the master narrative of the GDR's development. On 30 November 1975, Berghaus told the Union of Theater Practitioners that Brecht's eightieth birthday was not only a matter for the BE, the Brecht Center, or Brecht specialists; it was a matter for the entire state.[72] There was a steady rise in the political ceremony associated with each anniversary: the opening ceremony was attended by the Deputy Minister of Culture in 1968, by the Minister of Culture in 1978, and by Erich Honecker in 1988. The public face of the 1988 commemorations was the unveiling of Fritz Cremer's statue of Brecht outside the BE, in the presence of Honecker and other members of the Politbüro.[73] This image is typical of the media coverage of anniversaries in the late GDR, when state ceremonies were inflated in an attempt to compensate for a decline in popular participation. Yet its prominence in the media is also ironic, given the traditional emphasis in the GDR on the fact that Brecht had intended "Ehrung durch Arbeit" to replace physical monuments. Brecht's poem "Die Teppichweber von Kujan-Bulak" had become such a regular feature of the GDR press coverage of his anniversaries that its critical impulse had been lost.

Despite the way in which the GDR authorities exploited anniversaries as an opportunity for strategic communication, the Ministry of Culture and Politbüro were relatively reluctant arbiters in the conflicts of the BE's transitional period. While the Ministry oversaw the BE's plans for the anniversaries of 1968 and 1973, it did not micromanage the events themselves. In 1968, the ITI actually complained that state institutions had not been sufficiently involved in the planning process, arguing that they should have provided constant advice in view of the high political risk associated with the "Brecht Dialogue."[74] Even though the state had claimed the right to control Brecht's legacy in 1971, it initially made no attempt to use its authority over performance rights, and Berghaus was left to urge Hager, a member of the Politbüro, to make preparations for the 1973 anniversary. Directors who wanted to secure permission to stage Brecht's plays called on the state to exercise its powers; in February 1976, Matthias Langhoff reportedly told Radio DDR that the SED had nationalized Brecht by declaring that he was part of the national heritage, but that it was not making proper use of its powers — a remarkable comment from a director who had himself been on the receiving end of Party disciplinary proceedings.[75] When Berghaus's position as the BE's manager finally became untenable, it was because she had lost the trust of Brecht's heirs, not because she had lost the authorities' confidence in her political commitment or artistic ability. But even then, it was Brecht's forthcoming anniversary that spurred the Ministry of Culture and Politbüro into action, as they strove to meet the expectations generated by the GDR's culture of commemoration.

Notes

[1] Geoffrey Cubitt, *History and Memory* (Manchester: Manchester UP, 2007), 221.

[2] BBA 1646/48, quoted in Werner Hecht, *Brecht Chronik 1898–1956* (Frankfurt a.M.: Suhrkamp, 1997), 1252.

[3] "Inhaltsverzeichnis zum Tonband der Leitungssitzung vom 28.11.69," Helene-Weigel-Archiv (henceforth HWA) 164.

[4] Manfred Wekwerth, *Notate: Zur Arbeit des Berliner Ensembles 1956–1966* (East Berlin: Aufbau, 1967), 12–14.

[5] *Dokumente zur Kunst-, Literatur- und Kulturpolitik der SED 1971–1974,* ed. Gisela Rüß (Stuttgart: Seewald, 1976), 287.

[6] Jeffrey K. Olick notes that "part of the context for any new commemoration is the residue of earlier commemorations." See Olick, "Genre Memories and Memory Genres: A Dialogical Analysis of May 8, 1945 Commemorations in the Federal Republic of Germany," *American Sociological Review* 64 (1999): 381–402, here 382.

[7] "Gespräch zwischen Berghaus, Hecht, Kupke, Mickel, Pintzka, Schall," 5 November 1971, Berliner-Ensemble-Archiv (henceforth BEA) "Brecht-Woche der DDR 1973."

[8] "Brecht-Ehrung 1963," HWA 71; letter from Joachim Tenschert to Karl-Heinz Hafranke, 1 August 1966, BEA "Dramaturgie Durchschläge für Frau Weigel."

[9] HWA 71.

[10] Copy of a letter from Weigel to Joe [Losey], 24 January 1968, HWA 188.

[11] Wolfgang Jeske, "'Ich habe meinen Geburtstag erst am zwölften bemerkt . . .': Vom Briefschreiber Bertolt Brecht," *Junge Welt* (Berlin), 5 February 1998.

[12] Werner Hecht, "Information über die internationale Brecht-Veranstaltung," 5 April 1967, BEA "BRECHT: Internationales Brecht-Colloquium."

[13] Copy of a letter from Weigel to "liebe Freunde," 24 February 1967, BEA "BRECHT: Internationales Brecht-Colloquium."

[14] Letter from Weigel to Hecht, 8 April 1967, BEA "Briefwechsel Hecht. Allgemeines. Brecht-Dialog."

[15] Wolf Ebermann, "BRECHT-DIALOG 1968: Ergänzende Bemerkungen des iTi-Sekretariats," BEA "Korrespondenz A–K Brecht-Dialog."

[16] "Kurzer Bericht über die Sitzung des iTi-Direktoriums am 8.10.1967," BEA "BRECHT: Internationales Brecht-Colloquium."

[17] Ibid.

[18] Werner Hecht, "Internationale Brecht-Veranstaltung," 18 April 1967, BEA "BRECHT: Internationales Brecht-Colloquium."

[19] "INTERNATIONALES BRECHT-SYMPOSIUM: Beratung im Ministerium für Kultur am 10. März 1967," BEA "BRECHT: Internationales Brecht-Colloquium"; letter from Weigel to "liebe Freunde," 24 February 1967.

[20] In her discussion of anniversaries in Israel, Yael Zerubavel argues: "Each commemoration reconstructs a specific segment of the past and is therefore fragmentary in nature. Yet these commemorations together contribute to the formation of a *master commemorative narrative* that structures collective memory." Zerubavel, *Recovered Roots: Collective Memory and the Making of Israeli National Tradition* (Chicago: U of Chicago P, 1995), 6.

[21] E.g. w. h., "Politik auf dem Theater: Streiflichter vom Brecht-Dialog 1968 in Berlin," *Der Neue Weg* (Halle), 13 March 1968; Joachim Scholz, "Die Wunder des Menschen zeigen: Nachbemerkungen zum 'Brecht-Dialog 1968,'" *Berliner Zeitung,* 21 February 1968.

[22] Michael Stone, "Brecht und doch ein Ende?" *Christ und Welt* (Stuttgart), 23 February 1968.

[23] Klaus Völker, "Immer noch ein unbequemer Dichter," *National-Zeitung* (Munich), 21 February 1968.

[24] Werner Hecht, "Brecht-Dialog 1968: Versuch einer kritischen Auswertung," 1–2, BEA "BRECHT: Internationales Brecht-Colloquium."

[25] Hecht, "Brecht-Dialog 1968," 5 and 10; Werner Hecht, "Bemerkungen zur 'Vietnam-Diskurs'-Probe im Brecht-Dialog 1968," BEA "BRECHT: Internationales Brecht-Colloquium."

[26] Copy of a letter from Joachim Tenschert to the Ministry of Culture and Magistrat von Groß-Berlin, 27 May 1966, BEA "DRAMATURGIE '65–'69."

[27] Hecht, "Brecht-Dialog 1968," 10.

[28] Manfred Wekwerth, *Erinnern ist Leben: Eine dramatische Autobiographie* (Leipzig: Faber & Faber, 2000), 227.

[29] Wekwerth, *Erinnern ist Leben*, 232–33; "Versuch des Vorschlags einer Konzeption für die Weiterführung des Berliner Ensemble," 16 March 1968, Landesarchiv Berlin (henceforth LAB) C Rep. 902 2860.

[30] Hecht, "Brecht-Dialog 1968," 6.

[31] Copy of a letter from Ruth Berghaus, Uta Birnbaum, Guy de Chambure, Manfred Karge, Matthias Langhoff, and Hans-Georg Simmgen to Weigel, Giersch, Wekwerth, and Tenschert, 6 March 1968, in LAB C Rep. 902 2860.

[32] Stefan Mahlke, ed., *"Wir sind zu berühmt, um überall hinzugehen": Helene Weigel; Briefwechsel 1935–1971* (Berlin: Theater der Zeit, 2000), 208.

[33] "Dramaturgie-Sitzung am 19.9.1969," BEA "DRAMATURGIE '65–'69."

[34] See Laura Bradley, *Cooperation and Conflict: GDR Theatre Censorship, 1961–1989* (Oxford: Oxford UP, 2010), 95–110.

[35] "Ergänzendes Protokoll zur Beratung über die Berliner Theatersituation am 23.10.1969 beim Genossen Kurt Hager," Bundesarchiv (henceforth BArch) DY 30 IV A 2/2.024/30; see Laura Bradley, *Brecht and Political Theatre: "The Mother" on Stage* (Oxford: Clarendon, 2006), 98.

[36] Wekwerth, *Erinnern ist Leben*, 238.

[37] "Beschluß über die Sicherung, die Pflege und den Schutz des dramatischen und literarischen Werkes und des Nachlasses von Bertolt Brecht sowie des Nachlasses von Helene Weigel," in *Dokumente zur Kunst-, Literatur- und Kulturpolitik der SED 1971–1974*, ed. Gisela Rüß (Stuttgart: Seewald, 1976), 269–70.

[38] Copy of letter [from Berghaus] to Kurt Hager, 7 December 1971; "Aktennotiz," 21 November 1972. Both in BEA "Brecht-Woche der DDR 1973."

[39] "Aktennotiz."

[40] Berghaus, "Bericht und Einschätzung."

[41] Letter from Klaus Gysi to Ruth Berghaus, 18 December 1972, BEA "Brecht-Woche der DDR 1973."

⁴² "Gespräch zwischen Berghaus, Hecht, Kupke, Mickel, Pintzka, Schall."

⁴³ Manfred Wekwerth, "Die Lebendigkeit des Bertolt Brecht," *Neues Deutschland* (East Berlin), 10 February 1973; Manfred Wekwerth, "Gesichert und nicht diskutierenswert scheint mit [*sic*] die Frage, wo Brecht eigentlich zu Hause ist," in *Material zum Theater: Beiträge zur Theorie und Praxis des sozialistischen Theaters* 26, no. 8 (1973): 38–55.

⁴⁴ Ruth Berghaus, "Das Berliner Ensemble ist beinahe ein Vierteljahrhundert alt," in *Material zum Theater* 26, no. 8 (1973): 65–66, here 65.

⁴⁵ Werner Mittenzwei, "Zur Brecht-Forschung und -Rezeption in der DDR," BEA "Brecht-Woche der DDR 1973."

⁴⁶ Berghaus, "Das Berliner Ensemble," 65.

⁴⁷ "Plan des Berliner Ensembles für die Spielzeit 1972/73," February 1972, BEA "Berghaus Protokolle (Verwaltungs-Mat. 1971–3)."

⁴⁸ Berghaus, "Bericht und Einschätzung."

⁴⁹ Verband der Theaterschaffenden der DDR, "Bemerkungen zur Brechtwoche," 20 May 1973, BEA "Brecht-Woche der DDR 1973."

⁵⁰ Hecht, "Überlegungen zur Auswertung der Brecht-Woche der DDR für das Berliner Ensemble," BEA "Brecht-Woche der DDR 1973."

⁵¹ M[artin] L[inzer], "Weiße Flecken (2)," *Theater der Zeit* 45, no. 7 (1990): 28.

⁵² See Bradley, *Cooperation and Conflict*, 118–19, 149.

⁵³ "Protokoll zur Leitungssitzung am 19.8.1976," BEA "Protokolle, Leitungssitzung 1973–76."

⁵⁴ "Bericht der Akademie der Künste über die Brecht-Woche 1973," 13 June 1973, BEA "Brecht-Woche der DDR 1973."

⁵⁵ "Protokoll zur Leitungssitzung am 21. Oktober 1976," BEA "Protokolle, Leitungssitzung 1973–76."

⁵⁶ "Protokoll zur Leitungssitzung am 25.5.1976," BEA "Protokolle, Leitungssitzung 1973–76."

⁵⁷ Ibid.

⁵⁸ "Gedächtnis-Protokoll eines Gespräches zwischen dem Minister für Kultur und Frau Barbara Schall am 29.9.1976," 30 September 1976, BArch DY 30 IV B 2/2.024/102.

⁵⁹ Letter from Berghaus to Honecker, 12 January 1976, BArch DY 30 IV B 2/2.024/102.

⁶⁰ "Protokoll der Regie- und Dramaturgiebesprechung am 3.6.1976," BEA "Protokolle, Leitungssitzung 1973–76."

⁶¹ Ibid.

⁶² H. Kießig, "Information für Genossen Konrad Naumann," 23 June 1976, LAB C Rep. 902 3622.

⁶³ "Gedächtnis-Protokoll," corrected at the request of Frau Brecht-Schall.

[64] "Notiz über ein Gespräch des Ministers für Kultur, Hans-Joachim Hoffmann, mit Frau Barbara Schall am 14.4.1977," BArch DY 30 IV B 2/2.024/102.

[65] Letter from Hoffmann to Hager, 5 July 1976, BArch DY 30 IV B 2/2.024/102.

[66] "Protokoll zur Leitungssitzung am 6. Januar 1977," BEA "Protokolle, Leitungssitzung 1973–76."

[67] Ibid.

[68] "Protokoll zur Leitungssitzung am 17. März 1977," BEA "Protokolle, Leitungssitzung 1973–76."

[69] Kurt Hager, "Aktennotiz über die Frage der Leitung des Berliner Ensembles," 29 March 1977, LAB C Rep. 902 4573.

[70] "Konzeption zur Würdigung des 80. Geburtstages von Bertolt Brecht," BArch DY 30/IV B 2/9.06/87.

[71] "Vereinbarung über die Zusammenarbeit zwischen dem Berliner Ensemble und dem Brecht-Zentrum der DDR," LAB C Rep. 902 4573.

[72] "Diskussionsbeitrag von Ruth Berghaus auf dem Kongress der Theaterschaffenden," BEA "Berghaus Protokolle (Verwaltungs-Mat. 1971–3)."

[73] ADN, "Ein neuer Blickpunkt in Berlin: das Brecht-Denkmal Fritz Cremers," *Neues Deutschland* (East Berlin), 11 February 1988.

[74] Ebermann, "BRECHT-DIALOG 1968."

[75] Karl Wörmann, "Das 'Berliner Ensemble' in Schwierigkeiten," *Neue Zürcher Zeitung*, 26 February 1976; Bradley, *Cooperation and Conflict*, 96.

Brecht's Dependable Disciple in the GDR: Elisabeth Hauptmann

Paula Hanssen, Webster University

THE ROLE OF Brecht's collaborators has been discussed in many scholarly works and biographies, and his female collaborators have received particular attention.[1] During each phase of his career, Brecht had colleagues who helped to write and edit plays and short stories — such as Elisabeth Hauptmann in the Weimar Republic and then in the GDR, Margarete Steffin and Ruth Berlau during the years traveling and writing in exile, and Benno Besson and Käthe Rülicke-Weiler in the GDR. This essay focuses on Hauptmann, whose role was in some ways typical of Brecht's other collaborators, but who merits particular importance because of her longstanding role in the creation and public promotion of his works. Whereas much scholarship on Hauptmann has focused on her collaboration with Brecht in the Weimar years, this essay investigates her influence on the staging and publication of his texts in the GDR, and her contributions to new plays and adaptations. Hauptmann was more than simply the editor of Brecht's works in the GDR: behind the scenes, she quietly provided inspiration and guidance to Brecht and his assistants at the Berliner Ensemble (BE), as well as to Helene Weigel as the theater's managing director. As we shall see, members of the BE paid tribute to Hauptmann's importance, but her coauthorship of specific works often went unacknowledged there.

From Exile to East Berlin

Well-known for her editorial influence as well as her authorial role in Brecht's early works up until 1933, when they left Germany — Hauptmann to St. Louis and the greater New York City area, and Brecht to Scandinavia — Hauptmann maintained contact with Brecht in exile and often met with intellectuals to find opportunities to produce his plays.[2]

In letters to Brecht she offered critique, commentary, and suggestions for his works in progress. After Brecht had brought his family and Ruth Berlau to the United States in 1941, settling in Santa Monica to work in the film industry, he relied initially on Berlau to find opportunities for productions in the New York City area. Yet in 1944, when Brecht hired Eric Bentley to translate his works into English, he promptly recruited Hauptmann to edit and oversee the translations, even giving her the right of *plein pouvoir* over the texts. This was her first chance to manage the political message of his plays, and Bentley argues that she was not slow to use this power. In fact, he claims that "with her, policy and ideology came before facts and loyalty to them."[3] For example, instead of portraying the Communists and Social Democrats as the adversaries that they were in a scene from *Furcht und Elend des Dritten Reiches* (Fear and Misery of the Third Reich, 1937–38), Hauptmann insisted that they should be portrayed as friends in the English-language version *The Private Life of the Master Race* (1942). She changed the text, with Brecht's approval, and thus saved his reputation as a supporter of the Popular Front of Communism and Social Democracy, which the Comintern had proclaimed in 1935.

When Hauptmann finally moved to southern California in 1945 to work with Brecht and the composer Paul Dessau, whom she married, Brecht was thrilled and made plans for her to work with him in postwar Germany. He wrote to Hauptmann from Switzerland in September 1947, assuming that she, as an American citizen, would have no trouble getting papers for the American zone in Germany. He chided her in his letter for delaying her departure, promising her a working relationship and even royalties:

> Ich selber habe jetzt endlich Schweizer Reisepapiere und betreibe die Berliner Reise mit größter Beschleunigung. Sie sollten so schnell wie möglich abreisen. [. . .] Ich rechne sehr damit, dass wir irgendein Arrangement treffen können und wieder zur Arbeit gelangen. Reden Sie sich nichts mit der Gesundheit ein, das ist nur eine Frage der Beschäftigung; Sie sind ausersehen, 90 Jahre alt zu werden und werden sich darüber noch oft beklagen. [. . .] Die *Dreigroschenoper* soll Albers auf Tournee nehmen, das ist auch Geld [als Tantiemen] für Sie. Packen Sie also. (*BFA* 29:467–68)

> [I finally have Swiss travel documents and am organizing the trip to Berlin as fast as possible. You should set off as soon as you can. [. . .] I'm really counting on us coming to some kind of agreement and starting to work together again. Don't talk yourself into ill health; it's just a question of keeping busy. You've been chosen to live to the age of 90

and you'll be complaining enough until then [. . . Hans] Albers is supposed to be taking *The Threepenny Opera* on tour; that'll mean money [in royalties] for you too. So get packing.]

In fact, Hauptmann did have health issues, and she lacked the financial means for the long trip. Both factors delayed her departure to Germany until late in 1948. Exhausted, she recuperated for a few weeks in Braunschweig at the home of Horst Baerensprung, a friend who had also spent the Hitler years in the United States. Hauptmann finally traveled through the Soviet sector to Berlin in February 1949, arriving by car with Walter Janka, who worked briefly for the new German film studio, DEFA, and went on to manage the publishing house Aufbau. By 1949, Brecht had started to work with other writers and actors and Paul Dessau had begun a relationship with an actress. Yet in the years that followed, Hauptmann succeeded in carving out a niche for herself in the GDR as a member of the Socialist Unity Party (SED), as a dramaturge and consultant working with young directors at the BE, as an advisor to the BE on administrative matters, and as the editor of Brecht's works. From 1949, Hauptmann edited the *Versuche* (Experiments) series, which Brecht had started in the Weimar Republic, and she would go on to edit his *Gesammelte Werke* (Collected Works). They were published by Suhrkamp in West Germany and by Aufbau in the GDR.

Hauptmann and the Berliner Ensemble

Hauptmann's role at the Berliner Ensemble is not easy to reconstruct, because she was not employed there officially until 1954 and often worked behind the scenes editing, writing, and discussing Brecht's ideas with his young assistants and dramaturges. Yet two key long-term members of the BE have written about the importance of Hauptmann's role at the theater. Werner Hecht, who joined the BE in 1959 and went on to become director of the Brecht Center and to write numerous books and articles about Brecht and his colleagues, explains:

Wer zu ihr kam, die Mitarbeiter des Berliner Ensembles und andere Ratsuchende, bekam mehr als erwartet. Sie gab wichtige Hinweise für die Interpretation von Stücken und Gedichten und verwickelte dabei ihre Partner sofort in Arbeits- und Denkprozesse. In den Gesprächen mit ihr wurde Brecht lebendig.[4]

[Those who came to her, colleagues from the Berliner Ensemble and others seeking advice, received more than they bargained for. She gave important tips on interpreting plays and poems, and she immediately engaged her conversation partners in the work and the thinking behind it. Brecht came alive in conversations with her.]

Manfred Wekwerth, who joined the BE as Brecht's assistant in 1951 and went on to become the company's chief director and manager, writes that it was Hauptmann's encouragement that dissuaded him from leaving the theater soon after his arrival. Both Wekwerth and Hauptmann were renting tiny rooms in the same building, so small that he describes them as broom closets. He had packed to leave Berlin in 1951 but happened to run into Hauptmann in the building. Wekwerth poured out his frustration to Hauptmann, discouraged by the absence of collegiality or interest in his ideas at the BE and by his lack of direct access to Brecht. Hauptmann put on a pot of coffee and invited him in, encouraging him by recounting her long struggle in 1927 to convince Brecht to work on her translation of John Gay's *The Beggar's Opera* (1728), which became their most successful play, *Die Dreigroschenoper* (The Threepenny Opera, 1928). She assured Wekwerth that afternoon that she, too, had ideas for the new BE, which she would be presenting to Brecht.[5] In his reflections on the BE, Wekwerth praises Hauptmann for her knowledge and influence at the theater, insisting that she was the best Brecht student and the best teacher, and claiming that most of Brecht's students could also be called hers. Sitting on wicker chairs on her balcony, Hauptmann, Wekwerth, and the other young dramaturges at the BE in the 1950s would discuss Brecht's theories and their practical application. Wekwerth claims that Hauptmann's insights and mentoring were then reflected in the plays that he and the other students directed.[6]

When she arrived in Berlin in 1949, however, Hauptmann seemed to have little connection to Brecht and other former collaborators from the Weimar Republic. Working for DEFA, she attempted to develop ideas for films that went nowhere: a new version of *Hansel and Gretel*, or a new adaptation of *Till Eulenspiegel*, the prankster from the late Middle Ages. Often alone, separated from Paul Dessau and not yet integrated into the Brecht circle, Hauptmann became despondent. Brecht wrote to encourage her, using the intimate form of address "du" instead of his usual more formal "Sie," and including his nickname "bidi" as his signature. Both Paula Banholzer, Brecht's girlfriend from his youth in Augsburg, and Margarete Steffin had used this nickname in their letters to Brecht. Its usage in Brecht's letter to Hauptmann signifies his attempt to lend her emotional support through intimacy. But the main form of help was practical: Brecht offered Hauptmann work — "our work" — to take her mind off things:

Liebe Bess,
    die beiden Aufträge, damit Du nichts vergißt, wenn Du allein bist und vielleicht geht es leichter, wenn Du etwas für unsere Arbeit tust. [. . .]
    [. . .] Bis sich alles besser eingelaufen hat, mußt Du Dich vor allen Dingen um die *Versuche* kümmern und den Kontakt zu Suhrkamp halten. Der Vertrag sieht ein kleines Entgelt für beides vor, aber das kann mit den Jahren sehr viel mehr werden, betrachte das mit der DEFA als *vorübergehend.*
    b.i.d.i. liebe, liebe bess. Immer.

b

Schreib an Theater. (*BFA* 29:538)

[Dear Bess,
    Here are two jobs, so that you won't forget anything when you're alone, and perhaps it'll be easier for you if you are doing something for our work. [. . .]
    [. . .] Until everything has been established on a more secure footing, you must first and foremost take care of the *Versuche* and maintain contact with Suhrkamp. The contract includes a small payment for both tasks, but this payment may become a very great deal larger in the future; consider the work with DEFA as *temporary.*
    b.i.d.i. dear, dear Bess. Always.

b

Write to the theater.]

Although Hauptmann was initially working unofficially as a dramaturge at the BE, she began to collaborate with Brecht and Weigel in other capacities. She not only served as a translator for letters to England, the US, and France, and as consultant to Weigel and the directors at the theater, but was also involved in most aspects of their work. One key task consisted of finding plays suitable for performance or adaptation for the new "socialist" stage. For example, Hauptmann was in contact with the American socialist playwright Herb Tank, who worked with a group in New York called the "New Playwrights."[7] Tank had written the play *Tanker Nebraska*, about a mutiny provoked by an officer's cruelty to a black sailor. Hauptmann translated the play into German and convinced Weigel and Brecht to produce it in March 1952. The production was well received and was then repeated by other Eastern-bloc companies, such as the Polish Teatr Nowy in Łodz in 1952.[8]

Hauptmann was also closely involved in productions of Brecht's own plays. She and Brecht traveled to Frankfurt am Main in September 1952 for the rehearsals for the November 1952 production of *Der gute Mensch von Sezuan* (The Good Person of Szechwan, 1941), directed at the Städtische Bühnen by Harry Buckwitz. When Hauptmann took a short holiday from the rehearsals to visit her old friends in Braunschweig, Buckwitz sent her a telegram saying that Brecht needed her back to help with new cuts.[9] Later Brecht dedicated the 1952 production of *Puntila and His Man Matti* to "E.H." (EHA 322). Hauptmann also accompanied Brecht to Milan for Giorgio Strehler's production of *The Threepenny Opera* in February 1956.

Shortly before her death, Hauptmann described her work with Brecht and the BE for the film crew of the documentary *Die Mitarbeiterin* (The Female Collaborator, 1972). The film deals particularly with her work as part of the collective that wrote *Pauken und Trompeten* (Trumpets and Drums) in 1955, for performance later that same year. Both Brecht and Besson are credited as authors of the script, which was adapted from George Farquhar's play *The Recruiting Officer* (1706). However, Hauptmann also received royalties at the same percentage as Besson: they each received thirty percent, and Brecht took the remaining forty percent.[10]

Hauptmann's notes indicate that she did indeed make extensive contributions to *Pauken und Trompeten*, even though she was not acknowledged as coauthor. The Brecht Archive has seven versions of the play, all of which list either Brecht alone or Brecht and Besson as authors. While Hauptmann's handwriting is evident in these typescripts, the most telling evidence of her work is the translation of Farquhar's original text in the Elisabeth Hauptmann Archive. The handwritten title page lists Hauptmann and Besson as translators, and credits Brecht, Hauptmann, and Besson for the adaptation (EHA 220/1). Comparison of one version of *Pauken und Trompeten* from the Brecht Archive,[11] one scene credited to Hauptmann in another version (BBA 981/4–50), and the published text in Brecht's *Gesammelte Werke* reveals that the text typed by Hauptmann contained many lines for the female characters that added depth to their roles, especially that of the female lead, Victoria.[12] In Hauptmann's scene 8 (BBA 981/4–50), Victoria, who has disguised herself as a male officer in order to spy on her beloved, Captain Plume, delivers a monologue about women's weakness, then encourages herself to act: "Nun, Victoria, hast du nicht ein Offizierspatent in der Tasche? [. . .] Victoria, auf zum Kampf, auch du hast jetzt Hosen an!" (BBA 981/08; Now, Victoria, don't you have officer's papers in your pocket? [. . .] Victoria, off to battle, you too have pants on now!). In the finished version some of the lines were cut, but the sentiment from the

Hauptmann version survived: "Auf zum Kampf, Victoria, auch du hast Hosen an!" (*GW* 6:2688; Off to battle, Victoria, you too have pants on!).

It is where Hauptmann discusses the appropriation of the cultural heritage, the "Aneignung des Erbes," that her conclusions about the transformation of a classical comedy such as *The Recruiting Officer* into a socially critical comedy, *Pauken und Trompeten*, are especially interesting. SED policy stipulated that the cultural heritage — literary works in particular — from the period prior to the GDR should be adapted according to the needs of the new socialist society. The SED recommended the "Überprüfung, Entwicklung und Anwendung [des Erbes] je nach den konkreten geschichtlichen Aufgaben der Gegenwart, je nach den objektiven Kriterien des gesellschaftlichen Fortschritts" (vetting, developing, and using the cultural heritage according to the concrete historical tasks of the present, according to the objective criteria for social progress).[13] Hauptmann fulfilled this mission. She wrote that *The Recruiting Officer* had been transformed "aus einer verspielten Komödie mit gesellschaftskritischen Zügen in eine gesellschaftskritische Komödie" (from a light comedy with some elements of social critique into a socially critical comedy), adding that "eine der wichtigsten Fragen in den Theatern ist die sogenannte Aneignung des Erbes" (one of the most important questions in the theaters is the so-called appropriation of the cultural heritage).[14]

In addition to *Trumpets and Drums*, Hauptmann adapted several other works for the BE. They included *Die erste Reiterarmee* (The First Cavalry, 1952) by Wsewolod Wischnewski; Hauptmann adapted the play in 1952, and Brecht subsequently considered producing it in the Soviet Union during a visit in 1955.[15] In October 1953, Hauptmann was working with Besson on a German version of the eighteenth-century English play by Ben Jonson, *Volpone*, and the publisher Henschel subsequently printed the manuscript for the BE.[16] Hauptmann was drawn to plays that could be didactic; Jonson, like Brecht, wrote in such a vein, seeing it as "the office of a comic poet to imitate justice and instruct to life."[17] Undoubtedly, another attraction of *Volpone* for Hauptmann was that its parody on vice and virtue was similar to the parody on criminals and the police in *Die Dreigroschenoper*.

These were not the only new projects in which Hauptmann was involved. *Hirse für die Achte* (Millet for the Eighth), a political farce from Mao Tse-tung's China directed by Brecht and performed by the BE, was based on Hauptmann's adaptation of the play *Lebensmittel* (EHA 419; Food, 1954).[18] Although she is not given printed credit as collaborator, other clues, such as her letter to a friend on 6 October 1954, support her authorship: "What am I doing? What I am generally doing — translating, 'bearbeiten' [adapting], writing notes on this or that theatrical production for a 'Programm-Heft' [program booklet] for a short Chinese play which I dug up and [which] runs under the name of *Hirse für die Achte*, a wonderful shorter play" (EHA 419). On 31 August 1955, Brecht wrote to "Comrade" Yüan Miau-tse of the success of the play: "*Hirse für die Achte* spielen wir immer noch. Das Stück macht dem Publikum viel Vergnügen" (*BFA* 30:371; We're still performing *Millet for the Eighth*. The audience really enjoys the play).

It was not just in the Weimar Republic, then, that Hauptmann did not receive full acknowledgment for works written by Brecht and his collaborators. Divergent claims of authorship have also been made about the adaptation of Molière's *Don Juan*, the play that "opened" the renovated "Theater am Schiffbauerdamm" on 19 March 1954. In a letter of 12 May 1964, Hauptmann wrote to a Professor Goldsmith at the University of Colorado that she and Besson had written the first version (EHA 387). Yet in an interview with his biographer André Müller, Besson claimed to have undertaken the adaptation himself.[19] Other evidence indicates that Hauptmann did indeed contribute to the play: a German translation of *Don Juan* by Eugen Neresheimer is in Brecht's library with notes by Hauptmann;[20] moreover, a comparison of the Neresheimer translation and the BE's finished text reveals close similarities, suggesting that the translation was used for the adaptation. A typescript of Besson's version is held in the Elisabeth Hauptmann Archive, with handwritten corrections by Hauptmann. And after the premiere of *Don Juan* at the BE, Hauptmann wrote to Benno Besson asking for 250 marks in payment for her work on the program.[21]

Hauptmann's contributions to the BE's productions were clearly invaluable as the new company continued to expand its repertoire. In 1954, she was finally made an official member of the company as a "literarische Mitarbeiterin und Dramaturgin" (literary collaborator and dramaturge), a position that she held until her death in 1973. Her official letters detail some of her work at the BE, including her dealings with publishers, like Suhrkamp in the West and Aufbau in the East, and her response to Weigel's requests for advice on personnel and on performance rights. The correspondence shows just how important Hauptmann was to Brecht and Weigel as an English-speaking agent representing them and herself with royalty agencies. For example, Hauptmann reassured Weigel in a short letter of 2 February 1955 that she would keep up the pressure on the William Morris Agency responsible for their royalties in the US (BBA 773/100). In addition, Hauptmann was often called upon to correspond with foreign theaters and discourage those that were not deemed suitable from presenting Brecht's plays. Here is a response that she received from Hans Hess, the Artistic Director of York Art Gallery in England:

> 21 Jan 1957
>
> Dear E H,
> Many thanks for your letter of the 12th of January which reached me exactly at the right moment, namely, the day before my meeting with John Fernald of the Royal Academy of Dramatic Art. In view of everything you have said about *Simone Machard*, I think it is best to decide here and now that the play could not be performed owing to all the difficulties you have pointed out . . . (EHA 387)

But Hauptmann was also responsible for correspondence about international publications and productions beyond the English-speaking world; a letter from Suhrkamp in March 1956 reports on a Spanish translation for Argentina and an agency collecting royalties in Yugoslavia (BBA 790/37).

At the same time as Hauptmann was acting as an external agent for Brecht and Weigel, she also acted as an advisor on administrative matters at the BE. In 1956, for example, she commented on a draft contract between the actors, staff, and management of the theater. Her comments reflected her keen understanding of the pedagogical thrust behind the BE's work, an aspect that David Barnett has highlighted earlier in this volume. Hauptmann emphasized the need to include motivation, goals, and methods in the preamble to the contract, rather in the manner of a course syllabus: "in der Präambel [sollte] stehen, in welcher Richtung wir arbeiten, für wen und auf welche Weise" (the preamble to the contract [should] contain information about the thrust/purpose of our work, for whom we are working, and how).[22] In the same letter, Hauptmann went on to suggest ways in which the draft preamble could be edited and improved, pointing out that the fourth paragraph could be omitted because the idea had already been expressed earlier.

Hauptmann's letters also show that her work for the BE was frustrating at times. In May 1954, some members of the theater accused her of sitting on the script of *Hirse für die Achte*, claiming that it was taking much too long to prepare it for production. Hauptmann wrote to Weigel in mid-May 1954, defending herself and her work:

> Aber ich will nicht im einzelnen auf die nie abreissende Diskussion über das Stück in meiner Wohnung, die Recherchen nach [einem] Über-

setzer, Verhandlungen wegen der Rechte eingehen, das Aufnotieren des Inhalts, Analyse der Dialektik usw, das Ansammeln von Material zur Information und für [das] Programmheft bei mir. (BBA 737/34–35)

[But I don't want to go into detail about the never-ending discussion about the play in my apartment, the search for a translator, negotiations over the rights, note-taking on the content, analysis of the dialectic etc., the collection of background material for our benefit and for the program, all of which happened at my place.]

Hauptmann's frustrations grew particularly acute when she thought that she had not been consulted over projects that she had worked on, and when she needed income. In an undated letter to Brecht, she complained of precisely these issues, yet went on to assure him that she regretted her anger during a recent telephone conversation:

Nach so was ist mir, als ob ich den ganzen Mund voll Sand habe, so ekelhaft ist mir so ein Gespräch. [. . .]
Mit meinem "Lebensunterhalt" wäre ich normalerweise auch nicht im argen; ich hatte nur die sehr teure Op[eration] und jetzt eine Zahnsache, für die die Kasse nicht aufkommt. [. . .] Sie tun mir den Gefallen und bemühen sich nicht um ein Stück für mich, wenigstens nicht mit meinem Namen bei Verlagen oder Theatern. Ich möchte das nicht. [. . .]
Das Beste in diesem Jahre war die Kamelie, die Ingwer-Schokolade und die zwei Wochen Buckow, vielen Dank dafür. Auch die Stritt-matter-Aufführung (bis auf den Schluss, den ich noch nicht verändert gesehen habe).
Hauptmann (BBA 654/85)

[After something like that I feel as if my whole mouth were full of sand; that's how disgusting a conversation like that feels to me. [. . .] I wouldn't normally have trouble meeting my "living costs" but I had that very expensive operation and now a tooth problem that the insurance won't cover. [. . .] Do me a favor and don't look for a play for me, at least do not mention my name to publishers or theaters. I don't want that. [. . .]
The best parts of this year were the camellia, the ginger chocolate, and the two weeks at Buckow, thanks so much for them. And the Strittmatter production (except for the ending, which I haven't seen in the changed version yet).
Hauptmann]

The reference here at the end is to a production of Strittmatter's *Katz-graben* from 1953, extensive notes for which were found in Hauptmann's papers, bound and ready for publication. These notes suggest that she was rather more involved in that production than has been officially recorded.[23] The references in Hauptmann's letter to gifts that she had received from Brecht provide further evidence of their close personal and working relationship.

Hauptmann as Editor

Both during and after this last phase of Brecht's life, Hauptmann's major responsibility was editing Brecht's works: his collected plays, *Stücke*, started to appear in 1953 and his poems, *Gedichte*, were published between 1960 and 1965. Eventually, the collected works, *Gesammelte Werke*, were published in 1968 under her supervision. During this process, Hauptmann had the difficult task of sorting out the various corrections and amendments that had been made to the manuscripts over the years. Scholars such as Erdmut Wizisla have criticized her editorial work: the versions of texts she chose to include in the edition were verified only by her, and they were put together in the order of which she approved. Hauptmann's editorial principle was the "Prinzip der Ausgabe letzter Hand," whereby the latest extant version of each text was published.[24] Editors of the more recent *Berliner und Frankfurter Ausgabe* have published multiple versions of texts and set out their historical development and significance.[25] Hauptmann considered herself a coauthor and not just an editor, which makes her interventionist approach more understandable.

As editor Hauptmann had great influence on the selection of texts to be published, and she displayed the same political commitment to maintaining Brecht's reputation as a Marxist and a reformer as she had done in her earlier work with Eric Bentley. Gerhard Seidel highlights Hauptmann's omission of texts that could be seen as critical of the GDR; the texts that were not published included "Lebensmittel zum Zweck" (Foodstuffs for the Cause, 1950), a poem that presents the USA's donation of food parcels to West Berlin as an attempt to influence the populace of East Berlin rather than as an act of charity. Earlier in this volume, Erdmut Wizisla refers to a letter in which Hauptmann suggested to Weigel that the GDR edition could dispense with texts that seemed offensive in the versions published by Suhrkamp. But there are other examples too: in July 1967, Hauptmann wrote a letter to the BE's secretary, Frau Ebel, advising her on how to respond to an enquiry about a volume for the West German book club Bertelsmann-Lesering. Hauptmann urged that Brecht's famous poem "Die Lösung" (The Solution,

1953) should be omitted from the volume because it criticized the GDR government. Hauptmann argued that Brecht's comments applied only to a particular phase of the GDR's history, euphemistically referring to the problems in the GDR as those of a developing country instead of as systemic flaws, as Brecht's poem suggested. She recommended poems that were critical of Nazism instead:

> Aus Band 7 würde ich nicht "Die Lösung" nehmen, dieses drüben ach so sehr beliebte Gedicht aus den *Buckower Elegien*, sondern "den Blumengarten" und "Vor acht Jahren." Was das letztere angeht, so gehört es zu den vielen Elegien, in denen Brecht noch die Anwesenheit von Nazis und Nazigeist beklagt. Diese Seite wird fast immer in den *Buckower Elegien* unterschlagen. Statt dessen hetzt man einige andere kritische Gedichte Brechts aus den *B.E.* zu Tode, um immer wieder zu beweisen zu versuchen, was man gern bewiesen haben möchte. (Daß Brecht bei dem schwierigen Aufbau von etwas ganz Neuem auch mal zu kritschen Bemerkungen kam, ist nur zu selbstverständlich, Prinzipielles wurde dadurch nicht in Frage gestellt.) Deshalb, meine ich, sollte man das Zu-Tode-Hetzen "Der Lösung" drüben nicht fördern.[26]

> [From volume 7 I wouldn't take "The Solution," that poem from the *Buckow Elegies* that is oh so beloved in the West, but rather "The Flower Garden" and "Eight Years Ago." As for the latter, it is one of the many elegies in which Brecht still criticizes the presence of Nazis and Nazi thinking. This aspect of the *Buckow Elegies* is almost always suppressed. Instead, some other critical poems of Brecht's from the *B.E.* are thrashed to death, as people try again and again to prove what they want to have proven. (The fact that, during the difficult process of constructing something entirely new, Brecht sometimes made critical comments is only to be expected. But he never questioned matters of principle.) That's why, in my opinion, we shouldn't encourage people in the West to carry on rehashing "The Solution" to death.]

This demonstrates again how Brecht and Hauptmann's shared political vision influenced her editorial work, which started in 1945 in New York with her supervision of Eric Bentley's English translations and continued in East Berlin.

Conclusion

Hauptmann seems to have served in almost all capacities for Brecht and the BE, and she was highly regarded by her colleagues as well as by Brecht. Besides her constant contributions to adaptations and discussions of plays to be performed, and her research on plays that would be appropriate for their socialist theater, Hauptmann was constantly engaged as an editor of Brecht's works, as a writer and teacher for the BE, and as a supporter of Brecht's legacy. In this way her contributions, though often behind the scenes, were manifold at the BE, and they included correspondence with publishers within and beyond the German-speaking world. The BE's assistant directors and dramaturges, as well as Brecht, Weigel, and the audience at the theater, all reaped the benefits of Hauptmann's involvement in the management of Brecht's legacy.

In 1961, Hauptmann received the Lessing Prize, the highest award for literature in the GDR, for her work editing and writing with Brecht and other members of the BE. Yet it was only after Hauptmann's death that her own collected works appeared in print. In the epilogue to the volume, the critic Fritz Hofmann summed up her contribution to the cultural life of the GDR:

> Als Dramaturgin am Berliner Ensemble, als Übersetzerin und Bearbeiterin klassischer und moderner Stücke, als Herausgeberin des Werkes von Brecht stellte Elisabeth Hauptmann ihre reichen Erfahrungen, ihre literarische Einfühlungskraft, ihre intime Kenntnis des Brechtschen Werks in den Dienst des kulturellen Wiederaufbaus und einer neuen, sozialistischen Theaterkultur.[27]

> [As a dramaturge at the Berliner Ensemble, as a translator and adaptor of classical and modern plays, as the editor of Brecht's works, Elisabeth Hauptmann placed her rich experience, her literary sensitivity, her intimate knowledge of Brecht's works in the service of cultural renewal and a new socialist theatrical culture.]

Hauptmann was not striving to be the most objective editor and translator of Brecht's works; she saw herself as a partisan defender of both Brecht and the GDR. She was unquestionably a strong force in the control of Brecht's papers, his plays, and even productions in other theaters and countries. She was also a coauthor of adaptations attributed to Brecht and his assistant directors, and she translated newer plays by other playwrights into German. But Hauptmann was only able to exercise this influence because Brecht, Weigel, and their collaborators and staff acknowledged her as the expert on all things Brechtian. As Brecht's most longstanding continuous collaborator, and as the coauthor of many of his key works, she wielded substantial intellectual authority in the management of his published legacy after his death. The full scope of her contribution to Brecht's work and legacy has still to come to light and receive full acknowledgment, even now.

Notes

[1] See e.g. *Brecht Yearbook* 19 (1994): *Focus: Margarete Steffin*; Sabine Kebir, *Bertolt Brecht: Ein akzeptabler Mann? Brecht und die Frauen* (East Berlin: Der Morgen, 1987) and *Ich fragte nicht nach meinem Anteil: Elisabeth Hauptmanns Arbeit mit Bertolt Brecht* (Berlin: Aufbau, 1997).

[2] Hauptmann had worked with Brecht on almost all his Berlin texts, writing plays and musicals that were subsequently performed in the GDR, such as *Mann ist Mann* (Man Equals Man, 1925), *Mahagonny* (1928), and then the *Lehrstücke* or teaching plays such as *Der Jasager* (He Who Says Yes, 1929–30), *Der Neinsager* (He Who Says No, 1931), and the antifascist play *Die Rundköpfe und die Spitzköpfe* (The Roundheads and the Peakheads, 1933).

[3] Eric Bentley, *The Brecht Memoir* (Evanston: Northwestern University Press, 1985), 12.

[4] Werner Hecht, "Die Mitarbeiterin," in *Brecht: Vielseitige Betrachtungen* (East Berlin: Henschel, 1978), 151–52.

[5] Manfred Wekwerth, *Erinnern ist Leben: Eine dramatische Autobiographie* (Leipzig: Faber & Faber, 2000), 64–65.

[6] Manfred Wekwerth, *Schriften: Arbeit mit Brecht* (East Berlin: Henschel, 1975), 27.

[7] Elisabeth Hauptmann, program for a production of *Tanker Nebraska* at the BE, premiered on 22 March 1952.

[8] Kazimierz Braun, *A History of Polish Theater, 1939–1989: Spheres of Captivity and Freedom* (Westport, CT: Greenwood Press, 1996), 48.

[9] Telegram from Buckwitz to Hauptmann, 12. November 1952, Elisabeth-Hauptmann-Archiv (henceforth EHA) 211/7. Where no further explanation of sources is necessary, subsequent references to this archive are included in the main text. The EHA was being recatalogued when this essay went to press, so file references may change.

[10] Kebir, *Ich fragte nicht nach meinem Anteil*, 206–7.

[11] Text of *Pauken und Trompeten* (1955) in BBA 198/1–179. Where no further explanation of sources is necessary, subsequent references to this archive are included in the main text.

[12] Bertolt Brecht, *Gesammelte Werke in 20 Bänden* (Frankfurt a.M.: Suhrkamp, 1967), 6: 2617–2710. Subsequent references to this volume are included in the main text using the abbreviation *GW* 6 and page number.

[13] Hartmut Zimmermann, Horst Ulrich, and Michael Fehlauer, *DDR-Handbuch*, 3rd edn. (Cologne: Wissenschaft und Politik, 1985), 1:766.

[14] Elisabeth Hauptmann, "Über die Bearbeitung von Farquhars Komödie *Der Werbeoffizier*," EHA 280.

[15] Werner Mittenzwei, *Das Leben des Bertolt Brecht oder der Umgang mit den Welträtseln* (East Berlin: Aufbau, 1987), 2:631.

[16] See Hauptmann's personal papers, EHA 419, and translator's notes to *Volpone*, EHA 219/5.

[17] Ben Jonson, *Volpone, or the Fox*, ed. J. Creaser (New York: New York UP, 1978), 71.

[18] *Hirse für die Achte: Ein chinesisches Volksstück; Deutsche Fassung für das Berliner Ensemble von Elisabeth Hauptmann und Manfred Wekwerth nach der Übersetzung aus dem Chinesischen von Yuan Miaotse* (Leipzig: Friedrich Hofmeister VEB, 1954).

[19] André Müller, *Der Regisseur Benno Besson* (East Berlin: Henschel, 1967), 18, 26.

[20] John Fuegi, "Whodunit: 'Brecht's' Adaptation of Moliére's *Don Juan*," *Comparative Literature Studies* 60, no. 2 (1974): 158–72.

[21] Letter from Hauptmann to Benno Besson, March 1954, EHA 419.

[22] Letter from Hauptmann to Herr Rietorf, 21 January 1956, BBA 773/109.

[23] Matthew Philpotts, "'Aus so prosaischen Dingen wie Kartoffeln, Straßen, Traktoren werden poetische Dinge!': Brecht, *Sinn und Form*, and Strittmatter's *Katzgraben*," *German Life and Letters* 56, no. 1 (2003): 56–71.

[24] Jan Knopf, *Bertolt Brecht: Ein kritischer Forschungsbericht; Fragwürdiges in der Brecht-Forschung* (Frankfurt a.M.: Fischer Athenäum, 1974).

[25] Erdmut Wizisla, "Editorial Principles in the Berlin and Frankfurt Edition of Bertolt Brecht's Works," *The Drama Review* 43, no. 4 (1999): 31–39.

[26] Letter from Hauptmann to Frau Ebel, 7 July 1967, EHA 682.

[27] Elisabeth Hauptmann, *Julia ohne Romeo: Geschichten, Stücke, Aufsätze, Erinnerungen*, ed. R. Eggert and R. Hill (East Berlin: Aufbau, 1976), 242.

III. Creative Responses to Brecht's Work

Musical Threnodies for Brecht

Joy H. Calico, Vanderbilt University

KURT WEILL MAY be the most famous of Brecht's musical collaborators, but Hanns Eisler and Paul Dessau were the two composers with whom Brecht enjoyed his most enduring and most prolific artistic relationships. This essay focuses on their literary and musical responses to his death on 14 August 1956. At that time Eisler was perhaps Brecht's oldest close friend; their partnership had been forged in Weimar-era Berlin, had weathered European and American exile, and continued in East Germany. When Eisler's *Johann Faustus* libretto drew fire from the SED in 1953 Brecht was his staunchest defender, and Eisler is said to be the composer with whom the author was most compatible artistically and personally. Dessau began working with Brecht in 1943 and became a valued collaborator in California and the GDR; his music is the definitive sound of Brecht's late works. Together they staged ten premieres and withstood the 1951 controversy over their *Lukullus* opera, and Brecht held Dessau in high enough esteem to negotiate performance rights on his behalf for *Mutter Courage und ihre Kinder* (Mother Courage and Her Children, 1939), *Der gute Mensch von Sezuan* (The Good Person of Szechwan, 1941), and *Der kaukasische Kreidekreis* (The Caucasian Chalk Circle, 1944) in Switzerland, Austria, and West Germany.[1] When Brecht died, both composers marked his passing by returning to texts he had written in the 1930s, but their treatments differ considerably. Karen Leeder has shown in her survey of fifty years of poetry about Brecht's death that initial poetic responses tended to be traditionally mournful while later responses were more variegated,[2] and these composers' works bear that out. Eisler, disillusioned and wounded by East German cultural politics, responded with despair and nostalgia. Dessau's response, however, represents a strand of modernist elegy that, beginning in the 1950s, says Leeder, "permitted a much more robust reckoning with the deceased" and is "not solace as traditionally understood." In the words of Jahan Ramazani, quoted by

Leeder, modernist elegies offer "not answers but memorable puzzlings."[3] This essay investigates the composers' responses as representative of each end of that spectrum.

Hanns Eisler

Eisler's initial public responses to Brecht's passing were not musical; they were short pieces of prose and poetry for the press. The first was part of a series of tributes published in the GDR newspaper *Neues Deutschland*, the official organ of the SED Central Committee. On 16 August 1956 it marked Brecht's death by devoting parts of three pages, including the front page, to statements from the Party leadership and key cultural figures.[4] On 17 August its coverage continued with condolences from abroad, excerpts from West German obituaries, and a few personal notices, including Eisler's first public statement:

> Der Tod Bertolt Brechts, des größten Dichters und Dramatikers nicht nur unseres Jahrhunderts, ist ein entsetzlicher Verlust für die Menschheit. Ihn ehren, heißt seine Werke lebendig halten. Dafür will ich mich bemühen, so gut ich es kann und solange ich lebe.[5]
>
> [The death of Bertolt Brecht, the greatest poet and playwright not just of our century, is a terrible loss for mankind. To keep his works alive is to honor him. I will strive to do that as well as I can and for as long as I live.]

True to the deceased's aphoristic style, Eisler's text is conspicuously shorter and less sentimental than the others alongside which it appears.

Eisler published his second newspaper notice on 26 August 1956 in Vienna's *Österreichische Volksstimme*, the official organ of the Austrian Communist Party (KPÖ),[6] even though Brecht's ties to Vienna were nominal. Eisler, on the other hand, had lived there from childhood until 1926 and moved frequently between East Berlin and Vienna from 1948 to 1955. When he was considering where to settle down after his return to Europe in 1948, Vienna was a strong frontrunner.[7] Eisler's homage in the *Österreichische Volksstimme* appears to have been at least as much an acknowledgment of Eisler's loss as of Brecht's death. At any rate both men received Austrian passports in 1950 (Brecht by virtue of his marriage to the Viennese Helene Weigel) and retained them until their deaths. All the while Brecht and Eisler served as cultural icons for the GDR yet declined to join the SED. Presumably fifteen years in exile teaches one to always have an exit strategy.

The *Österreichische Volksstimme* published two verses of a poem Eisler wrote entitled "Kantate auf den Tod Bertolt Brechts" (Cantata on the Death of Bertolt Brecht).[8] The accompanying musical incipit was said to be the beginnings of a cantata Eisler was writing based on this text, but it was never completed. The editors provided some context for Eisler's relationship to Brecht with a reference to the "Einheitsfrontlied" (Song of the United Front), the most famous song they had written together and a favorite memento of the mid-1930s. Eisler subsequently published an expanded version of his poem on 23 September 1956 in *Neues Deutschland*, where it is conspicuously situated. It is framed by an article first published two days earlier in the West German *Süddeutsche Zeitung* that recounts a controversy elicited by plans to stage Brecht's *Mutter Courage* at the Göttingen National Theater in the 1956–57 season. Theater manager Heinz Hilpert had endorsed Brecht's open letter opposing the instatement of conscription in both Germanys, and his public support of the East German playwright's position brought Hilpert into conflict with some theatergoers as well as with city officials.[9]

Eisler's poem consists of five verses, the first and last of which had first appeared in the *Österreichische Volksstimme* piece above. Those two are modeled after the corresponding stanzas in Brecht's poem "Kantate zu Lenins Todestag" (Cantata on Lenin's Death, 1935), and Eisler's adaptation substitutes Brecht for Lenin. Certainly the use of extant work by others honored one of the poet's favorite working methods, although neither newspaper noted the relationship between Eisler's poem and Brecht's text. The first verse of Brecht's poem is based on an anecdote about a soldier on Lenin's death watch who tried to rouse him by crying out "the exploiters are coming!" When Lenin did not respond to that most urgent of calls, the soldier accepted that his leader was truly dead:

Als Lenin gestorben war
Sagte, so wird erzählt, ein Soldat der Totenwache
Zu seinen Kameraden: Ich wollte es
Nicht glauben. Ich ging hinein, wo er liegt, und
Schrie ihm ins Ohr: "Iljitsch
Die Ausbeuter kommen!" Er rührte sich nicht. Jetzt
Weiß ich, daß er gestorben ist. (*BFA* 12:57)

[When Lenin had died
A soldier of the death-watch, so the story goes,
Said to his comrade: "I couldn't
Believe it. So I went inside where he lies and
I screamed into his ear, ILYTCH,
THE EXPLOITERS ARE COMING!"

He didn't move, and then
I knew he was dead.[10]]

In Eisler's poem, written in the first person and addressed to Brecht using his first name just as the soldier used Lenin's first name, the composer tests the deceased Brecht with the same exhortation. Framing this poem with a report about West German resistance to Brecht was surely meant to suggest that the exploiters were, in fact, still at the door — or at least at the border:

Als Brecht gestorben war
Da wollt ich es nicht glauben.
Ich ging hinein
Und sprach zu ihm:
"Bert
die Ausbeuter kommen!"
Er rührte sich nicht.
Da wußt ich, daß er gestorben war.
        (*Neues Deutschland*, 23 September 1956)

[When Brecht had died
At the time I didn't want to believe it.
I went in
And said to him:
"Bert!
The exploiters are coming!"
He did not move.
Then I knew he was dead.]

Brecht's "Lenin" poem concludes with a quotation from Marx's writing on the Paris Commune, in which he wrote that the "martyrs are enshrined in the great heart of the working class." Brecht substituted "Lenin" for "martyrs" in his verse:

Lenin ist eingeschreint
In dem großen Herzen der Arbeiterklasse.
Er war unser Lehrer.
Er hat mit uns gekämpft.
Er ist eingeschreint
In dem großen Herzen der Arbeiterklasse. (*BFA* 12:60)

[Lenin is enshrined
In the great heart of the working class.
He was our teacher.
He fought alongside us.

He is enshrined
In the great heart of the working class.[11]]

Eisler's poem further substituted the familiar "du" form in addressing
Brecht directly:

Und du bist eingeschreint
in dem großen Herzen
der Arbeiterklasse. (*Neues Deutschland*, 22 September 1956)

[And you are enshrined
In the great heart
Of the working class.]

If, as Katharine Hodgson asserts, Brecht's original poem "comes very
close to a Soviet-style panegyric,"[12] then Eisler's appropriation comes
closer still, unabashedly vaunting the poet as peer of the revolutionary
icon. If official-style monumentality is averted, it is only by his use of the
familiar "du" form that both humanizes Brecht and hints at Eisler's
personal loss.

The composer's contributions to the special issue of *Sinn und Form*
dedicated to Brecht, published in early 1957, are far more intimate.
Whereas the aforementioned items had appeared in newspapers for a
general readership, *Sinn und Form* was the literary publication that had
essentially served as a "house journal" for Brecht in the cultural-political
battles he and his circle had waged with the SED authorities in the early
1950s.[13] Stephen Parker and Matthew Philpotts call the 1957 special
issue a "landmark in literary history"; it featured some of Brecht's
previously unpublished works alongside essays and memoirs by
prominent friends from around the world.[14] Eisler contributed an essay
and a song, each telling in its own way. The essay, entitled "Bertolt
Brecht und die Musik," began with a quotation from Xenophon's
Symposium asserting that a person's nature is revealed not only in
important works but also in the humorous and quotidian.[15] As proof of
this, Eisler presented a vignette from each of the three geopolitical phases
of their 30-year relationship: the Weimar Republic, exile, and the GDR.

The first recalled the performance of *Lehrstück* at the 1929 Baden-
Baden festival (later revised as *Das Badener Lehrstück vom Einverständnis:
The Baden-Baden Lesson on Consent*), at which a prominent music
critic grew faint during the scene in which two clowns sawed off the
limbs of a third. In Eisler's vignette Brecht scoffed at this, saying "der
Mann wird doch auch nicht ohnmächtig in einem Sinfoniekonzert, wo
doch immer gesägt wird, nämlich die Geigen. (Brecht haßte Geigen.)"

([that critic] certainly won't faint at a symphony concert where things are being sawed all the time, namely the violins. [Brecht hated violins.]) Eisler then told of taking Brecht to meet his former teacher Arnold Schoenberg in Hollywood in 1942. He was justifiably uneasy about how Brecht would behave when he met the elderly composer, but "es ging besser, als ich dachte" (it went better than I expected), probably because Schoenberg had no idea who Brecht was. The two men swapped stories about donkeys, and Eisler claimed that Brecht wrote a poem about the donkeys in honor of Schoenberg's seventieth birthday.[16] The third episode concerns what Brecht jokingly referred to as "Misuk," and begins with Eisler lamenting thirty years of futile attempts to persuade Brecht that Beethoven was a masterful composer. He admitted that he remained skeptical of Brecht's insistence on reason in music, given the reality of lived musical experience. There are no odes to genius, no war stories, no sycophantism; just three anecdotes representing three decades of friendship.

Eisler's musical contribution is even more intimate. The song, entitled "Zu Brechts Tod," is composed for solo voice and has a very sparse accompaniment for four French horns. It is a mere twelve measures long. The text is a modified version of Brecht's poem "Der Anstreicher spricht von kommenden großen Zeiten" (The Housepainter Speaks of the Great Times to Come) from the *Deutsche Kriegsfibel* (German War Primer), which first appeared in *Das Wort* in Moscow in the spring of 1937 (*BFA* 12:349). By definition, a primer teaches one how to read, using appropriately simple vocabulary and syntax. This particular primer is "a most elementary instruction about war, since the current preparations for war indicate [that the Germans] have plainly learnt nothing from the wars of the past."[17] Therefore "The Housepainter" (Brecht's nickname for Hitler) is quite unlike the monumental, multi-stanza "Lenin Cantata." Each line has the same grammatical structure, and the nouns trace a progression from wilderness via rural life to an urban setting and its human inhabitants:

> Die Wälder wachsen noch.
> Die Äcker tragen noch.
> Die Städte stehen noch.
> Die Menschen atmen noch. (*BFA* 12:10)

> [The forests still grow.
> The fields still bear.
> The cities still stand.
> The people still breathe. (*Poems* 287)]

The version Eisler set to music is slightly modified (this was not unusual; Eisler routinely altered Brecht's poems when he set them to music):

Die Wälder atmen noch.
Die Wälder wachsen noch.
Die Äcker tragen noch.
Die Menschen atmen noch.

[The forests still breathe.
The forests still grow,
The fields still bear.
The people still breathe.]

Eisler omitted the line about cities — after all, in the mid-1950s, many of the cities to which Brecht might have referred when he wrote the poem were *not*, in fact, still standing. The focus shifts entirely to the natural and away from the man-made metropolis, once a hallmark of civilization, and whose absence now connotes the barbarity of war. He also creates a frame by using the verb "breathe," a return to the most fundamental of life functions, in the first and last lines. Some version of life does indeed continue after the death of a loved one.

The musical phrases are in A A B C form. Five of the twelve measures are sung a cappella, and the chordal accompaniment provides minimal harmonic grounding. The text setting is mostly syllabic in steady quarter notes until the first syllable of the final verb "atmen" (breathe), when the voice soars to a sustained high A. The distinctive instrumentation of four-part French horns underneath is mellow, somber. Eisler's song was never published except in this autograph form in *Sinn und Form*, suggesting that it was not meant for performance but for contemplation only.

Both poems Eisler used for commemoration date from the 1930s, and both represented previous collaborations with Brecht. Eisler had published a setting of the last stanza of the "Lenin" poem as "Zu Lenins Todestag" (On Lenin's Death) in 1932, and then set almost the entire text to music in 1937 as *Lenin Requiem*.[18] He had also composed a cantata entitled *Gegen den Krieg* (Against War) based on earlier versions of poems from *Deutsche Kriegsfibel* in 1936, although the one he used for "Zu Brechts Tod" (On Brecht's Death) was not included. Brecht published both poems in the collection *Svendborger Gedichte* (Svendborg Poems, 1939); perhaps Eisler returned to it seeking inspiration. That collection represented shared exile experience and intensive artistic collaboration, but perhaps even more importantly it came from a much simpler time, politically speaking. The mid-1950s in the GDR were far murkier. Heroes were sometimes indistinguishable from villains; Stalinization and de-Stalinization had betrayed the ideals of Marxism; artists who had made their careers as leaders of the opposition were now allied with the ruling Party. The composer was devastated by Brecht's passing. He wept when he told a friend "Brecht is tot, meine Jugend ist gestorben" (Brecht is dead, my youth has died);[19] to another he wrote "Es ist eine entsetzliche Leere um mich und ich bin gebrochen" (There is a horrible emptiness around me and I am crushed).[20]

Paul Dessau

Dessau also contributed an autograph manuscript to the commemorative issue of *Sinn und Form*. It was "Das Lied vom Rauch" (The Song of the Smoke), from *Der gute Mensch von Sezuan*, and it bore the inscription "Los Angeles 1948." He composed music for the play from August 1947 to September 1948 on his peregrination from Hollywood to Zurich and Paris, before settling in East Berlin with his new wife, Brecht's collaborator Elisabeth Hauptmann.[21] As with Eisler's choices, a song from *Der gute Mensch* marks a return to both exile-era literature (Brecht had written the play with Ruth Berlau and Margarete Steffin between 1939 and 1941) and to a prior collaboration (Dessau and Brecht worked closely together on it in California before Brecht returned to Europe).

"The Song of the Smoke" is scored for voice with a repetitive pattern in the piano accompaniment and features Dessau's trademark irregular meter in the verse; the refrain is in a steady duple meter. The text setting is syllabic and the vocal line sits squarely in the middle range, as befits a song to be performed by actors. A poor family sings of the futility of living in a cruel, corrupt world. Dessau's autograph score in *Sinn und Form* includes just the first of the poem's three verses:

> Einstmals, vor das Alter meine Haare bleichte
> Hofft mit Klugheit ich mich durchzuschlagen.
> Heute weiß ich, keine Klugheit reichte
> Je, zu füllen eines armen Mannes Magen. (*BFA* 6:192)

> [Once I thought intelligence was sure to aid me.
> I was quite an optimist when younger.
> Now I realize it never paid me:
> How can our intelligence compete with hunger? (*Plays* 6:18)]

The recurring refrain advises giving up and selling out, since in the end human life is as ephemeral and insignificant as smoke in the wind:

Darum sag ich: laß es!
Sieh den grauen Rauch
Der in immer kältre Kälten geht: so
Gehst du auch. (*BFA* 6:192)

[Therefore I said: drop it!
Like smoke twisting gray
Into ever colder coldness you
Will blow away. (*Plays* 6:18)]

Dessau took Brecht at his most literal, unsentimental word. Unlike Eisler's poignant and wistful song, written specifically for this occasion, Dessau's choice of this extant piece seems utterly matter-of-fact in this context: Brecht is dead, gone like so much smoke on the wind.

By late December 1957 Dessau had also completed his elegy *In memoriam Bertolt Brecht*.[22] He conducted the premiere at the Metropol-Theater in East Berlin on what would have been Brecht's sixtieth birthday (10 February 1958). It is a three-movement orchestral work later described by the composer as a "Requiem ohne Worte"[23] (requiem without words):

Movement I: "Lamento" (40 measures)
Movement II: "Der Krieg soll verflucht sein!" (165 measures)
Movement III: "Epitaph" (51 measures)

It produces the effect of A B A1 C form, however, because the second movement ends with a brief reprise of the first. The outer movements have titles traditionally attached to commemorative works and appropriately slow tempi. They are also dodecaphonic, using the twelve-tone compositional method pioneered by Schoenberg (and used by Eisler in the *Lenin Requiem*, among other pieces) that tends to generate highly dissonant harmonies and disjunct melodies. Twelve-tone music remained controversial in the GDR in 1957 because it was associated with formalism, so Dessau's decision to employ it in what was sure to be a high-profile composition was a bold one.

The use of dodecaphony was not the most conspicuous aspect of the piece, however; the centerpiece was the substantial, raucous, and referential second movement. Its motto, "Der Krieg soll verflucht sein" (war should be cursed), comes from a climactic moment in *Mutter Courage*. Brecht had written the play with Margarete Steffin in 1939, and, as with *Der gute Mensch*, Dessau composed the score after the war and across two continents (begun in California in 1946 and completed in East Berlin in 1948). This was not just a tribute to their work in exile. The production of *Mutter Courage* with Dessau's music and Weigel in the title role at the Deutsches Theater in 1949 was a landmark in postwar German theater. Its success "prepared the ground" for the founding of the Berliner Ensemble, and the image of Weigel's Mother Courage with her wagon became iconic; the BE performed the work in that production over 400 times before 1961.[24] This movement uses the tune from "Mutter Courages Lied" (Mother Courage's Song) in cantus firmus style, meaning that a melody is presented prominently in long note values while accompaniment figures and/or counter-melodies swirl around it. Dessau also compared the movement to a chorale fantasy, in which the theme is treated contrapuntally.[25] Due to the pitch content of the pre-existing melody the second movement is not dodecaphonic (although it is polytonal).

Employing the melody from "Mutter Courages Lied" is even more significant when one considers that the origins of the song lie in a tune Brecht himself adapted and published in the appendix of the *Hauspostille* (Domestic Breviary) in 1927. Brecht appropriated an old French romance entitled "L'Étendard de la Pitié" for his own "Ballade von den Seeräubern" (Ballad of the Pirates), and nearly twenty years later he asked Dessau to use that as the basis for his own song. Initially the composer had reservations about the process and the potential of such a banal melody, but was eventually persuaded to comply with Brecht's request.[26]

Despite the fact that *In memoriam* is a "requiem without words," the recognizable tune prompts the listener to recall the lyrics of "Mutter Courages Lied," which would have been familiar in East Berlin in the 1950s. Geiger has shown that the chorale fantasy setting had roots in the finale of *Mother Courage*, where Dessau set the last verse for male chorus in cantus firmus style.[27] The lyrics may have triggered compositional decisions for the composer as well. Consider the text of the refrain:

> Das Frühjahr kommt. Wach' auf, du Christ!
> Der Schnee schmilzt weg. Die Toten ruhn.
> Doch was noch nicht gestorben ist.
> Das macht sich auf die Socken nun. (*BFA* 6:10)

> [The spring is come. Christian, revive!
> The snowdrifts melt. The dead lie dead.
> And if by chance you're still alive
> It's time to rise and shake a leg. (*Plays* 5:136)]

This recalls the German chorale "Wachet auf" (known in English as "Sleepers Awake"), a staple of the Lutheran repertoire written by Philipp Nicolai in 1599 and made famous by J. S. Bach's exquisite cantata setting BWV 140. This is no accident; Brecht knew the chorale genre and its cultural significance well enough to skewer it quite skillfully, as in his "Hitler Chorales." The chorale fantasy Dessau invoked to describe the second movement is a genre strongly associated with Bach, who applied the term to organ works in which a chorale tune was presented as a cantus firmus in the bass.[28] Bach, musical icon of Leipzig because of his seventeen years in its employ, featured prominently in the cultural politics of the early GDR. The 250th anniversary of his death in 1950 was marked by festivities on a par with those that had surrounded Goethe's 200th birthday the year before.[29]

Because Dessau composed this central movement first (about which more below), perhaps its Bach allusions suggested the B-A-C-H cipher as the constitutive motif of the tone row used for movements I and III. Composers have long used the letters of Bach's name rendered in the German spelling of pitches (B = B-flat, A, C, H=B-natural) as a kind of homage; Dessau had used it before, too.[30] Virtually alone among such composers, Dessau had the advantage of a similar construction in the cipher for his own name, D –Es (D – E-flat). When inverted and extended to four notes, Dessau's motif is identical to Bach's, albeit transposed (Es = E-flat, D, F, E). This motif has the additional symbolic advantage of containing two descending half-steps (B-flat to A, C to B-natural for Bach; E-flat to D, F to E for Dessau) — desirable because this interval is a traditional musical emblem of mourning.[31] Constructing a tone row replete with such intervals, and using it as the basis for two movements entitled "Lamento" and "Epitaph," virtually guarantees that an audience will attend to the sigh motifs throughout. Dessau also manipulated the row to generate an allusion to the famous "Dies irae" chant incipit from the requiem mass, that ominous fragment that has entered the pop culture lexicon as shorthand for death. It is featured unaccompanied in measure 8 of the "Lamento," lest the listener miss it.

Brecht's admiration for the music of Bach (and Mozart) is well known, but like many modernists, he cultivated disdain for the Romantics, as witnessed by his rejection of Beethoven above, and his love-hate relationship with the legacy of Wagner.[32] And yet Dessau's musical homage takes the form of a large, programmatic orchestral work — a decidedly Romantic genre, replete with the hallmarks of nineteenth-century monumentality in which the essential property of excess vacillates between the sublime and the absurd.[33] And it was marked as such from its very first performance. The first half of that concert featured two Brecht works: *In memoriam*, and Wolfgang Fortner's 1947 cantata *An die Nachgeborenen* (To Those Born Later). Fortner's work, also on a grand scale, is noteworthy because he was West German and had expressed reservations about allowing his cantata to be performed in the GDR. He, too, composed some dodecaphonic pieces, although *An die Nachgeborenen* is not one of them.[34]

The second half of the program was given over to Beethoven's Symphony No. 3. Its legend is well known: the original dedicatee was Napoleon, but once he declared himself emperor, Beethoven rescinded the dedication and rendered it instead as *Sinfonia eroica, composta per festeggiare il sovvenire d'un grand'uomo* (heroic symphony, composed to celebrate the memory of a great man). The *Eroica* (Heroic), as it is commonly known, has a second movement entitled "Marcia funebre" (funeral march). Dessau referred to the second movement of his *In memoriam* as a march, too, a multivalent genre designation that might derive from the martial quality of the original *Mother Courage* material and its wartime setting, or from the funereal purpose of this commemorative work, also composed, apparently, to celebrate the memory of a great man.

The "great men" analogy was established by the music programmed for the concert, but it quickly runs up against an uncomfortable historical reality. Beethoven's revised dedication meant that Napoleon had been a great man until he turned his back on his revolutionary ideals to satisfy his own ego. Even if the concert theme was supposed to be only superficial ("musical works in memory of great men"), one would not have had to extrapolate too far along that line of reasoning to wonder what was implied by pairing Brecht with Napoleon. There have always been those who viewed the East German Brecht as a man colluding with a corrupt state in the role of privileged and protected gadfly. And there is no small irony in the fact that *In memoriam* was premiered at a concert that also featured an iconic work by Beethoven, a Romantic composer that Brecht detested, as Eisler noted above.

The second movement of *In memoriam* evokes an additional symphonic association from the Romantic era, one that seems quite obvious to this listener's ear but which Dessau did not mention and has remained unremarked in the literature. It is Berlioz's *Symphonie fantastique: Episode de la vie d'un Artiste* (Fantastic Symphony: An Episode in the Life of an Artist) of 1830. If Beethoven's *Eroica* launched the early Romantic programmatic symphony, Berlioz's *Symphonie fantastique* is its most extreme manifestation. Without sung words, but with the aid of program notes and highly imaginative instrumentation, Berlioz's symphony tells the story of an artist's futile obsession with a woman that devolves, in movement four, into an opium-induced hallucination in which the protagonist imagines he has murdered her and witnesses his own execution at the guillotine. This movement is known as the "Marche au supplice" (March to the Scaffold). In the fifth and final movement, entitled "Songe d'une nuit de sabbat" (Dream of a Witches' Sabbath) he finds himself in the afterworld, where the beloved appears as a grotesque parody of her human self. The finale is notorious for its tolling funeral bells and the blasphemous use of the "Dies Irae" tune as a primary theme, presented cantus firmus style à la chorale fantasy. A noisy march, cantus firmus in the brass surrounded by woodwind figuration and schlepping percussion effects — these are definitive features of the second movement of *In memoriam*, as well. The quotation of the "Dies Irae" motif appears in Dessau's first movement and is not treated as a major theme in that piece, but its conspicuous presentation made this listener predisposed to hear the second movement in the context of the *Symphonie fantastique*.

One could argue that these likenesses are merely coincidental and ultimately irrelevant because the tone of *In memoriam* is so different. But how much of that difference is perceived because we are told the serious function of the work in its title? Berlioz's symphony, generously aided by its colorful program notes and movement titles, is grandiose fun, while Dessau's piece, also supported by an overdetermined programmatic title, is somber and resolute. It would be reasonable to assume that such a grave piece was composed solely in response to Brecht's death. In fact, the composer wrote the first and last movements expressly for *In memoriam*, but the entire second movement — the only part with an explicit musical link to the dedicatee — was a ten-year-old piece. Tischer uses "ready-made" to describe the manner in which Dessau repurposed this work, which he had composed in 1947–48.[35] The movement began as a self-contained piece of chamber music variously titled *Marschphantasie*, *Kriegsmusik Suite*, and *Suite für 15 Instrumente nach der Musik zu "Mutter Courage und ihre Kinder"* (March-Fantasy, War Music Suite, Suite for 15 Instruments on Music from "Mother Courage and her Children").[36] His original stage music for *Mother Courage* was scored for two flutes, piccolo, trumpet, guitar, harmonica, percussion, and prepared piano; the version used for the Berlin production added an accordion. The only change Dessau made when he recycled the piece as the central movement of *In memoriam* was to its instrumentation, which is consistent across all three movements. In fact, the orchestra's excessive size and range is comparable to that of the *Symphonie fantastique*: expanded woodwinds, eleven-part brass, nine pieces of percussion, accordion (in place of Berlioz's harps), and four-part strings — including prominent violins. Why feature the one instrument Brecht so famously despised? Better yet, why compose an instrumental homage to a poet and play-wright whose words the composer had set countless times in the past? Contrast this with Fortner's cantata, which also used an enormous orchestra but omitted the violins, and set one of Brecht's most beloved poems.

Dessau experienced two major moments of artistic emancipation in his career: the first when he began working with Brecht in 1943, and the second when he stopped working with Brecht in 1956.[37] In the interim Dessau was devoted to him, and strongly influenced by everything from his politics to his aesthetics. By the mid-1950s, however, Dessau's pursuit of a more complex, dissonant musical language had become a source of contention. They had a falling-out about Dessau's score for *Der kaukasische Kreidekreis* in 1955, and tensions appear to have lingered. Two weeks before Brecht's death Dessau indicated that his plans for an opera based on *Puntila* were not contingent upon the play-wright's participation: "man [braucht] keine 'Genies' zu Texten (s. Weber und Beethoven)" (one doesn't need "geniuses" to write an opera libretto [see Weber and Beethoven]).[38] Dessau's output in the late 1950s and 1960s reveals a complete reorientation toward large-scale orchestral works and away from the vocal music he had composed since he began working with Brecht, and this new course began with *In memoriam*. It is also the first in a series of pieces increasingly composed in the spirit of late Schoenberg, in which Dessau sought ways of reconciling dodecaphony with tonality (and, I would add, non-serial atonality) in his compositions.[39]

The new course did not come easily. Sixteen months passed between Brecht's death and the completion of *In memoriam*, a piece only thirteen minutes in duration. Dessau wrote "Lamento," about three minutes of music, in the first eight weeks and recycled some seven minutes of music for the second movement, but the last three minutes ("Epitaph") took much longer to materialize.[40] Geiger attributes the protracted process to an "emotionale Ambivalenz zwischen Trauer und Erleichterung" (emotional ambivalence between sorrow and relief).[41] This seems plausible, and not just because it took Dessau a long time to write the score; the music contains plenty of ambivalence as well. The absence of text in an homage to a man of letters, the excesses of the giant Romantic symphony and allusions to two of its masterpieces for a man who claimed to reject Romanticism, prominent violins for a man who despised them. Violins even have the last word; together with the violas they declaim the final melody in "Epitaph," and therefore in the entire piece, before the texture dissolves into quiet percussion over a pedal point. The only greater affront would have been a solo for *Heldentenor*, the high, stentorian voice associated with the excesses of Wagner's operas (Fortner's cantata did, in fact, feature a tenor soloist).

Dessau did not compose *In memoriam* as an insult or a joke, and I do not propose hearing it as such; instead, I suggest listening to its multivalent "memorable puzzlings" as a modern elegy. As such it is, in Karen Leeder's formulation, "tempered by the skepticism of a critical present and thus encompass[es] disagreement, accusation or disaffection,"[42] not to mention wit, in addition to nostalgia and mourning. (Perhaps there were hints of this complexity in Dessau's contribution to *Sinn und Form*, as well. After all, from all the songs he had composed for *Der gute Mensch* he chose "The Song of the Smoke," whose message is to give in and sell out.) *In memoriam* honors Brecht's penchant for appropriating and repurposing material (by himself or by others), Dessau's work with him in exile, and their greatest postwar success in the GDR, but it is not hagiography. Eisler's commemorations are more conventional modes of lament, yet he also appropriated and recycled extant texts, in this case from a much earlier, politically simpler time (the 1930s). The way in which each composer mourned the passing of his favorite collaborating poet proved prophetic. When Eisler died in 1962 he had composed relatively little since Brecht's death, although he did set a few of the poet's other, older texts between 1957 and 1959.[43] Dessau, on the other hand, was galvanized by the new critical course of *In memoriam*; he lived until 1978, composing prolifically and relishing his status as elder statesman of East German art music.

Notes

I am grateful to the following people for their assistance: Anouk Jeschke, archivist of the Hanns-Eisler-Archiv, and Daniela Reinhold, archivist of the Paul-Dessau-Archiv, both of the Akademie der Künste in Berlin; Alexander Colpa, Elaine Kelly, Günter Mayer, Laura Silverberg, Despina Stratigakos, Kira Thurman, and Matthias Tischer.

[1] William Grange, "Choices of Evil: Brecht's Modernism in the Work with Eisler and Dessau," in *Brecht Unbound*, ed. James K. Lyon and Hans-Peter Breuer (Newark: U of Delaware P, 1995), 147–57, here 152. Grange's assertion that Dessau's music for these plays was difficult because Brecht was interested in non-Western music is false

and reveals a common bias in research about Brecht's musical collaborations, which is that Brecht was responsible for all the innovations.

[2] Karen Leeder, "'Nachwort zu Brechts Tod': The Afterlife of a Classic in Modern German Poetry," *Brecht Yearbook* 32 (2007): 333–54, here 337.

[3] Leeder, "'Nachwort zu Brechts Tod,'" 350.

[4] These included Pieck, Ulbricht, Zweig for the Akademie der Künste (Academy of Arts), Becher for the Ministerium für Kultur (Ministry of Culture), and nine signatories for the Union of Soviet Writers.

[5] "Sein Werk lebendig halten," *Neues Deutschland* (East Berlin), 17 August 1956. *Neues Deutschland* continued to feature excerpts from Brecht's works and tributes from international figures daily until 20 August 1956.

[6] The editor-in-chief, Erwin Zucker-Schilling, was an acquaintance of Eisler's. At the time of Brecht's death Zucker-Schilling was married to Steffi Wolf; in 1958 she would divorce him, move to Berlin, and marry Eisler.

[7] Regarding Eisler's re-emigration and postwar activities in Vienna see Peter Schweinhardt, *Fluchtpunkt Wien: Hanns Eislers Wiener Arbeiten nach der Rückkehr aus dem Exil* (Wiesbaden: Breitkopf & Härtel, 2006).

[8] "Kantate auf den Tod Bertolt Brechts," *Österreichische Volksstimme* (Vienna), 26 August 1956.

[9] "Beim Pförtner hing ein Brief von Brecht," *Neues Deutschland* (East Berlin), 23 September 1956. The original was published in *Süddeutsche Zeitung* (Munich), 21 September 1956. Stephan Buchloh describes this as a case of FRG censorship in *Pervers, jugendgefährdend, staatsfeindlich: Zensur in der Ära Adenauer als Spiegel des gesellschaftlichen Klimas* (Frankfurt a.M.: Campus, 2002), 167–77. Buchloh identifies the author of the quoted article as Josef Schmidt (it is unattributed in *Neues Deutschland*). Hilpert had been artistic director of the Deutsches Theater in Berlin under Goebbels.

[10] Verses 1–4 translated as "Cantata for Lenin's Death," by George Tabori in *Brecht on Brecht: An Improvisation* (London: Samuel French, Inc., 1967), 51.

[11] Katharine Hodgson, "'Exile in Danish Siberia': The Soviet Union in the Svendborg Poems," in *Brecht's Poetry of Political Exile*, ed. Ronald Speirs (Cambridge: Cambridge UP, 2000), 66–85, here 74.

[12] Hodgson, "'Exile in Danish Siberia,'" 74.

[13] Stephen Parker and Matthew Philpotts, *"Sinn und Form": The Anatomy of a Literary Journal* (Berlin: Walter de Gruyter, 2009), 231. As a member of Brecht's inner circle, Eisler also had longstanding ties to the journal. *Sinn und Form* had defended Eisler in 1953 when his *Faustus* libretto was under attack, and would honor him posthumously with a special issue in 1964.

[14] Parker and Philpotts, *"Sinn und Form,"* 232.

[15] Xenophon, *The Symposium*, trans. H. G. Dakyns (n.d.; Project Gutenberg, 1998), http://www.gutenberg.org/etext/1181, accessed 13 January 2011.

[16] When he told the story in 1958 Eisler claimed to have been very harsh with Brecht: "I said: 'If you lose control and are rude to Schoenberg, I declare I shall immediately

break off relations with you, regardless of our friendship. You must not do that [. . .] [O]therwise our friendship will be a thing of the past.'" Hanns Eisler, "Ask Me More about Brecht: Conversations with Hans Bunge; Four Excerpts," trans. Wolfgang Pick, in *Hanns Eisler: A Miscellany*, ed. David Blake (Chur, Switzerland: Harwood, 1995), 413–40, here 414. He also says he encouraged Brecht to write the birthday ode "What I learned from a donkey," and that the text is among Brecht's papers, but it has not been found.

[17] Ronald Speirs, "Introduction," in *Brecht's Poetry of Political Exile*, 1–15, here 3.

[18] "Zu Lenins Todestag" appeared on the front page of the *Illustrierte Rote Post* in January 1932, in a special issue commemorating Lenin. Eisler's *Lenin Requiem* was not known at the time of Brecht's death because it was not premiered until 22 November 1958. It then played a significant role in debates regarding the role of modernist music in the GDR in the mid-1960s. See Laura Silverberg, "Between Dissonance and Dissidence: Socialist Modernism in the German Democratic Republic," *Journal of Musicology* 26, no. 1 (2009): 44–84.

[19] Jürgen Schebera, *Hanns Eisler: Eine Biographie in Texten, Bildern und Dokumenten* (Mainz: Schott, 1998), 261.

[20] Undated letter from Eisler to Ernst Hermann Meyer. Hanns-Eisler-Archiv of the Akademie der Künste in Berlin (hereafter HEA) 6222.

[21] Paul-Dessau-Archiv of the Akademie der Künste in Berlin (hereafter PDA) 1.74.0316.1–2.

[22] The essential study from the GDR is Gerd Rienäcker, "Analytische Anmerkungen zu Orchestermusik 'in memoriam Bertolt Brecht' von Paul Dessau," in *Musikalische Analyse in der Diskussion*, ed. Mathias Hansen (East Berlin: Akademie der Künste der DDR, 1982), 69–82. Important recent scholarship includes Friedrich Geiger, "*In memoriam Bertolt Brecht* von Paul Dessau," in *Fokus: Deutsches Miserere von Paul Dessau und Bertolt Brecht; Festschrift Peter Petersen zum 65. Geburtstag*, ed. Nina Ermlich Lehmann, Sophie Fetthauer, et al. (Hamburg: von Bockel, 2005), 217–37; and Matthias Tischer, *Komponieren für und wider den Staat: Paul Dessau in der DDR* (Cologne: Böhlau, 2009), especially 104–25. Geiger's study disentangles the piece from the ideology of previous East German analyses, and Tischer situates the work within numerous intertextualities.

[23] Notes for the Musica Viva festival program in Munich for a concert on 16 December 1966. PDA 1.74.1675. See also Tischer, 110–15.

[24] Gitta Honegger, "Gossip, Ghosts, and Memory: Mother Courage and the Forging of the Berliner Ensemble," *The Drama Review* 52, no. 4 (2008): 98–117, here 99.

[25] Honegger, "Gossip, Ghosts, and Memory," 99.

[26] Dessau recounted this collaborative process in PDA 1.74.1677.1. For Brecht's version see the appendix in his *Hauspostille* (Berlin: Propyläen, 1927), 149–50. For a side-by-side comparison of all three tunes see Albrecht Dümling, *Laßt euch nicht verführen* (Munich: Kindler, 1985), 91–92. Regarding the appropriation of extant works, which Dessau initially rejected as plagiarism, see *Paul Dessau: Aus Gesprächen* (Leipzig: VEB Verlag für Musik, 1974), 74–75; and Dessau, *Notizen zu Noten*, ed. Fritz Hennenberg (Leipzig: Reclam, 1974), 41–43.

[27] Geiger, "*In memoriam Bertolt Brecht* von Paul Dessau," 231–33. Geiger argues that Dessau's implicit textual allusion is therefore to the last verse of the song, which mourns the horror of war, and not to the first, which praises Mother Courage's business sense, as previously claimed.

[28] Tischer discusses the chorale fantasia designation at some length, but does not associate it with the refrain of the original song lyrics. Tischer, *Komponieren für und wider den Staat*, 110–11.

[29] For a useful overview of the literature on this topic see Tischer, *Komponieren für und wider den Staat*, 164–68.

[30] See Peter Petersen, "In Paris begonnen, in New York vollendet, in Berlin verlegt: *Les Voix* von Paul Dessau," in *Musik im Exil: Folgen des Nazismus für die internationale Musikkultur*, ed. Hanns-Werner Heister, Claudia Maurer Zenck, and Peter Petersen (Frankfurt a.M.: Fischer, 1993), 438–59.

[31] Geiger, "*In memoriam Bertolt Brecht* von Paul Dessau," 223–25, and Tischer, *Komponieren für und wider den Staat*, 104, 119–21.

[32] Regarding Brecht's engagement with Wagner see Calico, *Brecht at the Opera* (Berkeley: U of California P, 2008), particularly the introduction and chapter two.

[33] Regarding monumentality as a stylistic property of nineteenth-century orchestral music see Alexander Rehding, *Music and Monumentality: Commemoration and Wonderment in Nineteenth-Century Germany* (Oxford: Oxford UP, 2009).

[34] In an email to the author dated 13 August 2010, Fortner scholar Alexander Colpa described the tonality of the cantata as indebted to Hindemith and built on a "'diminished seventh' tetrachord D – F – A-flat – B and several whole-tone collections."

[35] Tischer, *Komponieren für und wider den Staat*, 104 and 106–7.

[36] The earliest version, dated Hollywood 1947, is found in PDA 1.74.308. Other versions and portions of versions are found in PDA 1.74.0286.1 and PDA 1.74.0286.2.

[37] Karl Mickel, "Zu seinem 100. Geburtstag am 19.12.1994: Gesprächsrunde – Wiederentdeckungen und Neubewertungen des Komponisten," *Theater der Zeit* 50, no. 1 (1995): 23. Cited in Daniele Reinhold, *Paul Dessau 1894–1979: Dokumente zu Leben und Werk* (Berlin: Henschel, 1995), 83.

[38] See Geiger, "*In memoriam Bertolt Brecht* von Paul Dessau," 235–36. Brecht apologized to Dessau in a letter dated 2 March 1955 (*BFA* 30:315). A bit of Dessau's perspective can be gleaned from letters he wrote at this time to his friend and mentor in Paris, Rene Leibowitz, reprinted in *Let's Hope for the Best: Briefe und Notizbücher aus den Jahren 1948 bis 1978*, ed. Daniela Reinhold (Hofheim: Wolke, 2000), 44–49.

[39] Tischer, *Komponieren für und wider den Staat*, 115.

[40] Geiger, "*In memoriam Bertolt Brecht* von Paul Dessau," 233–34.

[41] Geiger, "*In memoriam Bertolt Brecht* von Paul Dessau," 234.

[42] Leeder, "'Nachwort zu Brechts Tod,'" 350.

[43] Schebera identifies four large-scale pieces as commemorative of Brecht: the cantata *Die Teppichweber von Kujan-Bulak* (The Carpet Weavers of Kujan-Bulak, 1929–30); a setting of "Legende von der Entstehung des Buches Taoteking auf dem Weg des Laotse in die Emigration" (Legend of the Origin of the Tao Te Ching during the Exile of Lao-Tze, 1938); music for *Schweyk im zweiten Weltkrieg* (Schweyk in the Second World War, 1943/1955); and *Bilder aus der Kriegsfibel* (Images from the War Primer). Schebera, 261–62. I have focused on texts the composer explicitly identified as responses to Brecht's death.

.

The Legacy of Brecht
in East German Political Song

David Robb, University of Belfast

T HE SED'S INSTANT appropriation of Brecht as a revolutionary cultural icon after his death in 1956 was always too easy and one-sided. It ignored the thematic and formal contradictoriness in Brecht's work as well as the writer's problematic reception in the GDR in the 1950s, when his perceived formalistic tendencies sat uneasily with the tenets of Socialist Realism. In the field of political song this one-sided perception was cemented by the reception of the Brecht and Eisler *Kampflied* (battle song) tradition from the late 1940s onward, notably by Ernst Busch and the choirs of the Free German Youth movement (FDJ), the schools, and the army. By the early 1960s, however, the more subversive aspects of the poet's work were being seized on by the singer and poet Wolf Biermann, who frequently adapted Brechtian lyrical motifs to comment critically on GDR political reality. Biermann was to revive a vibrant relationship to Brecht by consciously setting himself in a line of tradition with him, particularly the literary grotesque of his early work. For this the GDR cultural authorities charged Biermann with literary decadence and eventually banned him from performance and publication from 1965 to 1976.

The Brechtian influence could also be seen in Biermann's use of music, especially the aesthetic of musical montage that Kurt Weill and Hanns Eisler had pioneered in their work with Brecht. After the expatriation of Biermann from the GDR in November 1976, this aesthetic became key to new developments in GDR political song. These developments included the unique cabaret form known as *Liedertheater* (song theater), initiated by Hans-Eckardt Wenzel, Steffen Mensching, and their group Karls Enkel. Their interdisciplinary art form represented among other things a creative appropriation of the theatrical tradition that the GDR claimed as its own progressive heritage. This included the montage aesthetic of agitprop revue, Brechtian theater, and Eislerian song as well as socially critical clowning from commedia dell'arte through to the Munich clown Karl Valentin. What is intriguing about the art forms of both Wolf Biermann and Wenzel and Mensching is how a genre that their forefathers had deployed in the Weimar Republic to criticize the capitalist state now encountered a basic contradiction within a communist state (East Germany). Originally intended as an art form of resistance, it was now expected to work for the promotion of the state itself. The ways in which GDR performers such as Biermann and Wenzel and Mensching subverted these expectations in order to expose the hollowness of the state's revolutionary aspirations will be the focus of this essay.

In the early postwar period, the tradition of German workers' songs was already being promoted in the Soviet occupied zone. Ernst Busch had become famous as an actor and recording artist in the early 1930s for performing Brecht and Eisler's *Kampflieder* such as the "Solidaritätslied" (Solidarity Song, 1930) and "Einheitsfrontlied" (Song of the United Front, 1934). Busch made further recordings after the war and edited a songbook entitled *Internationale Arbeiterlieder* (International Workers' Songs, 1949).[1] Inge Lammel, a researcher at the Workers' Song Archive of the Academy of Arts in East Berlin, continued nurturing this tradition from the 1950s onward in her numerous editions of song pamphlets and books. The culmination of this pro-state political song activity was the formation of the GDR *Singebewegung* (youth singing movement) in 1968. From then onwards, the repertoire of international freedom songs, including those by Brecht and Eisler, was increasingly complemented by original material. Under the slogan *DDR-Konkret*, the FDJ encouraged young students and workers to write new songs dealing with their everyday lives. But these were not supposed to criticize the workers' state. Inge Lammel explained:

> Die neuen Lieder werden für die Politik von Partei und Regierung geschaffen. Sie sind nicht mehr Kampfmittel einer unterdrückten Klasse gegen eine Klasse von Ausbeutern, sondern Ausdruck der gemeinsamen Interessen aller Werktätigen.[2]

> [The new songs are created to support the policies of the Party and the government. They are no longer the means of resistance of an oppressed class against a class of exploiters, but rather the expression of the common interest of all workers.]

This immediately presented a contradiction with the traditional gesture of "going against the grain" in political song (as well as in Brechtian theater itself). It had an inhibitive effect, as reflected in the tame, often obsequious songs of the *Singebewegung*. But alongside this there existed an alternative culture of singers and songwriters (*Liedermacher*). It is here that one encounters a more critical use of the Brecht and Eisler inheritance designed to expose the contradictions between the claims of the state and reality.

The most prominent of these artists was Wolf Biermann, who came over to East Berlin from Hamburg of his own free will at the age of seventeen in 1953. As the son of a communist Jew murdered in Auschwitz, Biermann had initially been feted by the GDR establishment. His brand of art was a montage of various styles from high and low culture. Musically his influences ranged from Eisler (who had discovered the young singer at the Berliner Ensemble in the late 1950s) to the French *chanson* and the German street ballad. Lyrically he was highly influenced by François Villon and Bertolt Brecht among others. In his use of motifs and imagery from such plebeian poetic traditions we encounter a subversive and creative approach to the dominant communist literary heritage, an approach that performers such as Wenzel and Mensching would continue in the 1980s. In his early poem "Herr Brecht" (1965) Biermann indicates his irreverent approach to the GDR state's obsession with its cultural legacy, in his friendly critique of the monotonous ongoing work in the Brecht Archive. He describes the dead poet taking a walk along Friedrichstraße from his burial place in the Huguenot Cemetery and meeting some employees of the archive. Here Biermann imagines the dead Brecht's reaction:

> Was, dachte er,
> das sind doch die Fleißigen
> vom Brechtarchiv.
> Was, dachte er,
> seid ihr immer noch nicht fertig
> mit dem Ramsch?
>
> Und er lächelte
> Unverschämt-bescheiden und
> war zufrieden.[3]
>
> [Well well, he thought,
> that's that keen lot
> from the Brecht archives
> Well well, he thought,
> are they still sorting out
> all that mess?
>
> And he smiled his
> insolent-modest smile
> and was content.]

Biermann frequently communicated his views through the use of literary role-play. In many songs he identifies strongly with Villon, the anarchic fifteenth-century vagabond poet.[4] With his references to Villon, Biermann was latching onto a tradition in German political song that had begun in the literary cabarets of the Weimar Republic, where Villon had been a role model for poets such as Brecht and Walter Mehring. Brecht's poem "Vom François Villon" (Of François Villon, 1918) used sensual body imagery to depict the hedonistic and dangerous lifestyle of Villon:

Er mußte Menschen mit dem Messer stechen
Und seinen Hals in ihre Schlinge legen.
Drum lud er ein, daß man am Arsch ihn leckte
Wenn er beim Fressen war und es ihm schmeckte. (*BFA* 11:56)

[His fate it was to stab men with his knife
And stick his neck into the traps they set.
So let them kiss his arse while he was trying
To eat some food that he found satisfying. (*Poems* 17)]

In *Rabelais and His World* Mikhail Bakhtin defines such Villonesque activities as feasting, defecation, beatings, cursing, and laughter as popular motifs of the carnival of the Middle Ages.[5] These had an anti-authoritarian, utopian aspect in their symbolism of a world temporarily turned on its head with the "suspension of all hierarchical precedence."[6] Included in this is the motif of the grotesque body, which, according to Bakhtin, symbolizes a world that is not fixed or constant but continually renews itself.[7]

Biermann made no secret of his admiration for Villon, Heinrich Heine,[8] and Brecht, consciously embracing their profane poetic tradition. While professing loyalty to the ideals of the GDR state, he adopted an impudent, plebeian tone that attacked the way in which these ideals were being corrupted. His singing style was correspondingly physical and irreverent, grotesquely elongating vowel sounds or cutting up words. The depiction of women in Biermann's songs of the early 1960s conforms to this profane tradition, which accentuates the sensual and bodily, and is again reminiscent of Heine and the early Brecht. The symbolism of renewal and transformation inherent in such imagery clashed with the rigidity of GDR state policy and ideology. In "Lied auf das ehemalige Grenzgänger-Freudenmädchen Garance" (*AL* 57–58; Song for the Former Cross-Border Call-Girl Garance) of 1961, Biermann sings about a prostitute who is forced to give up her occupation because of the building of the Berlin Wall. The song implies that this, and not her sexual promiscuity, is her downfall: "Aber du, Garance, bist die Schönste! / Die Unzucht hat deinen Leib nicht gefressen / Die Unzucht nahm nicht deine Lieblichkeit." (But you Garance, are the most beautiful! / It wasn't the fornication that used up your body / It wasn't the fornication that took your loveliness.)[9]

With his reference to Brecht's *Buckower Elegien* in "Die alten Weiber von Buckow" (The Old Wives from Buckow, 1962) Biermann again consciously places himself in the Brechtian literary tradition. Here he presents an image of old women standing in the rain cursing the GDR state because they cannot buy fish, while the young fishmonger is in bed with his girlfriend:

Ein Fischer jung und stark
— ein junges Weib von Buckow
Verschläft mit ihm bis acht
Das hat die Weiber von Buckow
So bös und nass gemacht. (*AL* 68)

[A fisherman young and strong
— a young wife from Buckow
Oversleeps with him until eight
That made the wives of Buckow
All angry and wet.]

Such imagery in the work of Biermann was the antithesis of the requirements of Socialist Realism and led to the charge of literary decadence. In this respect he was following in the footsteps of both Brecht and Eisler who, despite their elevated status in the GDR, had also been criticized for formalist decadence by the cultural authorities in the early 1950s.

In Biermann's appropriation of the Villon motif in his "Ballade auf den Dichter François Villon" (Ballad of the Poet François Villon) forty years after Brecht's poem, a similarly vibrant language and imagery of the body clashes with the images of GDR officialdom. The profane imagery contrasts with the reverential tones with which socialism was treated in the GDR media and public life. Biermann, in typically immodest fashion, begins the song by establishing the line of heritage from Villon through Brecht up to himself. He alludes to the watchful, intrusive eyes of the GDR secret police (Stasi) as he shelters his grotesquely decaying guest Villon in his flat. There is further grotesque imagery in Biermann's description of Villon's fat wife Margot, who makes him curse, and in the way he ingratiates himself with his superiors:

> Die Eitelkeit der höchsten Herrn
> Konnt meilenweit er riechen
> Verewigt hat er manchen Arsch
> In den er mußte kriechen. (*AL* 121)

> [The vanity of the rulers he
> Could smell from miles around
> He had to crawl right up their arse
> In rhyme to set it down. (*PB* 85)]

Villon's carnivalism forms a counterpoint to rigid authority. The stinking Frenchman drinks wine and vodka and struggles with the official language of the Party newspaper. When he is shot at while walking along the Berlin Wall, red wine flows from his wounds. He coughs up the lead cartridges, spits, and curses. The fact that the police can only find his skeleton in Biermann's cupboard is significant: the spirit of Villon will always haunt the authorities — he is synonymous with the utopian spirit of the carnival crowd and its subversion of hierarchy.

Further Brechtian influences in Biermann's use of the grotesque can be seen in songs from the early 1960s. "Soldat, Soldat" (Soldier, Soldier), an antiwar song from 1963, is reminiscent of Brecht's "Legende vom toten Soldaten" (*BFA* 11:112–15; Legend of the Dead Soldier, *Plays* 1:391–93) in its references to the facelessness and interchangeability of soldiers: "Soldaten sehn sich alle gleich / lebendig und als Leich" (*AL* 103; Soldiers are identical / The quick, the dead and all, *PB* 41). His "Ballade vom Mann" (The Ballad of the Man), also from 1963, parodies the self-defeating policies of the SED: a man steps in a pile of feces and finds a solution in chopping off his foot. But he cuts off the wrong foot, and then, in his rage, cuts off the other one too. Biermann, who was expelled from the Party in 1963, makes the parallel clear:

> Es hackte die Partei
> sich ab so manchen Fuß
> so manchen guten Fuß
> abhackte die Partei. (*AL* 99)

> [The party has chopped off
> a good few of its feet
> a few of its good feet
> the party has chopped off. (*PB* 77)]

But at this early stage in his career, Biermann holds onto the possibility of reform, singing that unlike this man's, the Party's foot can still grow back on.

It is highly likely that the grotesque imagery in "Ballade vom Mann" was influenced by the dismemberment of the character Herr Schmitt by two clowns in Brecht's play *Das Badener Lehrstück vom Einverständnis* (The Baden-Baden Lesson on Consent, 1929). This had been intended as an abstract portrayal of the brutality of power relationships in capitalist society — in short: to demonstrate that people do not help one another. The slapstick, which Brecht had learned from his Bavarian compatriot, Karl Valentin, contributed to the development of Brecht's estrangement technique, the *Verfremdungseffekt*.[10] The intention was to use artificial (unnaturalistic) performance techniques to prevent the audience's identification with the characters and thereby keep its attention focused on the political message. We see this technique in Biermann's "Ballade vom Mann" in the song's function as a parable (here of how the Party cuts its own nose off to spite its face), in the aforementioned grotesque lyrical imagery, but also on the level of performance: in the singer's exaggerated fricative on every repetition of the word "Fuß" and the jarring elongations of certain vowels, for example, the "ei" in "Partei." These guide the audience toward the parodic intent.[11]

The musical approach of Weill and Hanns Eisler played a significant role in Biermann's work. While he did not write Eislerian *Kampflieder* — his ballads reflected an altogether more subjective style[12] — he had learned, as one of Eisler's most famous pupils, "daß die Musik nicht nur ein Transportmittel sein soll" (that music should not be just a means of transport).[13] Biermann's songs illustrate the Eislerian practice of using music to promote dialogic interplay between different textual levels. In his 1969 song "Enfant perdu," Biermann's lament for political dissident Robert Havemann's son Florian, who had abandoned the GDR for the West in the wake of the Soviet crushing of the Prague Spring, the churchlike tonality of the harmony in the minor key expresses the sadness of loss.[14] This mood is abruptly broken up, however, by a change in rhythm to a staccato pulse, as Biermann acknowledges the fact that for many in the GDR emigration is never far from their thoughts: "Abgang ist überall" (*AL* 217; Departure is everywhere).

The use of music to support parody is evident in Biermann's song "Acht Argumente für die Beibehaltung des Namens 'Stalinallee'" (*AL* 160–63; Eight Arguments for the Retention of the Name "Stalin-Allee," 1965). Here the singer mocks the changing of the name of the street to Karl-Marx-Allee after the revelations of Stalin's crimes at the Soviet

Union's Twentieth Communist Party Congress in 1956. For Biermann the name should stay as a monument to the legacy of the Stalinism that had so corrupted the GDR. The air-pumping effect of the harmonium conjures up the sound of a carousel and street party celebrations.[15] Through this use of music Biermann caricatures the abandon with which the Party renames streets and towns in order to manipulate history.

When Biermann was refused reentry into the GDR in November 1976 after a concert in West Germany this caused a storm of protest and resulted in a renewed clampdown in the arts. It was as a reaction to the ensuing crisis in political song in the GDR that the new form of *Liedertheater* emerged in the late 1970s. Political singers were now faced with a dilemma. On the one hand young musicians were increasingly rejecting the singing groups of the FDJ such as the Oktoberklub, who propagated the SED line in their songs.[16] For more critical singers on the other hand it was clear that direct subversion in the style of Biermann would simply be censored on the GDR stage. Other artistic ways therefore had to be found to express criticism.

New experiments were conducted by groups whose origins lay in the FDJ singing club movement. The group Schicht emerged from the Song Group of the TU (Technical University) of Dresden and Gerhard Gundermann's Brigade Feuerstein from the Singing Club of Hoyerswerda. They developed a new multimedia approach using text, drama, costumes, masks, and electronic music. The trend caught on and until the late 1980s numerous *Liedertheater* groups formed throughout the GDR at amateur and professional levels, producing a scene distinct from cabaret. Wenzel and Mensching's group went by the name Karls Enkel (Karl's Grandchildren), an allusion to Karl Marx. The group began experimenting with theatrical techniques in 1978, thereafter rehearsing at the Berlin Volksbühne under director Heiner Maaß, who had previously worked with Heiner Müller. Maaß was of a critical political disposition. In 1973 he had been sacked from his position at the Magdeburg theater for his involvement in a controversial production of Müller's *Mauser*.[17] He helped Karls Enkel free itself from what Wenzel considered to be the redundant personality cult of the *Liedermacher*, whereby the lyrics and style of delivery directly matched the emotions and personal concerns of the performer. Wenzel stated in 1984 that their costumes, masks, and makeup helped them to create a playful distance that relativized their textual utterances.[18] The group researched the techniques and costumes of "low" plebeian and alternative theatrical forms such as commedia dell'arte and the proletarian revues of the 1920s, in order to investigate possible parallels with the present day.[19]

The music now had a theatrical function too. Once again a montage aesthetic drawn from Weill and Eisler meant that diverse musical styles with their respective associations could be juxtaposed to the text in a dialectical and often parodic way. Any form of music could be utilized in this manner, from the international *Kampflied*, the street ballad, and the chanson to German *Schlager* (easy listening hits), rock, or even operetta. In their production *'s geht los! — Aber nicht mit Chassepots* (Let's Go! — But not with Rifles, 1980)[20] they sang forbidden Social Democratic songs from the period of the Anti-Socialist Laws instituted by Bismarck in 1878. In *'s geht los!* the melodies were broken up and defamiliarized in order to point ironically to parallels between censorship in the Bismarck period and in the GDR. Out of this formal approach emerged Karls Enkel's montage aesthetic, which set theatrical and musical technique against text, contributing to an expression of philosophical ambivalence seldom witnessed in GDR political song. It confused the censors and was enthusiastically received by the group's insider following, consisting mostly of students, academics, and music fans.

In Karls Enkel's theatrical aesthetic there was already evidence of Weill's approach in *Der Aufstieg und Fall der Stadt Mahagonny* (The Rise and Fall of the City of Mahagonny, 1928), whereby a form is used ironically to undermine the cultural traditions and practices associated with it. In *Mahagonny* Weill had combined the concept of *Zeitoper* (Opera for Our Time) with Brecht's emerging theory of estrangement effects. Music, text, and performance now had to shake audiences out of their passive consumption of art, to lead them to a critical awareness of its themes. Weill's compositions supported Brecht's satire on the illusionist consumer paradise represented by the city Mahagonny. A musical montage technique was employed in which elements of opera, popular ballad, jazz, and sea shanty (as well as rhythmic influences from Stravinsky) formed dissonances with one another or created tension with the content of the lyrics to produce an alienation effect.[21] In the early 1980s in the GDR Karls Enkel were to take a similar ironic approach to the sacred left-wing tradition of agitprop theater. For example, while they based their *Liedertheater* on the proletarian revue structure, they turned the revue on its head to reveal the contradictions within the so-called proletarian society of the GDR itself. The pinnacle of this experiment was the *Hammer-Rehwü*[22] of 1982, a coproduction by Karls Enkel, Wacholder, and Beckert & Schulz. It was highly ironic that they adopted the artistic form and structure of Erwin Piscator's *Roter Rummel* (Red Revue) of 1924[23] in order to parody the real-existing socialism of the 1980s. While the *Roter Rummel* had propagated a distinct political moral and been used as support platform for the Communist Party before the elections of 1924, the *Hammer-Rehwü* was consciously anti-ideological. If the hero of Piscator's revue was the worker, the hero of the *Hammer-Rehwü* was the clown, who parodied a glorified image of the worker. Other customary figures of the proletarian revue such as the policeman, the capitalist, and the pastor were replaced by social "types" of the GDR such as the general, the dictator, and the fellow traveler, all of whom were parodied in a controversial manner.[24] In the final scene the speaker of the Brechtian epilogue emphasized the main difference between the two revues, concluding: "die Moral, es ist fatal, / Nicht mitgeliefert wurd in diesem Fall." (The moral, it is clear to see, / is lacking here unfortunately.) Instead of being presented with an explicit moral, the audience was confronted with comic relativity, slapstick, and carnivalesque exuberance with a marked emphasis on the body — the antithesis of a dry, ideology-crammed FDJ singing group concert.

The music of the *Hammer-Rehwü* often had, as with Weill, an ironic function in its undermining of the textual content. An example of this is the arrangement of the poem "Égalité." The prudish associations of the rococo style emphasize the feigned innocence of Wenzel's performance. All of this, however, contradicts the text, which paints a mocking picture of political leaders sitting on the toilet with their trousers down. The performance also used the revue technique of *Demontage* (dismantling) whereby, according to Christa Hasche, traditional associations are satirically disrupted "in the cutting up of plays or the quoting of documents."[25] In the *Hammer-Rehwü* this can be seen in the parodic recasting of motifs from Brecht and Weill's *Mahagonny*. Since Brecht's inheritance was revered and highly nurtured in schools, and indeed throughout GDR society, an educated audience would have understood the parodic appropriation of these quotations. For example, the lines from Paul's song in *Mahagonny* "Laßt euch nicht verführen" (literally: Don't let yourself be seduced) now become: "Du, laß dich nicht bescheißen!" (Don't let yourself be shat on). The new version laughs at the utopian belief in a future communist paradise and implies that the government uses people as mere objects in the pursuit of that goal. The original *Mahagonny* lines read:

> Laßt euch nicht verführen
> Zu Fron und Ausgezehr
> Was kann euch Angst noch rühren
> Ihr sterbt mit allen Tieren
> Und es kommt nichts nachher. (*BFA* 2:358)

[Take not as your teacher
The tyrant or the slave.
And do not dread the preacher:
The end for every creature
Is nothing but the grave. (*Plays* 2:198–99)]

In the version by Karls Enkel, these lines are adapted to become:

Du, laß dich nicht einwickeln
Von Liebe, Fron und Ehr
Wir sind Verbrauchsartikel
Und sterben wie Karnickel.
Und es kommt nichts nachher.[26]

[Don't let yourself be wrapped
In love, slavery, or honor
We are articles for consumption
And end up like rabbits
In nothing but the grave.]

If the contradiction in *Mahagonny* lies in the fact that Paul's appeal to enjoy life to the full ends in the self-destruction of society, it is clear from the *Hammer-Rehwü* that the theme of living life in the now is a basic existential longing of the younger generation in the GDR. The consolation of a utopia in the distant future, as propagated by the government, is no longer taken seriously. The production of the *Hammer-Rehwü* thus concludes with a verse from Erich Mühsam in which a lust for "a life in the now" is apparent in the face of false comforts and superficial contentment:

Ich möchte vom Glücke gesunden.
Die Seele sehnt sich nach harten Streichen,
Die Seele sehnt sich nach frischen Wunden,
Nach Kämpfen und Bängnissen, ohnegleichen.[27]

[I'd like to recover from happiness.
My soul is longing for hard blows,
My soul is longing for fresh wounds,
For battles and ordeals unparalleled.]

These texts reflected a general trend among young writers in the GDR who felt cut adrift from the progressive historical continuum that their socialist forefathers had believed in. Referring to a text by Ralph Grüneberger, Karen Leeder writes: "Far from casting themselves in the role of Brecht's 'Nachgeborenen,' (Those Born After) [. . .] the young writers place themselves much further down an attenuated and sorry line: 'Wir, die Nachundnachgeborenen' (born after bit by bit)." [28]

While Brecht had explained the corruptibility of man in terms of the dehumanizing forces of capitalism in plays such as *Mahagonny, Die Dreigroschenoper* (The Threepenny Opera, 1928) and *Der gute Mensch von Sezuan* (The Good Person of Szechwan, 1941), Karls Enkel now investigated this theme controversially within their own context of a socialist society. For censorship reasons it was impossible to tackle this subject matter head-on, but in 1983 they managed to couch it within their theatrical adaptation of Karl Marx's *Achtzehnter Brumaire* (Eighteenth Brumaire) text from 1852, which they entitled *Die komische Tragödie des 18. Brumaire* (The Comical Tragedy of the Eighteenth Brumaire).[29] In this musical montage of quotations from the Marx text alongside poems and songs of their own, Karls Enkel implied that corruption was a basic feature of political life in the GDR. The actors together with dramaturge Heiner Maaß were concerned to show that it was the corruptibility of people that hindered the achievement of a real socialism. In this respect Brecht was a major point of reference. When I interviewed him in 1994, Maaß stated that the intention with *Die komische Tragödie* was to do a *Threepenny Opera* for the GDR and that it turned into the biggest bombshell ("der härteste Hammer") they had ever produced.[30]

In *Die komische Tragödie* the theme of Bonaparte's appeasing of the Parisian proletariat with petit-bourgeois comforts is set side-by-side with the famous lines from Marx's *Brumaire* about how history repeats itself: the first time as tragedy and the second time as farce.[31] A medley on this theme culminates in the "Farce-Lied" (Farce Song). Cast member Dieter Beckert, in the role of Louis Napoleon, sings: "Der Mensch ist viel zu leicht gemacht / Und viel zu schnell zu kaufen" (Man is made far too easily / And is far too easily bought). This is indeed reminiscent of "Das Lied von der Unzulänglichkeit menschlichen Strebens" (The Song of the Insufficiency of Human Endeavor) from *Die Dreigroschenoper* with its lines such as: "Denn für dieses Leben / Ist der Mensch nicht schlecht genug" (*BFA* 2:291; For this bleak existence / Man is never bad enough, *Plays* 2:152). *Die komische Tragödie*'s musical accompaniment, with its tango melody from *Carmen* and its decadent connotations gives a distinct *Dreigroschenoper* flavor. To make this connection clear, the music changes into Weill's "Salomo-Song" melody, which underpins Beckert's historical conclusion:

> Es lernten von Napoleon Bismarck und andre [*sic*] Fürsten,
> Wie er gekauft das Lumpenpack mit Schnäpsen und Würsten.

Das ist ein clevres Stück mein Kind,
Der Stoff ist bekannt, aber neu sind die Stars.
So endet manche Hungersnot
Das eine Mal als Tragödie, das andre Mal als Farce.[32]

[Bismarck and other princes learnt from Napoleon
How to buy off the proles with schnapps and sausage
That's a clever thing my child
The story is old but with brand-new stars.
That's how to end hunger
The first time as tragedy, the second time as farce.]

A similar Brechtian/Weillian epic treatment of a current political subject was evident in *Die Sichel-Operette* (The Sickle Operette)[33] of 1987. This successor to the *Hammer-Rehwü* was staged by Wenzel and Mensching together with former members of Karls Enkel and a larger ensemble of musicians and actors calling itself the Sichel-Kollektiv (Sickle Collective). Thematically, if the *Hammer-Rehwü* had been a carnivalesque ridiculing of GDR officialdom and *Die komische Tragödie* a satire of communism's failure to change mankind's base instincts, then the *Sichel-Operette* was quite simply a parody of the political cul-de-sac the GDR found itself in two years before the fall of the Wall, a period in which the aging Politbüro resisted Gorbachev's liberal reforms from Moscow and countless citizens (among them many actors and musicians) applied to leave for West Germany.

Similarly to *Mahagonny*, the *Sichel-Operette* plays thematically with the longings and illusions that are an intrinsic formal characteristic of the operetta. In this way, if *Mahagonny* counted as epic opera, then the *Sichel-Operette* can be seen to be epic operetta. Jan Knopf writes that the *Mahagonny* opera deals with the matter of its own genre, that is with opera as an expression of a heightened culinary stance, of illusionism, romanticism, and escape.[34] The spectator, however, is confronted with the destruction of these illusions, which thwarts an experience of enjoyment. A corresponding approach is apparent in the *Sichel-Operette*. The plot takes place in an imaginary country "in the East." It is based upon the love between the native Hans Sichel and Princess Tiffany of Monaco. This in itself is an allusion to the romantic notion of marrying a Westerner and then being able to leave the GDR. But this and all the other illusions are dashed, and the songs and musical leitmotifs are constantly interrupted by comic antics and clowns' dialogues. In both form and content, the operetta functions as a parody of socialist illusions in a country where petit-bourgeois comforts have become more important than political ideals. It also parodies the illusions of citizens applying to leave the GDR expecting to find a land of milk and honey in the West.

Ironical quotation or *Demontage*, as in the *Hammer-Rehwü*, also contributes to the contradictory effect. The passage from Offenbach's *Orphée* "Als ich noch Prinz war in Arkadien, / lebt ich in Reichtum, Glanz und Macht" (When I was a prince in Arcadia, / I lived in richness, splendor, and power) is now transformed by the "Kaiser" (played by Dieter Beckert) into: "Als ich in Binz war mit Bernhardy, / da schwammen wir zum Horizont" (When I was in Binz with Bernhardy, / we swam to the horizon). Binz is on the island of Rügen on the Baltic Sea just off the GDR coast, a place from which people frequently attempted to escape the GDR by swimming to Denmark. In this way the taboo theme of flight is set side-by-side with that of a self-indulgent, out-of-touch GDR leadership.

The dream is not fulfilled; the happy wedding between Hans and Princess Tiffany does not take place. "Das Volk," who sing their "Wir sind glücklich" (We are happy) rondo, finally mutiny, forcing a gro-tesque happy end in which Hans and Tiffany and the Kaiser and his wife go to the altar as crippled geriatrics. In view of the lack of political prog-ress in 1987 combined with the actual political discontent among the cast (the actor Horst Kotterba, who played Hans, had himself applied to leave the GDR) there was no chance of a victorious "happy world." Thus, as with the Brechtian *Mahagonny* model, the *Sichel-Operette* subverts the traditional form of the genre and in doing so uncovers a contradictoriness of reality denied in conventional operetta.

Brecht's use of the European theatrical clowning tradition was another formal aspect that inspired Wenzel and Mensching in their comical exposure of the political contradictions and human failings in everyday GDR life. This clown aesthetic served Wenzel and Mensching well in the *Da Da eR* productions that they mounted as a duo from 1982–90. From Brecht, for example, they had learned the dramaturgical usefulness of the clown mask in its malleability, its ability to represent diverse concepts. One clown's trait that Brecht had made use of was the mask of stupidity, for example, in the figures of Galy Gay and Schweyk. As Bakhtin writes: "Stupidity (incomprehension) [. . .] interacts dialogically with an intelligence (a lofty pseudo intelligence) with which it polemicizes and whose mask it tears away."[35] In the "Passport Scene" from *Neues aus der Da Da eR* (News from the Da Da eR, 1983), Weh is the fool who cannot understand the logic of a bureaucracy that prevents him from obtaining a passport photograph. Meh, the photographer, continually asks him: "Waren Sie denn schon da?" (Have you been there yet?), a veiled reference to the Stasi secret police. But Weh fails to understand this and replies repeatedly in an innocent voice: "Nein, ich war noch nicht bei Ihnen. Ich möchte doch ein Paßfoto" (No, I haven't been to you before. I just want a passport photo).[36] In this way they parody taboos surrounding travel restrictions to the West. Another example from this production is given in the "Scheißszene" (Shit Scene). Here, the clowns Weh and Meh are overwhelmed by the GDR blues. Meh cures Weh's misery by hammering a giant nail through his head. Weh, in turn, proceeds to wrap Meh up completely in cotton padding so that he may no longer perceive the causes of his affliction. The clowns' futile solutions to the problem are a comical abstraction of a no-way-out situation in the GDR. People are politically impotent in the face of an unchanging hierarchy, but simultaneously — through subservience and inner retreat — they also contribute passively to the problem. Like Herr Schmitt in the clowns' scene of Brecht's *Badener Lehrstück* and the characters of Karl Valentin, the suffering of Weh and Meh is comical and ludicrous because, as Lee Baxandall writes with reference to Herr Schmitt, it is "endured without comprehension of its causes."[37] But Wenzel and Mensching do not offer a solution, and here we see the main difference between *Neues aus der Da Da eR* and Brecht: it is clowns' theater as opposed to a didactic play. While the tension between the individual and the collective is exposed, the laughter resolves this tension. The audience is not invited, as with Brecht, to change society's structure, merely to laugh at the ridiculousness of it. At the same time the collective laughter at a commonly perceived plight in the GDR contributed to the promotion of an alternative consciousness that laid the basis for the movement for change in the late 1980s. In *Altes aus der Da Da eR* (Old News from the Da Da eR) from 1988–89, renamed *Letztes aus der Da Da eR* (Final News from the Da Da eR) after the fall of the Berlin Wall, the scenes and songs reflected the historical turning point. With a mixture of rage, grief, relief, and anticipation, the clowns and their audience laid the GDR to rest finally in a chorus of laughter.[38]

Both Biermann and Karls Enkel identified with the grotesque aspects of the early Brecht material — the language, the body motifs, and (in the case of Wenzel and Mensching) the clown attire and gestures familiar from productions of *Mann ist Mann* (Man Equals Man) in 1926 and *Das Badener Lehrstück* in 1929. Their identification with this material projected a different Brecht from the official image that the SED preferred to propagate. In both cases it was provocative — a tool to expose the stagnant state of the revolutionary ideals in the GDR. After the fall of the Wall the Brechtian *Gestus* no longer had a use in attacking the shortcomings of communism, but the dialectical aesthetic of Brecht's work remained a creative inspiration for Wenzel and Mensching. In June 1998 Wenzel staged *Hanswurst und andere arme Würste* (Hanswurst and Other Poor Sausages) ("Hanswurst" being the German theatrical variation of the Harlequin) at the Berliner Ensemble for the celebration of the hundredth anniversary of Hanns Eisler's birth. The production consisted of a collage of Eisler texts and music set alongside texts by Hölderlin, Brecht, and others, the montage effect emphasizing the uncomfortable, critical figure that Eisler had been both in his exile abroad and in the GDR.[39] As in the finale to *Neues aus der Da Da eR* from 1983, the conclusion to this production has no moral apart from silence:

> In meinem Alter wäre das Schweigen vielleicht viel gemäßer als das Reden. Deshalb höre ich jetzt auf zu reden, und lasse Sie darüber nachdenken, was ich jetzt zu schweigen habe.[40]

> [At my age it is perhaps far more appropriate to be silent than to speak. I'll therefore stop talking now and let you consider what it is I have to be silent about.]

Just as there seemed to be no way out of the deepest stagnation in the GDR, the capitalism of the post-reunification period appeared too powerful for one to believe that society could be changed by theater, music, or literature. Perhaps however, laughter, as a successful act of Brechtian alienation, still offers the possibility for artists like Biermann, Wenzel, and Mensching[41] to inspire critical thinking and to promote an alternative consciousness, if only among like-minded people.

Notes

[1] Ernst Busch, *Internationale Arbeiterlieder* (East Berlin: Lied der Zeit, 1949).

[2] Inge Lammel, *Das Arbeiterlied* (Leipzig: Reclam, 1970), 82. Quoted in Lutz Kirchenwitz, *Folk, Chanson und Liedermacher in der DDR* (Berlin: Dietz, 1993), 86.

[3] Wolf Biermann, "Herr Brecht," in *Alle Lieder* (Cologne: Kiepenheuer & Witsch, 1991), 49; "Herr Brecht," in *Poems and Ballads*, trans. Steve Gooch (London: Pluto, 1977), 25. Further references will be given as *AL* and *PB* in the text.

[4] See David Robb, "Narrative Role-Play as Communication Strategy in German Protest Song," in *Protest Song in East and West Germany since the 1960s*, ed. David Robb (Rochester, NY: Camden House, 2007), 67–96, here 83–89.

[5] See Mikhail Bakhtin, *Rabelais and His World* (Bloomington: U of Indiana P, 1984), 263–69.

[6] Bakhtin, *Rabelais and His World*, 10.

[7] Bakhtin, *The Dialogic Imagination* (Austin: U of Texas P, 1981), 192.

[8] See Biermann's own version of Heine's epic poem *Deutschland: Ein Wintermärchen* (1844): Wolf Biermann, *Deutschland: Ein Wintermärchen* (West Berlin: Klaus Wagenbach, 1972).

[9] Unless otherwise indicated, all translations into English are by David Robb.

[10] Walter Benjamin documented how Brecht credited Valentin with giving him the original idea of epic *Verfremdung*. In the rehearsals for *Eduard II* a comment of Valentin's inspired the artificial portrayal of the soldiers whereby their fear was accentuated by the chalking of their faces. Walter Benjamin, *Understanding Brecht*, trans. Anna Bostock (London: NLB, 1973), 115.

[11] Biermann, "Ballade vom Mann," on *Es geht sein' sozialistischen Gang*, LP © CBS 1977.

[12] Georg-Friedrich Kühn, "Kutsche und Kutscher: Die Musik des Wolf Biermanns," in *Wolf Biermann*, ed. Heinz Ludwig Arnold (Munich: edition text + kritik, 1980), 106–31, here 111.

[13] Biermann, *Frankfurter Rundschau*, 30 December 1972.

[14] Kühn, "Kutsche und Kutscher," 89.

[15] Kühn, "Kutsche und Kutscher," 124.

[16] See David Robb, "The Cat-and-Mouse Game with Censorship and Institutions," in *Protest Song*, ed. Robb, 228–54, here 229–35.

[17] Neidhardt Schreiber, "Hoffnungsloser Fall: Heiner Müller in Magdeburg," in *Zitadelle*, February 1996, 17.

[18] Karin Hirdina, "Präzision ohne Pingelichkeit: Wenzel und Mensching im Gespräch mit Karin Hirdina," *Temperamente* 4 (1984): 38.

[19] See David Robb, *Zwei Clowns im Lande des verlorenen Lachens: Das Liedertheater Wenzel & Mensching* (Berlin: Ch. Links, 1998). An earlier version of this section appeared in English as "Epic Operette and Anti-Culinary Clowning: Exposing the Illusion in the Liedertheater of Wenzel & Mensching," *Brecht Yearbook* 30 (2005): 335–52.

[20] Karls Enkel, "'s geht los! aber nicht mit Chassepots: Eine Collage über die Zeit des Sozialistengesetzes," unpublished manuscript and tape recording, 1980. Stiftung Archiv der Akademie der Künste (henceforth AdK) Liedertheater-Dokumentation, Forschungsabteilung Musik/Liedzentrum.

[21] Ronald Sanders, *The Days Grow Short: The Life and Music of Kurt Weill* (London: Weidenfeld and Nicolson, 1980), 145–53.

[22] Karls Enkel, Wacholder, Beckert und Schulz, "Hammer-Rehwü," unpublished manuscript and video recording, 1982. AdK Liedertheater-Dokumentation, Forschungsabteilung Musik/Lied-Zentrum.

[23] See Christa Hasche, "Bürgerliche Revue und 'Roter Rummel': Studien zur Entwicklung massenwirksamen Theaters in den Formen der Revue in Berlin 1903–1925" (PhD dissertation, Humboldt-Universität Berlin, 1980), 90.

[24] Robb, *Zwei Clowns*, 58–59.

[25] Hasche, 13.

[26] The "Du" at the start of the first line is also a clear reference to the banned Wolf Biermann song that begins "Du, laß dich nicht verhärten, in dieser harten Zeit." From "Ermutigung," *aah-ja!*, LP © CBS, 1974. Because Biermann's songs were strictly forbidden in the GDR it is possible that not everyone understood the reference, even though the *Hammer-Rehwü* audience consisted of many insiders of the *Liedermacher* scene.

[27] *Die Hammer-Rehwü*, from Erich Mühsam, *Auswahl: Gedichte Drama Prosa* (East Berlin: Volk und Welt, 1961), 51.

[28] Karen Leeder, *Breaking Boundaries: A New Generation of Poets in the GDR* (Oxford: Clarendon, 1996), 50.

[29] Karls Enkel, "Die komische Tragödie des 18. Brumaire des Louis Bonaparte nach Karl Marx oder Ohrfeige sind schlimmer als Dolchstöße," unpublished manuscript and video recording, 1983. AdK Liedertheater-Dokumentation, Forschungsabteilung Musik/Lied-Zentrum.

[30] Personal interview with Heiner Maaß, 23 March 1994.

[31] Karl Marx, *Der achtzehnte Brumaire von Louis Bonaparte* (East Berlin: Henschel Verlag, 1974), 15.

[32] Karls Enkel, "Die komische Tragödie," n. p.

[33] Das Sichel-Kollektiv, "Die Sichel-Operette," unpublished manuscript and video recording, 1987. AdK Liedertheater-Dokumentation, Forschungsabteilung Musik/Lied-Zentrum.

[34] Jan Knopf, *Brecht-Handbuch: Theater* (Stuttgart: Metzler, 1980), 67.

[35] Bakhtin, *The Dialogic Imagination*, 403.

[36] Wenzel and Mensching, "Neues aus der Da Da eR," unpublished manuscript and video recording, 1983. AdK Liedertheater-Dokumentation, Forschungsabteilung Musik/Lied-Zentrum.

[37] Lee Baxandall, "Bertolt Brecht's J.B.," in *Brecht Sourcebook*, ed. Carol Martin and Henry Bial (London: Routledge, 2000), 84–88, here 87.

[38] See David Robb, *Zwei Clowns*, 142–55.

[39] See David Robb, "The Demise of Political Song and the New Discourse of Techno in the Berlin Republic," in *Protest Song*, ed. Robb, 255–78, here 260–62.

[40] Hans-Eckardt Wenzel, *Hanswurst und andere arme Würste: Hanns-Eisler-Collage*, compact disc © Conträr Musik, 2001.

[41] Mensching's unpublished solo program *Amok* (2001) shows that he, like Wenzel, continued to pursue this aesthetic strategy after reunification.

Fatzer's Footprints: Brecht's *Fatzer* and the GDR Theater

Moray McGowan, Trinity College Dublin

O N 4 NOVEMBER 1989, at the historic demonstration on the Alexanderplatz in East Berlin, the text that playwright Heiner Müller initially planned to read from the podium was an extract from Bertolt Brecht's *Fatzer* that calls on the statesmen and their henchmen to release the state that no longer wants them.[1] Müller's view of the GDR as a failed experiment and his view of Brecht coalesce in his extended critical engagement with *Fatzer*, and both *Fatzer* itself and its simultaneous presence and near-absence in GDR theater are important elements in an understanding of Brecht in the GDR. Accordingly, this essay considers the distinctiveness of *Fatzer* even within Brecht's work and the influence this had on its delayed reception in the GDR, *Fatzer*'s importance for Heiner Müller and vice versa, those productions by GDR directors that did eventually take place, and finally the links between the GDR as a failed socialist experiment and the new significance *Fatzer* has acquired since 1989–90.

By his late twenties, in the middle years of the Weimar Republic, Brecht had seen the dramatic expansion and cyclical crises of industrial capitalism, war's brutalizing effects, the shortages that set in with the "Rübenwinter" (turnip winter) of 1917, military collapse, the revolution of 1918–19 and its ruthless suppression, economic turmoil, and Germany's acute version of the paramilitary lawlessness that was widespread in early 1920s Europe. In the cities of Weimar Germany, Brecht had encountered the anarchic, amoral potential and the sometimes nightmarish, sometimes liberating energy of violence displayed by human individuals, collectives, and masses struggling to survive in a world in the throes of dissolution and transformation. It is the grimly violent world of Max Beckmann's painting *Night* (1918–19) or of Alban Berg's dystopian intensification of Büchner's *Woyzeck* in his opera *Wozzeck* (1922). By the late 1920s, moreover, fascism, promising answers to these traumas of modernity, was on the rise.

This landscape of material and moral upheaval is the setting for Brecht's *Fatzer*, not a finished play but 500-plus manuscript pages of drafts, notes, and commentaries (*BFA* 10.1: 387–529). The common core of these overlapping, sometimes mutually contradictory fragments is a four-man tank crew that deserts toward the end of the First World War and goes to ground in Mülheim on the Ruhr, "dies finstere Viereck zwischen Kränen und Eisenhütten" (*BFA* 10.1: 463; this grim dark rectangle between cranes and ironworks). There the four men, called Fatzer, Koch, Büsching, and Kaumann in most of the drafts, plan to wait out the revolution that must surely happen any moment. The men's survival instincts interact and collide with a solidarity shaped by the brutal camaraderie of the front. It is Fatzer's anarchic refusal to die senselessly for an abstract ideal that inspires the tank crew to desert in the first place, to escape the maelstrom of the front, and thus to survive. But that same egotism comes to threaten the men's survival once it becomes clear that the revolution will not happen. Fatzer repays Kaumann's hospitality (the men are holed up in Kaumann's basement flat) by sleeping with his wife; having organized black market food he fails to rendezvous with the soldiers who are to supply it; and his brawls with a group of butchers make the four deserters dangerously visible. The other three therefore kill him shortly before dying themselves at the hands of the regular forces of order.

"The Highest Technical Standard":
Fatzer as Brecht's Most Brechtian Text

The sheer mass of fragments that constitute the *Fatzer* materials testifies to Brecht's prolonged wrestling with questions at the heart of his theater and its relationship to modern existence. As early as 1928 Brecht declared *Fatzer* to be "ein harter Bissen" (*BFA* 28:313; a tough mouthful). Indeed, though thirteen pages of the material were published in the first volume of Brecht's *Versuche* (Experiments) in 1930 — where they were announced as part 3 of *Der Untergang des Egoisten Johann Fatzer* (The Downfall of the Egotist Johann Fatzer) — and though in 1951 he considered including elements of *Fatzer* in a play about the model GDR worker Hans Garbe (*BFA* 27:324), *Fatzer* remained unfinished and unperformed at Brecht's death in 1956. His verdict of 1929, "fatzer

unaufführbar" (*BFA* 10.2: 1118; fatzer unperformable), already rang
with resigned finality.

Yet in 1939, from the vantage point of the exile in which he wrote
many of his canonical works, Brecht described not these "Great Plays,"
but *Fatzer* and its fellow fragment *Der Brotladen* (Breadshop, 1929–30)
as "der höchste Standard technisch" (*BFA* 26:330; the highest technical
standard). This being Brecht, he means it not in terms of a unified,
polished work, but precisely the opposite. The best structures with which
artists can engage with twentieth-century technological modernity are
fragments, kept open and unfinished so that they and others may
experiment further with them from different positions and perspectives as
this modernity continues to transform itself. (As a set of constantly
revisited questions of dramaturgy, politics, ethics, and ontology, Brecht's
Fatzer shares more with Goethe's *Faust* than simply the first name of
their title figures.) Tableaux are preferable to teleological plots, explorations of socially significant *Gestus*, that is, movement and language that
display the material circumstances of the figures, are preferable to those
of individual psychology.[2] Moreover, with the rise of totalitarianism,
which Brecht saw with an even grimmer clarity in 1939 than in the late
1920s, the fragment, resisting closure in order to offer utopian glimpses
of other possibilities, took on a new political significance.

Fatzer also develops further the stage forms and figures Brecht had
begun to explore, in plays such as *Im Dickicht der Städte* (In the Jungle
of Cities, 1922), to show human beings learning to live in modern cities.
On these urban battlefields, each figure is less an "Individuum"
(individual) than a "Dividuum," as Brecht characterized Galy Gay in the
1936 edition of *Mann ist Mann* (*BFA* 2:203; Man Equals Man). Each is
less a rounded character than a "ein Schauplatz von Widersprüchen
unsrer Gesellschaftsordnung" (an arena of contradictions in our social
order), as Walter Benjamin put it,[3] but also less schematic than, say, the
split figure of Shen Te/Shui Ta in Brecht's play *Der gute Mensch von
Sezuan* (The Good Person of Szechwan, 1941).

The *Fatzer* fragments are of many different text types, registers, and
styles, and the half-decade of their composition coincides with Brecht's
development in the latter 1920s from an iconoclastic, anti-idealist, but
politically unspecific materialism to a position informed by Marxism,
partially embracing but never subsumed by party dogma. But while one
of *Fatzer*'s central tensions is indeed "spontaneity versus doctrine," it
does not structure it in quite such simple binary terms.[4] Certainly, *Fatzer*
extends the exploration of asocial figures it shares with *Baal* (1918–20)
or *Trommeln in der Nacht* (Drums in the Night, 1919–22) by inves-

tigating their place in and conflict with the collective.[5] But while this
leads to a closer association with the didactic stance, and the formal
elements such as the chorus, of the *Lehrstücke* (learning plays), this
movement is not straightforwardly linear. Walter Benjamin noted
Brecht's goal in *Fatzer* as being to let the revolutionary figure emerge, of
his own accord and free of ethical motives ("ganz ohne Ethos von
selber"), from the bad, self-centered type ("aus dem schlechten,
selbstischen Typus").[6] Brecht's own view of this process and his success
in achieving its theatrical representation fluctuated over time and from
draft to draft.

Moreover, the didactic aspiration is not to hand down doctrines, but
to promote the critical study and practice of method: the "Fatzer-
dokument," one of the fragments, acknowledges that what the writer
learns in writing the text and what the "Schüler" (pupils) learn in
studying or performing it may be quite different (*BFA* 10.1: 514). The
"Fatzer-Kommentar" (*BFA* 10.1: 515–29; Fatzer commentary) is not a
guide to some putative model interpretation of the action or dialogue,
but a "diskontinuierliche Umschrift des Fatzer-Stoffs auf dem anderen
Schauplatz der Theorie" (discontinuous rewriting of the *Fatzer* material
in the other arena, that of theory).[7] Here *Fatzer* is aligned with the more
emancipatory aspects of the *Lehrstücke*, in that Brecht is striving for a
practice that combines performance with critical engagement: performance as experiential insight, not performance of pre-defined meaning.
The aim is to develop a participatory theater in which "der Denkende,"
the active thinker, would overcome the distinction that bourgeois
philosophy and bourgeois aesthetics make between "den Tätigen und
den Betrachtenden" (*BFA* 10.1: 524; the active participant and the
observer).[8] For the Brecht of 1930, this was "die große Pädagogik"
(*BFA* 21:396–98; great pedagogy), and his return in exile to the more
conventional approach of dramas that, for all their "epic" structures and
techniques, were to be performed by actors, at the behest of directors,
for spectators, was a pragmatic compromise and an aesthetic retreat.

The *Fatzer* material as a whole retains much of the transitional
ambivalence of *Mann ist Mann* (1926), though it explores this ambivalence with a darker intensity. *Fatzer*'s world is one where "unsere
Mutter ist ein Tank" (*BFA* 10.1: 453; our mother is a tank), a world
dominated by the need to secure "Obdach und Wasser und Fleisch"
(*BFA* 10.1: 440; shelter and water and meat). Brecht saw a new kind of
human being emerging from the conflicts between the elemental drives
of survival, hunger, shelter, sex, and companionship, interactions taking
place within the self, with others and with the material forces of a

transforming world. He saw too that the tensions these conflicts create between individual needs and desires, those of the group, and those of the larger collective such as the state generate disorientation and terror. Central to this is the idea of a "Furchtzentrum" of the play, where the elemental drives and the threats to them presented by other human beings and by the material environment are concentrated: "Furchtzentrum des Stücks. / Während der Hunger sie anfällt, geht das Dach über ihren Köpfen weg, verläßt sie ihr bester Kamerad und spaltet sie der Sexus" (*BFA* 10.1: 428; fear center of the play. / While hunger attacks them, they lose the roof over their heads, their best comrade abandons them, and sex divides them). This is compounded by the fact that the men are deserters, facing summary execution if caught, and thus in an intensely liminal situation, outside the law but not beyond its reach. It is compounded too by the role of fear as the harbinger of the emerging future, whose as yet indeterminate status, positive or negative, is in itself a motor of that fear: "Denn immer Furcht / Zeigt an, was kommt" (*BFA* 10.1: 465; for it is fear that always displays what is coming).

To call *Fatzer* "pre-ideological"[9] does not wholly escape the reductive dialectic that leads from these tensions to a resolution, be it socialism or any other ideology. In fact *Fatzer* is also post-ideological, extra-, and anti-ideological. Fatzer rejects "eure ungesunde lust / wie räder zu sein" (*BFA* 10.1: 463; your unhealthy desire / to be wheels [in the sense of cogs in the machine]) and the alienated self that is "nichts als unzerstörbar" (*BFA* 10.1: 464; indestructible, nothing else). Insisting that the human being is "kein Hebel" (not a lever), Fatzer begs his comrades:

Behaltet von allem, was an mir ist
Nur das euch Nützliche.
Der Rest ist Fatzer. (*BFA* 10.1: 495)

[Keep of me
Just that which is of use to you
The residue is Fatzer.]

"Der Rest ist Fatzer" does more than simply echo Hamlet's dying words, "the rest is silence." For Brecht, battling with his own contradictory impulses of radical individualism and collective utility, a central dilemma of the phase that embraces both *Fatzer* and the *Lehrstücke* was that of "Einverständnis," of insight into, and agreement with, at whatever personal cost, a course of action deemed socially necessary.[10] Without reinstating the anachronistic notions of the Schillerian moral individual,

Fatzer's partial refusal of "Einverständnis," his insistence on his irreducible residue of humanity, challenges both utilitarianism and the perversion of the Enlightenment dream of human progress into the pursuit of human perfectibility through selection.

In this respect, Fatzer's walks through the city of Mülheim, "aufhaltend das Rad" (*BFA* 10.1: 463; stopping the [turn of the] wheel), are literally insubordinate. With them he reclaims his right to the streets from both the law and the pragmatics of survival, both of which declare he should make himself invisible, and so rejects the subordination of the self to a social order and the power that underpins it. With Fatzer's walks Brecht creates a simple yet striking stage metaphor of refusal and revolt that resonates into the present.

Brecht was fascinated by the inseparable tension of the dystopian and the utopian in the *Fatzer* fragments, preferring it to models or parables, which often papered over these fundamental contradictions, even if they paid lip service to open form or "epic drama." But the dramatization of the energies of anarchic refusal, the emergence of the new as an inchoate process driven by and experienced with fear, and the prediction that for a long time there will be no more victors, only the vanquished (*BFA* 10.1: 427), did not sit easily either with the sanctioned, superficially Marxist narrative of progress or the narrative of Soviet victory over fascism. Reportedly, Brecht's professed goal on his arrival in the Soviet zone in the late 1940s was twenty years of "Ideologiezertrümmerung" (demolition of ideology), in which process *Fatzer*'s radical confrontation of freedom and discipline might have played a major role.[11] But there was, of course, no time for this in the GDR, even if there had been the will for it. As the Cold War intensified and the GDR's Western neighbor rebuilt, the GDR needed ideology, needed a set of ideals on which to build a society and reconstruct an economy, to renovate the house without having cleared the rubble in the cellar, as Heiner Müller put it (*FK* 32). Given, moreover, Brecht's other difficulties establishing, developing, and defending his theater and its aesthetic practice in the GDR, it is hardly surprising that he never seriously tried to stage *Fatzer* there.

Traces of *Fatzer* of at least two kinds can, though, be seen in Brecht's work after 1945. Firstly, there was the "Garbe-Stoff" (Garbe material): bricklayer Hans Garbe, by repairing a furnace while it was still operating, thus minimizing the loss of output, became a hero of socialist labor. A dramatization of the Garbe story might have won Brecht's theater more acceptance. Between 1951 and 1954 he worked fitfully on a stage version. Entries in his notebooks show that he intended to include material from the *Fatzer* fragments in this (indeed, Garbe was called Büsching in some drafts), and that the form too was to be "ein fragment in grossen, rohen blöcken" (*BFA* 27:324; a fragment in great, rough blocks). This was, though, the very opposite of the dramatic closure and resolution socialist realism required, especially since Brecht planned a whole act on Garbe's role in the June 1953 protests, and Brecht's Garbe project came to a standstill.

Secondly, the idea, expressed in the line "der Rest ist Fatzer," of the irreducibly human beyond functional usefulness and beyond ideology re-emerged in the *Antigonemodell 1948* (Antigone Model 1948). Brecht's revision, turning Antigone's brother Polyneikes into a deserter hung by the SS in spring 1945, gives the text an overtly antifascist stance, but the underlying motif remains the insistence on the right and duty of burial and thus the rescue of the human from the dictates of a dehumanizing state.[12]

Fatzer itself, though, remained unperformed at Brecht's death in 1956. Until well into the 1970s, it went unmentioned in histories of theater or studies of Brecht published in the GDR. Symptomatically, when in 1967 the Berliner Ensemble planned to stage the fragments Brecht had described as of "the highest standard technically," *Fatzer* was characterized in the preparatory discussions as a play about inactivity, fruitless waiting, and stagnation in a nihilistic world without social purpose,[13] and was abandoned in favor of *Der Brotladen*. Anticipating elements of *Die heilige Johanna der Schlachthöfe* (Saint Joan of the Stockyards, 1932), *Der Brotladen* is a farce on the crazy logic of capitalism and religion's role in diverting social unrest, with minimal power to unsettle a GDR audience.[14]

Perhaps unsurprisingly, then, *Fatzer* was first performed in the West, at the Schaubühne am Halleschen Ufer in West Berlin, in 1976, directed by Frank-Patrick Steckel.[15] However, shortly afterwards, *Fatzer* began its roundabout journey into the GDR theater. In 1977, one of the major figures of East German theater, Benno Besson, resigned as manager of the East Berlin Volksbühne, partly in frustration when the Brecht estate blocked a planned production of *Fatzer*.[16] With him went Manfred Karge and Matthias Langhoff, who had directed the Berliner Ensemble production of *Der Brotladen* and who now staged *Fatzer* in the West, namely in Hamburg in 1978, in an adaptation by the GDR playwright Heiner Müller.

Heiner Müller's Fascination with *Fatzer*: The Fragment as a "Text of the Century"

Fatzer's place in the GDR theater, and indeed its status in experimental theater internationally,[17] are inseparable from that of Müller. Its role for other GDR writers, such as Volker Braun, though significant, is secondary by comparison.[18] For Müller, Brecht's texts and theatrical practice were not models to be faithfully followed but, as he put it in 1983, a "Kläranlage" (purification plant), a set of processes, methods, ideas, and forms to be worked through critically in order to free theater from false accretions and discover new possibilities.[19] Müller's essay "Fatzer ± Keuner" (1979), whose title points to the multiple emphases that can be given to the *Fatzer* material depending on what is selected from it and how it is staged, ends with the much-quoted comment, "Brecht gebrauchen, ohne ihn zu kritisieren, ist Verrat" (*FK* 36; to use Brecht without criticizing him is betrayal). This is, certainly, dialectic deployed to secure as much freedom of action as possible while acknowledging a debt. But it is also dialectic in the spirit of Brecht: real respect for an artistic inheritance lies not in mummifying it but in extending it through experiment, doubt, and critique.

Fatzer's fragmentary form, and the aesthetics and politics that underpinned it, lent themselves optimally to Müller's approach. In his view, the intensity of *Fatzer*'s language and form made it a "Jahrhunderttext" (text of the century),[20] "der beste Text von Brecht überhaupt" (Brecht's best text of all), a high point in Brecht's work between "der junge Wilde" (the young savage) and "der Klassiker, stalinistisch gebremst" (the classic author held in check by Stalinism).[21] Müller alludes to or quotes *Fatzer* in countless interviews and essays. There are references to it in at least 140 of the files in the Müller archive of the Academy of Arts in Berlin, relating to many of his projects from the early drafts of *Die Schlacht* (The Battle) in the mid 1950s to *Quartett* (Quartet) in the 1980s. In 1967 Müller was involved in the unrealized plan to stage *Fatzer* at the Berliner Ensemble. He then himself adapted *Fatzer* for stage and radio (*HMW* 6:55–141), and finally directed it as part of a larger project in 1993, two years before his death. Perhaps inevitably, then, the Fatzer figure appears in Müller's parody of Brecht, of himself, and of his obsession with Brecht, *Nachleben Brechts Beischlaf Auferstehung in Berlin* (Brecht's Afterlife Intercourse Resurrection in Berlin, 1990).[22]

For Müller, who saw "Erfolg" (success) and "Wirkung" (impact) as inversely proportionate,[23] *Fatzer*'s unfinished and unfinishable form, its elemental starkness, and its focus on the emergence of the new as a moment of terror were its strengths. Its fragmentary structure reflected the character of German history (*HMW* 8:201), prevented "das Verschwinden der Produktion im Produkt" (the disappearance of the production process in the product),[24] and sustained glimpses of alternatives in and to an oppressively closed world. *Fatzer*'s language "formuliert nicht Denkresultate, sondern skandiert den Denkprozeß" (*HMW* 8:230; does not formulate the outcomes of thought, but scans [as in: rhythmically chants] the process of thought). Müller shared Walter Benjamin's preference for Kafka's parables over Brecht's, but saw *Fatzer* as Brecht's most Kafkaesque text. Being "eher fremd als verfremdend" (*FK* 31; more strange than estranging), that is, resisting what could all too soon become an unchallengingly familiar aesthetic device, *Fatzer* offered the theater practitioner Müller, who was only interested in theater that stepped beyond its own boundaries, the challenge of the radically unknown: "ftz experience — notwendigkeit die / stühle unter sich wegzusprengen die / einem untergeschoben werden" (ftz [*Fatzer*] experience — necessity of / blasting away the chairs that / are pushed in underneath us).[25]

The motif of Fatzer's resistance to exclusion is related, Müller suggests, to the lethal logic of selectivity as demonstrated in the Holocaust. "Das ist das FATZER-Problem, es ist das Grundthema des Jahrhunderts, und Auschwitz ist das Modell des Jahrhunderts" (That is the FATZER problem, it is the fundamental theme of the century and Auschwitz is the model of/for the century).[26] Selection leads to exclusion and, eventually, to elimination.

Alongside this, in the transformation, in Brecht's *Fatzer* drafts, of the figure of Koch, the fellow deserter who most strongly opposes Fatzer's asocial individualism, into the figure of Keuner, the pragmatic rationalist, Müller saw not only Brecht's "Kritik an der eigenen Person" (self-criticism),[27] but also the essence of the decay of revolutions into bureaucracies, the characteristic malady of communist parties (*FK* 36), and thus the stagnation and failure of the GDR as a utopian socialist project. The title "Fatzer ± Keuner" refers not only to those figures' inseparability but also to the inseparability of gain and loss: with the rise of the Keuners, the emancipatory energy latent in the Fatzers is lost to the socialist project.[28] The near-absence of *Fatzer* on the GDR stage goes hand in hand with the unspoken, indeed suppressed fact of the consequences in the GDR of the structures and processes it explores.

Fatzer ± Müller: Productions of *Fatzer* 1978–1993

Müller's stage adaptation of *Fatzer* (the one most widely used in subsequent productions of the play, East and West)[29] ranges widely across the unpublished material as well as that published in the *Versuche* in 1930. Müller often reassigns dialogue to different figures or repositions text to change the emphasis, and introduces extraneous material such as quotations from Nietzsche or the following lines from Brecht's notebooks, which stress the unfinished, experimental quality of the *Fatzer* project:

> Das Ganze, da ja unmöglich
> Einfach zerschmeißen
> Für Experiment (*HMW* 6:121; cf. *BFA* 10.2: 1120)

> [The whole thing, since it's impossible
> Simply smash it up
> For experiments]

At the same time, despite Müller's admiration for the fragment, his version aimed to be stage worthy and is significantly more coherent chronologically, indeed even in the psychology of the figures, than Brecht's, tracing the men's fate from their wartime desertion to their destruction. Where most of Brecht's drafts end with Fatzer's protest, Müller brings the violence more directly on stage, showing both the execution of Fatzer's executioner, Koch (in Brecht's drafts, it is usually Büsching who kills Fatzer), and the final explosion that destroys the men and the room that has been their refuge. Yet this ending is not simply nihilistic. It is accompanied in Müller's version by the text that closes Brecht's version in the *Versuche*, namely the verses entitled FATZER, KOMM (*BFA* 10.1: 511–13; *HMW* 6:140–42; FATZER, COME). To experiment is to fail, but freed of buoying illusions you sink to the bottom where the process of learning can begin:

> Fürchte dich! Sinke doch! Auf dem Grunde
> Erwartet dich die Lehre (*BFA* 10.1: 512)

> [Be fearful! Sink! At the bottom
> The lesson awaits you]

Müller shared Walter Benjamin's view of this aspect of *Fatzer*: "Im Hoffnungslosen soll Fatzer Fuß fassen. Fuß, nicht Hoffnung. [. . .] Zugrunde gehen heißt hier immer: auf den Grund der Dinge gelangen."[30] (Fatzer has to find his feet in hopelessness. His feet, not hope. [. . .] Sinking to the bottom here always means: getting to the bottom of things.)

For the premiere of Müller's adaptation of *Fatzer* in Hamburg in 1978, directors Manfred Karge and Matthias Langhoff paired it with Heinrich von Kleist's *Prinz Friedrich von Homburg* (Prince Frederick of Homburg, 1810), where a comparable insubordination is successfully disciplined. The production took place in the immediate aftermath of the "Deutscher Herbst" (German Autumn) of 1977, when a series of terrorist murders, hostage-takings, and hijackings by the Rote Armee Fraktion (Red Army Faction) and their successors, and the responses of the state and the security services to them, dominated the West German media and threatened to destabilize the Federal Republic as a constitutional state. The links made, in the adaptation, staging, and program notes, between *Fatzer* and this national trauma caused a minor controversy and the production only ran for seven performances.

Müller repeatedly drew parallels between *Fatzer* and the Rote Armee Fraktion.[31] In the behavior of the four deserters, he identified the internal dynamic of terrorist groups. Both survive battles, at the front or on the streets, then, radicalized by these very battles, turn on each other in the stillness of their hideouts. Once frustrated, their willingness for radical action leads to ruthless punishment of renegades among their own members. Müller also insisted on the importance of wresting the monopoly of political violence away from the state.[32] Despite the fact that the GDR state sometimes supported West German terrorists, this element of Müller's view of terrorism was no more welcome there than in the West. The East German periodical *Theater der Zeit*, which had devoted a long review to the Steckel production in West Berlin in 1976,[33] and whose response to Brecht's eightieth birthday in 1978 included coverage of his reception in the West, ignored the Hamburg production despite its strong GDR provenance.

Nine years later, in 1987, the Berliner Ensemble finally staged the official GDR premiere of *Fatzer*, in a version that was nominally Müller's. However, the production was directed by Manfred Wekwerth and Joachim Tenschert, and Müller disowned it. He had no direct involvement in the production, which may well have been intended to pre-empt the radio version he was preparing.[34] At a time of increasing skepticism about Brechtian models, especially in the canonized form preserved by the Berliner Ensemble, *Fatzer*'s open forms and unresolved tensions might have prompted a radical overhaul of the Berliner Ensemble's museal approach to Brecht. In the same year that Beckett's *Waiting for Godot* finally reached the GDR stage, and in a climate in which stagnation and nascent upheaval were in uneasy tension, the production did successfully emphasize the basic mood of waiting, in this case for revolution, which is ever-present in the *Fatzer* fragments.[35] But it avoided the challenge of Brecht's and of Müller's *Fatzer* by explaining, even explaining away, Fatzer's behavior as a symptom of the socio-economic and political circumstances.

Casting Ekkehard Schall, Brecht's son-in-law and a grand old man of Brechtian acting, in the role of the ex-soldier Fatzer (even though most soldiers in the First World War were conscripts and in their early twenties at most), appeared, as Loren Kruger suggests, "to legitimate the eponymous anti-hero as a national hero comparable with Faust and thus reinforced the status of the Brecht repertoire at a time when the BE had lost any pretensions to critique."[36] Crucially, despite using Müller's adaptation and thus profiting from his status as a critical voice in GDR theater, the production cut the closing words from "FATZER, KOMM" (see below), replacing them with the reappearance of Schall, as Fatzer, asserting his sense of self and resistance to erasure: "ich / Will nicht verrecken [. . .] Ich bin der Fatzer" (*BFA* 10.1: 449; I / Don't want to die like a dog [. . .] I am Fatzer).

In a note written after the first few performances, Wekwerth obliquely attacked Müller by bemoaning "den fatalen Respekt für den Fragment" (the fatal respect for the fragment), and insisted his production had treated *Fatzer* as a coherent drama.[37] This suggests an unbridgeable gap not only between his and Müller's conception of theater, but also between Wekwerth's and Brecht's. Wekwerth's removal from the Berliner Ensemble in 1991 had largely to do with his politically compromised position; but this production of *Fatzer* demonstrated also that his understanding of Brecht — once seen as authoritative — was irreparably outdated. The production was damned with faint praise in *Theater der Zeit* as a worthy if belated enterprise.[38] Even the reviewer in the Party newspaper *Neues Deutschland*, while praising Schall's perfor-mance as Fatzer, suggested that once again the Berliner Ensemble had converted the living energy of a Brecht play into a ponderous classic, out of touch with contemporary audiences' critical sensibilities.[39] Retros-pectively, it seems to have been an embarrassment even for Wekwerth, who leaves it unmentioned in the text of his autobiography *Erinnern ist Leben* (2000; Remembering is Living).

Simultaneously with the Berliner Ensemble premiere of *Fatzer* in June 1987, Heiner Müller and Michael Thalheim were recording their radio production, though since Brecht's heirs did not at first release the rights, it was not broadcast until February 1988. The cast included, ironically enough, Johanna Schall, Brecht's granddaughter and Ekkehard Schall's daughter, as well as performers from the experimental fringes of GDR theater, such as members of the theater group Zinnober, whose unofficial workspace served as temporary recording studio for the production. One of the very few alternative theater groups in the GDR, Zinnober's work in neglected spaces in Prenzlauer Berg represented a niche of autonomy within an all-embracing centralism. In this respect, it was comparable to Müller's use of the medium of radio, relatively overlooked within the GDR cultural apparatus, for his *Fatzer* adaptation. Radio, initially central to the propaganda strategies of the Soviet Zone and the GDR, gradually lost this significance, becoming "a medium on the margins of the apparatus."[40] Thus it offered Müller relative freedom, but also a form with which to challenge the one-dimensional narrative of official GDR historiography. Firstly, radio permitted a polyphonic and polysemic montage that did not privilege one voice or one sound over another, and therefore also did not privilege one text type (such as commentary) or one interpretation of or verdict on Fatzer's actions over another. Thus when Müller or Johanna Schall spoke passages of the "Fatzer-Kommentar," they did not function as privileged intervention but as counterpoint. And secondly, from the perspective of the listener, all the elements of this polyphony emanated from the same neutral technological object, the radio loudspeaker, practicing the much-advocated principle of leaving the individual listener to decide on the meaning, value, and relative significance of the elements of sound. The sound effects were minimal and generally avoided naturalistic markers of space. Sharp percussive noises functioned more as formal punctuation than naturalistic imitation, an effect intensified by the ambient industrial music soundtrack of the Berlin band Einstürzende Neubauten (Collapsing New Buildings).

The production emphasized the series of calls in the *Fatzer* text "FATZER, KOMM" for those in power and authority both to respect their own laws and to step down so as to allow democratic change that would respect the real needs of the people:

Du bist fertig, Staatsmann
Der Staat ist nicht fertig.
Gestatte, daß wir ihn verändern
Nach den Bedingungen unseres Lebens
[. . .]
Achte deine Gesetze, Gesetzgeber.
Laß dir die Ordnung gefallen, Ordner.
Der Staat braucht dich nicht mehr
Gib ihn heraus. (*BFA* 10.1: 513)

[You are finished, statesman
The state is not finished
Permit us to change it
According to the conditions of our lives
[. . .]
Respect your laws, lawmaker.
Put up with the order of things, steward
The state does not need you any more
Hand it over.]

After Mikhail Gorbachev initiated perestroika and glasnost in 1985, Müller was briefly optimistic that the reforms in Eastern Europe might lead to a better socialist future rather than back to capitalism. Even though the course of events by the time he took the platform on the Alexanderplatz on 4 November 1989 was eroding that optimism, it may still be audible in his initial intention to read the above section of *Fatzer* to the crowd. But disillusion rapidly returned, and (for example when accepting the Kleist Prize in November 1990: *HMW* 8:382), he now repeatedly cited or paraphrased a different passage from *Fatzer*: "Wie früher Geister kamen aus Vergangenheit / So jetzt aus Zukunft, ebenso" (*BFA* 10.1: 465; as once ghosts appeared from the past / now they come from the future too). Müller invokes *Fatzer* to understand what is happening as the GDR collapses and the new old future, that is, the return of the capitalism that socialism was meant to consign to history, approaches like a specter from the past.

The Kleist Prize speech is noteworthy too as a measure of Müller's changing view of socialism's prospects. A passage in Brecht's *Fatzer* shows the men awaiting the future:

Wir aber wollen uns
Setzen an den Rand der Städte und
Auf sie warten. Denn jetzt muß
Kommen eine gute Zeit; denn jetzt bald

Tritt hervor das neue Tier, das
Geboren wird, den Menschen auszulösen. (*BFA* 10.1: 427–28)

[We though want
To sit down on the fringes of the cities and
Wait for them. For now must
Come good times; for now, soon
The new beast will step forward, which
Is born to ransom humanity.]

In his 1978 adaptation, Müller precedes this with a projection of Lenin and a passage from a quite different section of Brecht's *Fatzer*, which ironically adopts a right-wing perspective to celebrate the smuggling of the "Spaltpilz" (divisive fungus) Lenin into Russia (*BFA* 10.1: 483). That is, in 1978, for all of Müller's criticism of Stalinism and the stagnation of socialism, the Soviet Union remained a source of potential progress. In 1990, in the Kleist Prize speech, he quoted, or rather misquoted, the same passage, preceding it with a claim that it was written "in der Erwartung von Hitler und Stalin, Auschwitz und Gulag" (in anticipation of Hitler and Stalin, Auschwitz and Gulag), giving "das neue Tier" (the new beast) a quite different, deeply pessimistic interpretation, awakening the echoes in "auslösen" (to ransom) of its near-homophone "auslöschen" (to wipe out).[41]

When Müller himself finally came to direct a stage production of *Fatzer* in 1993, the disorientation that characterized the social and political climate in the immediate aftermath of the end of the GDR was reflected in the drawn-out conception and rehearsal phase of the production, though this was also a result of Müller's view, which he retained to the end of his career, of theater as an experimental, learning process for the participants, where the outcome was secondary. In this respect, he was still working in the spirit of the Brecht of the *Fatzer* phase, though what emerged was a hermetic, almost private production in which a group of ex-GDR theater practitioners performed and explored their own loss of purpose. The production was almost universally slated by the critics, "drei ewige Stunden" (three endless hours) being one of the kinder comments.[42] The production went through numerous proposed titles and structures, such as *Fatzer 1 Germania 2*;[43] the title of Müller's last play *Germania 3* (1995) alludes both to this and to *Fatzer 3*, as the *Fatzer* fragments actually published in *Versuche* were entitled. Another plan was to couple *Fatzer*, with its reference to the final throes of the First World War, with Müller's *Die Schlacht*, set in a comparable phase of the Second World War. The production finally staged, the collage *Duell/Traktor/Fatzer*, linked *Fatzer*, set in 1917, to *Traktor* (Tractor, 1955–74), set in and immediately after the Second World War, and to two scenes from Müller's multi-part play *Wolokolamsker Chaussee* (The Road to Volokolamsk, 1984–86), namely *Der Findling* (The Changeling), a relocation of Kleist's story to the 1960s, and *Das Duell* (The Duel), set during the June 1953 workers' revolt. Into this collage Müller inserted his prose poem *Mommsens Block* (1993), about the creative crisis a writer faces when his object of investigation vanishes. Müller commented that these texts were all accounts of the failure of revolutions or social alternatives, deliberately performed in reverse order to challenge notions of linear progress.[44] On the stage, where a single red stripe ran front to back on an otherwise bare platform of metal plates, an oversized table mid-stage dwarfed the human figures that huddled at it, or on it, sitting trapped in spotlight beams like the victims of interrogations. Müller insisted that he was not interested in a critical retrospective on the GDR, but the images of stagnation and repetition and the silent surveillance of unnamed figures on the sidelines necessarily awoke just such associations, turning the production into a necrology for the GDR in particular and for ideologies of progress in general. This production's view of modern German history as social, political, and aesthetic petrifaction was a radical rejection of Wekwerth and Tenschert's *Fatzer*, which still extracted a linear purposefulness from the asocial energies of Fatzer and his destruction by the collective. The rehearsal notes show Müller determined to expunge all traces of the pre-1989 Berliner Ensemble style, even down to picking on and rejecting specific gestures that he believes the actors have acquired from Wekwerth's style of directing: "Die Geste ist von Wekwerth [. . .] Wekwerth vergessen" (that gesture is from Wekwerth [. . .] forget Wekwerth).[45]

Lazarus Walks: *Fatzer*, after Müller

For Müller, to emphasize the Brecht of *Fatzer* was to resist the posthumous canonization of Brecht as a monument of socialist rationality. Even when Brecht appears to embrace authoritarian positions or enter artistically damaging compromises with Stalinism or GDR cultural bureaucracy, Müller applies his principle that the text is always more clever than the author, and insists on the importance of elements of refusal and chaos in Brecht's work. This, finally, links to the sustained and even growing interest in *Fatzer* in the two decades since the GDR's collapse, for Fatzer's walk through Mülheim can also be understood in terms of new forms of resistance and refusal in the globalized contemporary world.

Since 2008, the Ringlokschuppen (engine shed), an experimental theater in Mülheim on the Ruhr, has been investigating the *Fatzer* materials through performances and workshops, such as the program *Traces of: Fatzer* during the Ruhr's reign as European City of Culture in 2010.[46] This, like the German-Italian *Fatzer* project in 2012, linking the Berlin Volksbühne and the Teatro Stabile in Turin, funded by the German Federal Culture Foundation, and involving multimedia festivals in both cities, might be written off as the integration into the cultural mainstream of one of Brecht's most resistant works.[47] The establishment of the Mülheimer Fatzer-Tage (Mülheim Fatzer Days) in 2011 could equally be dismissed as the conversion of Brecht's tenuous relationship with the city into a somewhat desperate attempt to stimulate tourism.

But the multiple formal possibilities of the *Fatzer* fragments make it possible still to use them to explore new forms of critical opposition. For a workshop entitled "Kommando Johann Fatzer" (Commando Johann Fatzer) at the Fatzer-Tage, Alexander Karschnia, co-founder of a German-Brazilian performance group, drew parallels with the Rote Armee Fraktion and the Brazilian urban guerrilla Carlos Marighela, and invoked the political theory of Michael Hardt and Antonio Negri, with its concept of the disorganized, resistant "multitude" in a globalized political economy,[48] to claim refusal, desertion, and mutiny as the initiating energies of radical revolt. The task of the "Kommando Johann Fatzer" is to emphasize productive contradictions, in the spirit of Brecht's wish to provoke a "Große Diskussion" (great discussion) as a precondition for the "'Große Produktion': Kommunismus" ("great production": communism).[49]

In the GDR, once Stalinism had stifled this discussion, it never revived, despite fitful phases of liberalization, and communism receded ever further into the future, before the collapse of the East European socialist states in 1989/90 consigned it, apparently lastingly, to the past. The matter is, though, not quite so final. In 1979, accepting the Mülheim Drama Prize for *Germania Tod in Berlin* (Germania Death in Berlin), Heiner Müller, while claiming to hope for a world in which plays such as *Germania* could no longer be written, because reality no longer provided dramatists with such negative material, also noted:

Seit dem RUNDGANG DES FATZER DURCH DIE STADT MÜLHEIM, der in bösen Sätzen den Zusammenhang von Krieg und

Geschäft reflektiert, hat sich an den Eigentümsverhältnissen in Mülheim wohl nicht viel verändert.[50]

[Since FATZER'S WALK THROUGH THE CITY OF MÜLHEIM, whose vicious sentences reflect the connection between war and business, I don't think much has changed in the structures of property ownership in Mülheim.]

In 1979, though the Ruhr's painful exit from heavy industry was underway, Mülheim was still in fact in the heart of a relatively prosperous, SPD-governed federal state committed to the social element of the social market economy. Three decades later, neoliberal economics, the erosion of the welfare state, and globalization have actually exacerbated differentials in income and ownership in the old Federal Republic, so that Müller's comment is more apposite still. Meanwhile, since 1990 the former GDR has been exposed to the same forces. *Fatzer*, once a play about the turbulent conditions from which socialism emerged and the irreducible human energies that resisted political resolution, has outlasted the state set up, one might say, to address the conditions and contradictions that *Fatzer* articulates. It has re-emerged as a set of materials for a new set of political and socioeconomic circumstances, in which Fatzer's Walk, the elemental representation of the destructive yet liberating energies of refusal, has not lost any of its relevance.

Notes

[1] He changed his mind at the last minute, reading an appeal for independent trade unions instead; see e.g. Heiner Müller, *Krieg ohne Schlacht*, 2nd edn. (Cologne: Kiepenheuer & Witsch, 1994), 354–55. For the *Fatzer* extract, see BFA 10.1: 513.

[2] See Hans-Thies Lehmann, "Versuch über Fatzer," in Lehmann, *Das Politische schreiben* (Berlin: Theater der Zeit, 2002), 250–60, here 251.

[3] Walter Benjamin, *Gesammelte Schriften* (Frankfurt a.M.: Suhrkamp, 1977), 2.2: 526.

[4] Andrzej Wirth and Martha Ulvaeus, "The Lehrstück as Performance," *The Drama Review* 43, no. 4 (1999): 113–32, here 114.

[5] See Frank Thomsen, Hans-Harald Müller, and Tom Kindt, *Ungeheuer Brecht: Eine Biographie seines Werks* (Göttingen: Vandenhoeck & Ruprecht, 2006), 76.

[6] Benjamin, *Gesammelte Schriften*, 2.2: 665.

[7] Judith Wilke, *Brechts "Fatzer"-Fragment: Lektüren zum Verhältnis von Dokument und Kommentar* (Bielefeld: Aisthesis, 1998), 10.

[8] See Reiner Steinweg, *Das Lehrstück: Brechts Theorie einer politisch-ästhetischen Erziehung* (Stuttgart: Metzler, 1972), 91.

[9] David Bathrick [drawing here on Heiner Müller], "Robert Wilson, Heiner Müller and the Preideological," *New German Critique* 98, no. 2 (2006): 65–76.

[10] See Günter Berg and Wolfgang Jeske, *Bertolt Brecht* (Stuttgart and Weimar: Metzler, 1998), 95–96; Michael Gratzke, "'Ihr habt verbreitet / Die Lehre der Klassiker': Bertolt Brecht und Heiner Müller lesen Kleists *Prinz Friedrich von Homburg*," *German Life and Letters* 64, no. 3 (2011): 455–71.

[11] See Heiner Müller, "Fatzer ± Keuner," in *Heiner Müller Material*, ed. Frank Hörnigk (Leipzig: Reclam, 1989), 30–36, here 32. Subsequent references to this essay are cited in the text using the abbreviation *FK* and page number. See also Joachim Biener, "'Ideologiezertrümmerung': Bertolt Brecht im Januar 1949 als Gast in der Vorlesung Professor Hans Mayers," in *Leipziger Brecht-Begegnungen 1923–1994*, ed. Alfred Klein, Roland Opitz, and Klaus Pezold (Leipzig: Rosa-Luxemburg-Stiftung Sachsen, 1998), 31–39.

[12] On *Fatzer* as a modern version of *Antigone*, see Lehmann, "Versuch über Fatzer," 255.

[13] "Notate zu *Fatzer* aus dem Berliner Ensemble," in Steinweg, *Das Lehrstück*, 253–55.

[14] Bertolt Brecht, *Der Brotladen: Stückfragment; Die Bühnenfassung und Texte aus dem Fragment* (Frankfurt a.M.: Suhrkamp, 1967).

[15] For two contrasting reviews of this production, see *Brecht in der Kritik: Rezensionen aller Uraufführungen*, ed. Monika Wyss (Munich: Kindler, 1977), 440–45.

[16] See Benjamin Henrichs, "Aufhaltsamer Abstieg," *Die Zeit* (Hamburg), 3 June 1977.

[17] See e.g. Andrzej Wirth, "Brecht's *Fatzer*: Experiments in Discourse Making," *The Drama Review* 22, no. 4 (1978): 55–66; *Asoziales Theater: Spielversuche mit Lehrstücken und Anstiftung zur Praxis*, ed. Florian Vaßen, Gerd Koch, and Reiner Steinweg (Cologne: Prometh, 1984); Wolfgang Storch, "Political Climate and Experimental Staging: *The Decline of the Egoist Johann Fatzer*," in *Bertolt Brecht: Political Theory and Literary Practice*, ed. Betty Nance Weber and Hubert Heinen (Manchester: Manchester UP, 1980), 106–12.

[18] In his notebooks, Braun explicitly links Fatzer with Hinze, the anarchic building laborer in his *Hinze und Kunze*, and, in 1977, as dramaturge at the BE, proposed *Fatzer* for the repertoire alongside William Shakespeare's *Julius Caesar*, Hanns Eisler's *Faustus*, and Christian Dietrich Grabbe's *Napoleon*: plays whose title figures embody transformative, albeit destructive energy. See Volker Braun, *Werktage 1: Arbeitsbuch 1977–1989* (Frankfurt a.M.: Suhrkamp, 2009), 25 and 111.

[19] Heiner Müller, *Gesammelte Irrtümer*, vol. 2 (Frankfurt a.M.: Verlag der Autoren, 1990), 27.

[20] Heiner Müller, *Werke*, 12 vols. (Frankfurt a.M.: Suhrkamp, 1998–2008), 9:242. Subsequent references to this work are cited in the text using the abbreviation *HMW* plus volume and page number.

[21] Heiner Müller, *Krieg ohne Schlacht: Leben in zwei Diktaturen* (Cologne: Kiepenheuer & Witsch, 1992), 226. *Fatzer* also features as a chapter heading in this autobiography (309).

[22] See David Barnett, "Heiner Müller as the End of Brechtian Dramaturgy: Müller on Brecht in Two Lesser-Known Fragments," *Theatre Research International* 27, no. 1 (2002): 49–57.

[23] See e.g. "Ein Brief," in *Heiner Müller Material*, ed. Hörnigk, 37–39.

[24] Heiner Müller, *Gesammelte Irrtümer*, vol. 1 (Frankfurt a.m.: Verlag der Autoren, 1986), 50.

[25] Unpublished document 3538 in the Heiner Müller Archive, Akademie der Künste Berlin; quoted from Levin Röder, "Theater der Schrift: Heiner Müllers Auto-biografische Dekonstruktion" (PhD diss., Humboldt Universität Berlin, 2007), 314.

[26] Heiner Müller, Frank Raddatz et al., *Jenseits der Nation* (Berlin: Rotbuch 1991), 27–28.

[27] Heiner Müller, "Notate zu Fatzer," *Die Zeit* (Hamburg), 17 March 1978.

[28] See Theo Girshausen, "Baal, Fatzer — und Fondrak: Die Figur des Asozialen bei Brecht und Müller," in *Dramatik der DDR*, ed. Ulrich Profitlich (Frankfurt a.m.: Suhrkamp, 1987), 327–43, here 335–37.

[29] See *Brecht-Handbuch*, vol. 1, *Stücke*, ed. Jan Knopf (Stuttgart and Weimar: Metzler, 2001), 175–76.

[30] Walter Benjamin, *Gesammelte Schriften* (Frankfurt a.M.: Suhrkamp, 1977), 2.2: 509; cf. Müller, *Gesammelte Irrtümer*, 2:58.

[31] E.g. Müller, *Gesammelte Irrtümer*, 1:25–26.

[32] Müller, *Krieg ohne Schlacht*, 312.

[33] Ernst Schumacher, "Lehrstück-Fragmente uraufgeführt," *Theater der Zeit* 31, no. 5 (1976): 45–47.

[34] See Loren Kruger, "Broadcasting (A)socialism: Brecht, Müller, and *Radio Fatzer*," in Kruger, *Post-Imperial Brecht: Politics and Performance, East and South* (Cambridge: Cambridge UP, 2004), 133–70, here 137 and 150.

[35] See e.g. Werner Mittenzwei's preparatory notes in *Bertolt Brecht: "Untergang des Egoisten Fatzer"* (East Berlin: Brecht-Zentrum der DDR, 1987), 17. This documentation displays the ambivalent spirit of genuine reformist intentions, opportunism, and desperation in which the "old guard" of the Berliner Ensemble undertook this production.

[36] Kruger, *Post-Imperial Brecht*, 138.

[37] Manfred Wekwerth, "Fatzer nach Ansehen der vierten Vorstellung," in *Theater nach Brecht: Baukasten für eine Theorie und Praxis des Berliner Ensembles in den neunziger Jahren* (East Berlin: Berliner Ensemble, 1989), 149.

[38] Dieter Krebs, "Noch und schon: Stirb und Werde; Brechts *Untergang des Egoisten Fatzer* in einer Fassung von Heiner Müller im Berliner Ensemble," *Theater der Zeit* 42, no. 9 (1987): 23.

[39] Anon., "Stück des jungen Brecht auf der Bühne," *Neues Deutschland* (East Berlin), 23 June 1987.

[40] Kruger, *Post-Imperial Brecht*, 147. See also Loren Kruger, "Heterophony as Critique: Brecht, Müller and Radio Fatzer," in *Brecht Yearbook* 17:234–51. This discussion of the radio version is indebted to Kruger's excellent articles.

[41] Heiner Müller, "Deutschland ortlos: Anmerkungen zu Kleist" (1990), quoted in Horst Domdey, *Produktivkraft Tod: Das Drama Heiner Müllers* (Cologne: Böhlau, 1998), 283.

[42] Gerhard Stadelmaier, "Abgestanden in Ruinen," *Frankfurter Allgemeine Zeitung*, 2 October 1993.

[43] For information on the rehearsals and the production, see Stiftung Archiv der Akademie der Künste, Zentrum für Theaterdokumentation, ID1037: Bertolt Brecht, Heiner Müller, "Duell Traktor Fatzer."

[44] "Probenbesuch 'Dialog Fatzer — Traktor' im Berliner Ensemble und Gespräch mit Heiner Müller," *Kulturspiegel*, Radio Berlin Brandenburg, 16 September 1993; *Müller MP3: Heiner Müller Tondokumente 1972–1995*, ed. Kristin Schulz (Berlin and Cologne: Alexander, 2011), track 107 of the accompanying CD.

[45] Quoted in Christoph Martin, "'Lasst euch nicht entmutigen': Probennotate," in *MÜLLER MACHT THEATER: Zehn Inszenierungen und ein Epilog*, ed. Stephan Suschke (Berlin: Theater der Zeit, 2003), 168–80, here 171 and 178.

[46] See: http://www.essen-fuer-das-ruhrgebiet.ruhr2010.de/en/twins/programme/ changing-stages/traces-of-fatzer.html, accessed 13 June 2011.

[47] http://www.kulturstiftung-des-bundes.de/cms/en/programme/internationale_ theaterpartnerschaften/fatzer_crosses_the_alps.html, accessed 13 June 2011.

[48] E.g. Michael Hardt and Antonio Negri, *Multitude: War and Democracy in the Age of Empire* (London: Hamish Hamilton, 2004).

[49] http://www.ringlokschuppen.de/ringlokschuppen/spielplan/veranstaltung/?txz 19mmevents_pi1[view]=detailview&tx_z19mmevents_pi1[item]=176, accessed 13 June 2011.

[50] "Mülheimer Rede," in *Heiner Müller Material*, ed. Hörnigk,100–101, here 101.

Reviving *Saint Joan of the Stockyards*: Speculation and Solidarity in the Era of Capitalism Resurgent

Loren Kruger, University of Chicago

CELEBRATED ON 10 February 1998, the centenary of Bertolt Brecht's birth anticipated the hundred-and-fiftieth anniversary of the *Communist Manifesto*, which appeared in late February 1848. The coincidence of Brecht's centenary and the anniversary of the *Manifesto* provided a timely opportunity to re-evaluate not only Brecht's legacy in the Berlin Republic and beyond but also his debt to Marx in his critique of capitalism.[1] Most explicitly, the Berliner Ensemble (BE) revived the rarely performed *Die Maßnahme* (The Measures Taken, 1930) and printed an annotated *Communist Manifesto* in the program in lieu of the play. Even where Marx was not mentioned, his ghost haunted revivals from Brecht's most anticapitalist period, from the Wall Street crash of 1929 to Hitler's seizure of power in 1933, as well as earlier versions of plays that matured in this period. They included *Der Brotladen* (Breadshop, 1929–30) at the Volksbühne and archival fragments such as *Jae Fleischhacker in Chikago* (Jae Meat Chopper in Chicago, 1926), a preliminary treatment of anticapitalist themes, at the BE. The fiftieth anniversary of Brecht's death in 2006 saw revivals that highlighted the conflicts of capitalist modernity, from Frank Castorf's version of *Im Dickicht der Städte* (In the Jungle of Cities, 1922) at the Volksbühne to the BE's *Mutter Courage* (Mother Courage, 1939), directed by Claus Peymann, who had already directed *Die Mutter* (The Mother, 1932) and *Die heilige Johanna der Schlachthöfe* (Saint Joan of the Stockyards, 1932) in 2003.

The revival of Brecht's anticapitalist plays not only acknowledges the history of Brecht productions in East and West Germany but also registers unease with the present and future of an unevenly united country. The division between East and West has not disappeared with unification but has become a shifting boundary between haves and have-nots, a boundary marked less by national treaties than by the fluctuating investments of transnational capital. In the twenty-first century, it is no longer the ghost of communism that haunts Europe but the specter of capitalism, profiting from speculation to the detriment of the common good. Despite this malaise, the crisis also presents an opportunity. The demise of the GDR ended the official sponsorship of Brecht and Marx but it also highlighted anew not only Brecht's anticapitalist drama but also Marx's critique of elite profiteering at the expense of the working majority. Marx's analysis of capitalism as a system of exploitation that "has left remaining no other nexus between people [*Menschen*] than naked self-interest, than unfeeling 'cash payment' [*die gefühllose 'bare Zahlung'*]" resonates in our era as wealth is manipulated for short-term gain by agents indifferent to social responsibility.[2]

While *Die heilige Johanna der Schlachthöfe* (hereafter, *Johanna*) has been described as Brecht's "most perplexing play," its critique of the turmoil wrought by capitalism's "uninterrupted convulsion [*Erschütterung*] of all social conditions, everlasting uncertainty and agitation" (*Manifest* 23; *Manifesto* 38, trans. mod.), in Marx's formulation remains as timely as ever.[3] Completed in the wake of the stock market crash of 1929 and the Great Depression thereafter, *Johanna* dramatized capitalist speculation and worker degradation in the stockyards of Chicago and beyond. Broadcast in part on Berlin radio in 1932 with Carola Neher as Johanna Dark and Fritz Kortner as her antagonist, the speculator Pierpont Mauler, it was unable to reach a wider audience before Hitler came to power in 1933, but even the abbreviated radio version received attention. The *Berliner Börsen-Courier* hailed it for its representation of "reale, meßbare, nüchterne Faktoren" (actual, measurable, sober factors) and for showing "die entscheidende Rolle, die Geld in der Fügung der Ereignisse spielt" (the decisive role played by money in the unfolding of events).[4] It received its first stage performance only in 1959 in Hamburg, directed by Gustav Gründgens with Brecht's daughter Hanne Hiob as Johanna.[5] Hannes Fischer directed the first GDR production in Dresden in 1961, which was followed the same year by Benno Besson's production in Rostock. Although performed approximately yearly in West Germany and elsewhere in Western Europe in the decade or so after the premiere, the play was revived in the GDR again only when it appeared at the BE for the first time in 1968, directed by Manfred Wekwerth and Joachim Tenschert, again with Hiob as Johanna. Criticized by GDR Brecht scholar Ernst Schumacher for supplying an overly historicist treatment of capitalism around 1900 rather than a necessary re-examination of capitalism in 1932 and in the present, this production never became part of the BE repertoire.[6]

The play commands attention now because it updates the struggle between capital and labor as well as the brutalization of workers and speculators in a world defined by the "cash nexus." Further, its dramatic structure tracks the kind of market manipulation, profit-taking, and sky-rocketing income of the very few at the expense of the many that has wreaked social and economic havoc in the so-called Great Recession, the era of deregulation, speculation, and crash that has made the ongoing crisis that began in 2008 seem like an uncanny but predictable repetition of the crisis of 1928–29.[7] Chicago inspired comparison with Berlin well before Brecht; in an 1893 visit, Mark Twain called Berlin "the German Chicago," which was echoed by Walter Rathenau's "Spree-Chicago."[8] While Chicago occupied an important place in the imagination of Brecht's generation, America as a whole exemplified the contradictions of capitalism. Anger about the Americanization of the German economy, epitomized not only by speculation but also by long-term unemployment and increasing inequality, resonated in more than a dozen revivals of *Johanna* from the BE in 2003 to Konstanz in 2010. The play's revival does more than simply re-activate comparisons between Berlin, Brecht's chosen domain, and Chicago, the imagined locus of *Im Dickicht der Städte, Der aufhaltsame Aufstieg des Arturo Ui* (The Resistible Rise of Arturo Ui, 1941), and *Johanna*. It also highlights the impact on Europe, including social democratic Germany, of the deregulation, market manipulation, and reduced social welfare following the so-called Washington consensus — the notion that unfettered markets generate prosperity and correct themselves without government intervention.[9] Cited in the program for the 2010 production in Konstanz, post-Soviet critic Boris Groys argued that, while Cold-War-era social democracies responded to the communist threat by softening the inequities of capitalism with social welfare paid for by high taxes, the unified German state, whether social democratic or officially pro-business, favors deregulation for capital and austerity for the poor.[10] While other revivals certainly deserve consideration, productions in Berlin by Peymann at the BE in 2003 and by Nicolas Stemann at the Deutsches Theater in 2009 invite particular attention because of Brecht's comparison of Berlin with Chicago, and Berlin's current status as capital of the Berlin Republic and magnet for global capital, especially real estate speculation, and for immigrant workers, from Asia and Africa as well as Eastern Europe.[11] Such transnational points of reference highlight the departure of these former GDR flagship theaters from the battles over the inheritance of Brecht that characterized the Cold War era, in favor, on the one hand, of a return to Brecht's anticapitalist plays from the capitalist crisis of the early 1930s and, on the other hand, in favor of a turn, in the current era of resurgent capitalism, to debates about equity, economic justice, and the relevance of socialism.

Before exploring the current resonance of *Johanna*, however, we should review the play's dramatization of economic processes historically. Brecht wanted the dramatic conflict between the meat-packing tycoon and market manipulator Mauler and the soldier of God and would-be activist Johanna to convey a "tiefgreifende und zum Handeln ausreichende Erkenntnis der großen gesellschaftlichen Prozesse unserer Zeit" (*BFA* 24:103; a profound and practically active awareness of the great social processes of our time, *Plays* 3.1: 119) including a critical understanding of production, exchange, and speculation. He also argued that his chosen mode of stylized representation was the most realistic way to reveal these processes (*BFA* 24:105; *Plays* 3.1: 118). While reading Marx, Brecht drew on American sources, including Bouck White's celebratory account of the charismatic capitalist Daniel Drew.[12] He also read the muckraking Chicago novels *The Pit* by Frank Norris (1903) and *The Jungle* by Upton Sinclair (1906). These novels condemned those who made fortunes by exploiting workers and cornering markets: that is, by monopolizing essential commodities like wheat and meat by buying up future stocks and thus inflating the price at the expense of workers and consumers.[13] In addition, he consulted the work of Germans who had visited Chicago, especially Egon Erwin Kisch's texts about speculation in the futures market and Erich Mendelsohn's photographs of the Board of Trade and the grain elevators that enabled the storage and rationalization of wheat supplies and thus the speculation on their future value.[14] From these documented sources and possibly also D. W. Griffiths' *A Corner in Wheat* (1909), a short but vivid film depicting a speculator who attempts to corner the market only to die crushed by wheat in his own grain elevator, Brecht generated the fragments *Dan Drew* (1924) and *Jae Fleischhacker* (1926), which dramatize speculation on the corner.

In *Johanna*, while the dramaturgy of market manipulation and its central agent Mauler drew on American capitalism, the title character and her milieu tapped other sources. Borrowing from colleague Elisabeth Hauptmann's transformation of the historical evangelical movement, the Salvation Army, into the fictional Black Straw Hats in *Happy End* (1929) as well as from Friedrich Schiller's *Jungfrau von Orleans* (Maid of

Orleans, 1801) and George Bernard Shaw's *Major Barbara* (1907), Brecht created a Johanna whose idealism and martyrdom recall Schiller's maid, while her naive belief in the power of justice against the force of money and her confrontation with a savvy manipulator of cash and charm recall Shaw's Barbara. But where Barbara makes peace with her arms-dealer father after finding no argument against the "beautifully clean workshops [. . .] and respectable workmen" of Andrew Undershaft's model munitions factory,[15] Johanna refuses Mauler's offer to buy off the Black Straw Hats and descends alone into the depths. There she suffers starvation along with dismissed workers, and comes to realize that

> dieses ganze System
> Ist eine Schaukel mit zwei Enden, die voneinander
> Abhängen, und die oben
> Sitzen oben nur, weil jene unten sitzen (*BFA* 3:197)

> [this whole
> System's a seesaw with two ends
> Depending on each other. Those on top
> Are where they are because the others
> Are down below (*Plays* 3.1: 78)]

But despite this insight into the logic of exploitation, Johanna finds the workers' call for armed resistance too cold and the sight of their leader in handcuffs evidence not of militance but of malice. Alarmed more by the potential of proletarian violence than the actual brutality of the police, she discards the strike notice and thus breaks the chain of solidarity. Despite her final attempt to separate the Black Straw Hats from the Beef Trust, both prefer her as a silenced saint rather than a vocal witness to their collusion. Johanna's death in the shadow of the slaughterhouses is not the classic tragedy of the crusading maid but the marketing of a martyr. The representation of Johanna as a suffering martyr rather than a critic of capitalism cements the alliance between the Black Straw Hats and the Beef Trust. The compliance of the Black Straw Hats allows the Beef Trust to proceed without opposition to secure the contraction of the supply of meat and with it the contraction of the labor force into a small group of disposable instruments, leaving a larger group of unemployed customers to depend on the ministrations of the Black Straw Hats.

The Hamburg premiere of *Johanna*, which took place in 1959, provoked responses divided along Cold War lines. In *Sinn und Form*, Brecht's dramaturge Käthe Rülicke-Weiler lauded the play's dramatization of capitalism's boom and bust cycles.[16] Drawing on Marx's

Capital and Lenin's *Imperialism as the Last Stage of Capitalism*, she argued that Brecht showed not only the power of monopoly capital to fix prices and reduce wages but also the potential counter-force of workers who, once fully aware of their power, would ultimately overcome capitalism and create "the good life."[17] In contrast, T. W. Adorno blasted the play for misrepresenting the "essence of capitalism." He argued that "events in the sphere of circulation, where competitors are cutting one others' throats, take the place of the appropriation of surplus value in the sphere of production," and that "the cattle-dealers' brawls over loot are epiphenomena that could not possibly bring about the great crisis on their own; [. . .] the machinations are not only childish, as Brecht no doubt wanted them to be, but also unintelligible by any economic logic."[18] Ironically, despite his opposition to orthodox Marxism-Leninism, Adorno's faith in the priority of production reproduces that orthodoxy without attending to Brecht's creative fusion of two elements: Marx's analysis of the expropriation of surplus labor value and American socialist insights into the devastating impact on workers' lives of the market manipulation that Adorno dismissed as an epiphenomenon.

Writing in 1986, Jan Knopf highlighted Brecht's interest in American as well as Marxist critiques of market manipulation. Without naming Adorno, he criticized those who claimed that the play simplified economic processes. He also dismissed Rülicke-Weiler's oversimplified parallel between Brecht's dramaturgy and Marx's crisis theory.[19] As Knopf suggests, Brecht's plot follows Mauler's attempt to corner the meat market in striking parallel to the cornering of the wheat market in Norris's *The Pit*.[20] It begins with Mauler's receipt of a "letter from New York" in scene 1 hinting that tariffs in the south would generate a glut of beef in the market and thus lower prices, goes on to his speculative and initially anonymous take-over of the market in scene 5 by selling short and then buying up predicted cattle stocks to bankrupt his competitors by forcing them in scene 8 to buy "das Fleisch [. . .], das sie uns / Schulden" (*BFA* 3:179; the meat they owe us, *Plays* 3.1: 58), and reaches an apparent crisis when the tariffs are lifted, the corner collapses, and the market crashes taking Mauler's profits down in scene 9. This scenario resembles *The Pit*, in which Curtis Jadwin, known in the Chicago exchange as a "bear," a trader profiting from downward pressure on futures, anonymously switches sides. As the "great Bull," he then drives up wheat prices to corner the market, but holds on too long and loses his fortune after high prices encourage farmers to plant more, which, in the perverse logic of the market, leads to the threat of renewed abundance and thus to drastically reduced future values. By choosing meat rather than wheat, Brecht gains not only images of the bloody slaughter of men and beasts made famous by *The Jungle*, but also the opportunity to present Mauler as a modern Faust, balancing precariously between identification with the objects of his speculation and canny conniving against rivals. Mauler feigns distaste with "dies blutige Geschäft" (*BFA* 3:129; this bloody business, *Plays* 3.1: 3) and empathy with "dieses Ochsen Ächzen" (*BFA* 3:30; the groaning of that steer, *Plays* 3.1: 4) to get Cridle to sign a promissory note of ten million dollars for a third of Mauler's packing company as a deal between friends, only to call in that debt when Cridle has sunk his capital into buying excess meat. Even though Mauler loses his assets when the corner collapses, as does Jadwin in *The Pit*, Brecht, more realistic than Norris in assessing the resilience of capital, has Mauler re-emerge from his brief descent to reclaim his position in the market in the penultimate scene. Mauler recovers not merely by following advice from New York to create a Beef Trust to limit livestock supply and depress wages but also by using the moral authority of the Black Straw Hats to "spread the gospel far and wide / That we were upright men, striving for the best / In evil times" (*Plays* 3.1: 96) and thus to persuade those excluded from the good life that their suffering is God's will.[21]

While Knopf rightly criticizes oversimplified parallels between Marx's analysis and Brecht's dramatization of speculation and its consequences for those "in the depths" of the slaughterhouses and other places of work and death, he underplays Brecht's debt to Marx. Nonetheless, Brecht deployed not only *Capital*'s analysis of industrial production but also the *Communist Manifesto*, whose critique of the reduction of people to commodities in the "cash nexus" and of the ever-greater exploitation of resources resonates globally today. Indeed, it was in reading Marx over the half-decade between *Dan Drew* and *Johanna* that Brecht found a critical matrix complex enough to accommodate the drama of the market manipulator Mauler and the tragedy of the fervent but naive crusader Johanna, whose death highlights capitalism's power to weather crises at the expense of the common good. In tracking the power of speculation to decouple exchange from use value, Brecht's play highlights the influence of those who manipulate the exchange value of essential commodities to highs and lows quite divorced from their use value to feed the world. By exposing the violence of institutions and their agents who reduce the value of the workers and farmers, whose livelihood depends on a fair price for their labor, to zero, and thus the bearers of this non-value to nearly nothing, that is to say death, Brecht caught precisely the "essence of capital" that Adorno claims he missed, the commodification of all human endeavor and with it the reduction of all human value to cold cash.

By the turn of the twenty-first century, the power of capital to undo the modest redistribution of wealth that was the legacy of organized labor and the welfare state and thus to treat all workers as dispensable commodities was demonstrably greater than it had been during the Cold War. As a survey commissioned in 2009 by transnational giant Bertelsmann indicates (see n. 9), this power reflects a majority whose skepticism about the future of a capitalist Europe driven by speculation on the American model has been deepening since unification, well before the acknowledged onset of the Great Recession of 2008.

By 2003, when Peymann's revival of *Die heilige Johanna* opened at the BE, the United States had invaded Iraq at the urging of multinationals like Haliburton (manufacturer of both military and oil development hardware) and representatives in the vice president's office.[22] Noting this collusion between capital and war, the BE program also highlighted the wealth gap between the rich and the global poor and indicted as cause for global unrest the exclusions of millions from the good life promised, but not delivered, by Western capitalism.[23] The anti-globalization rhetoric in the program might have reinforced the view, represented by the journal *Theater heute*, of Peymann as an old Western leftist whose representations of resistance generate mostly derisive laughter in the former communist East.[24] Nonetheless, however old-fashioned, this production highlighted, in the conflict between the Beef Trust and an increasingly isolated Johanna, whose canonization reflected the power of capital to commodify resistance, the difficulty of resisting capital in the era of its global penetration.

The sobriety of the set, a bare raked stage, and the relatively restrained performances by the two principals underscored this bleak picture.[25] Postponing Mauler's opening gambit in the speculation game, Peymann began with Johanna's speech from scene 2, which captures from the first line "In finsterer Zeit blutiger Verwirrung" the violent paradox of capitalism's "verordneter Unordnung / Planmäßiger Willkür / Entmenschter Menschheit" (*BE Johanna* 13; *BFA* 3:132–33; In a dark time of *bloody* confusion / Of ordained disorder / Of systematic lawlessness / Of dehumanized humanity, *Plays* 3.1: 7, modification in italics). Lighting designer Andreas Fuchs used cold blue light to signify the stockyard's depths of poverty, contrasting it with the red associated both with the stock exchange's bloody business and the Black Straw Hats' bright but unreal salvation. Opening the play with Johanna's direct appeal to the audience, which occurs in Brecht's text only after Mauler's plotting and the workers' protests, Meike Droste's fresh-faced activist invited sympathy even though her enthusiastic faith that her drum would raise up God in the slaughterhouses was undercut by her embarrassed admission that the deity may no longer find a place in the real world. Her character's sincerity highlighted by subdued makeup, Droste presented an affecting if naive picture offsetting the competing illusions of the speculators and the Black Straw Hats. Despite their initial opposition, these groups had in common vividly clownish makeup and sloganeering choruses accompanied with the exaggerated inflection and gesture associated with socialist satire since the 1920s.

Although sporting clownish makeup, Manfred Karge played Mauler with tactical coolness alternating with stylized displays of cunning in a manner true to his work at the BE in the 1960s and early 1970s (before he left the GDR in 1978). Reading the letter from New York slowly and with emphasis, he might have initially appeared slightly senile to some critics. However, the shifts in his performance show how Karge operated with several layers of estrangement. The first sudden shift occurred when Karge lamented the "bloody business" and offered a good deal to his "friend" Cridle (played likewise as a dissembler by Martin Seifert). When Cridle asked how cheap the deal would be, Karge switched attitude again as he briskly issued Mauler's cool response: "Darüber kann's bei alten Freunden / Wie du [*sic*] und mir kein langes Handeln geben" (*BE Johanna* 11; *BFA* 3:130; Old friends like us won't haggle / Over a little thing like that, *Plays* 3.1: 4). The BE rendered the reply even more brusque by cutting the intimacy implied by "wie du und mir." By establishing his sensitive soul as a crafty act from the outset, Karge presents Mauler as a consummate player of men and markets, who trusts no one and manipulates every person and every opportunity to maximize his profits. Rather than a mere carnival caricature of the evil capitalist, Karge plays a "caricature of the caricature" and thus presents a sharp critique not only of capitalists but of their theatrical oversimplification.[26] His performance, more than any other, highlights the critical force of the technique that the first translator of Brecht's *Verfremdung* aptly rendered as "dis-illusion."[27]

Although Droste's dis-illusioning of her character is more subtle, her Johanna mixes sincerity and self-righteousness. The introduction of the Salvationists, heralded by the hovering outline of an electric cross and a song echoing Hanns Eisler's dissonant *Bänkelsang* (music reminiscent of satirical folk ballads) more than the Salvation Army anthem "Onward Christian Soldiers," shows Johanna berating workers, blaming their poverty on their indifference to God and the spiritual life. Her naive enthusiasm leads her to applaud (as Droste claps her hands) Mauler's tale of being touched by the "other world," even as he encourages Slift (played with Mephistophelean relish by Veit Schubert) to show her the worst of the workers. Only when she descends into the slaughterhouses can she comprehend the logic of exploitation that divests workers of moral feeling, but Droste's performance plays with contradiction. Initially shocked by Mrs. Luckerniddle, a character borrowed from *The Jungle* who abandons her investigation of her husband's death by mincing machine in exchange for three weeks of canteen food, Johanna condemns not the wickedness of the poor that Mauler and Slift would have her see but their outright poverty. Johanna is moved to this conclusion by observing not only Luckerniddle and a man who takes her husband's clothes in return for food but also, at the start of the scene, the silent workers whose wan faces anticipate the matter-of-fact portrayal of the desperate Luckerniddle by Carmen-Maja Antoni (who played the lead in Peymann's *Die Mutter*). Armed with this insight that debasement of the poor is a commodity exploited by Slift on Mauler's instructions, Johanna interrogates the meat barons with righteous anger: "woher sollen sie denn eine Moral haben, wenn sie sonst nichts haben?" (*BE Johanna* 34; *BFA* 3:161; where are these people's morals to come from when they have nothing else? *Plays* 3.1: 38) and expels them when they attempt to bribe the church for $800. But, after being expelled in turn for depriving the church of this money, Droste's Johanna loses her righteous zeal as she wanders through the freezing yards in a shrunken, threadbare cardigan over an old dress. This abject picture may invite critics to see Johanna's insight that the power of the rich rests on the compliance of the poor as an expression of fear and of "Nichtausnocheinwissen" (*BE Johanna* 61; *BFA* 3:199; of not knowing a way out, *Plays* 3.1: 80, trans. mod.), and of her rejection of proletarian action against police violence, as resignation of Dickensian rather than Brechtian character.[28] But Droste's performance here and in the canonization scene, like her hand-clapping earlier, allows a sliver of estrangement to probe the gap between the Schillerian saint, whose abjectness measures her fall from idealism, and the play's *Grundgestus* (fundamental attitude) of critique.

In this production's final analysis, the market recovers not so much due to the latest advice from New York, which Peymann satirically delivers "ex machina" by flying postman, but rather because the capitalist class can still con the rest to consent to their own marginalization in order to save the system of buying and selling, even at the price of

"Maßnahmen, die hart erscheinen könnten / Weil sie einige treffen, ziemlich viele sogar / Kurz: [. . .] beinahe alle" (*BE Johanna* 74; *BFA* 3:214; Measures that may seem harsh because they / Hit some people — quite a few [. . .] / Pretty near everyone in fact, *Plays* 3.1: 96). In Mauler's plot to turn religious solace into a tool of pacification for the majority denied a good life, Johanna the saint stars because, once she is silenced, her "bloßes Aussehen / Vertrauen erweckt" (*BE Johanna* 75; *BFA* 3:216; *mere appearance* / Inspires trust, *Plays* 3.1: 98; modification in italics). This spectacle of the saint commodified may lack the appeal of a more militant heroine, an appeal strong enough that even the conservative *Frankfurter Allgemeine Zeitung* (or *FAZ*) indulged in the speculation, surprisingly generous for the German conservative paper of record, that "had she not died [. . .] she could have become a terrorist."[29] Nonetheless, Peymann's refusal to indulge this speculation by making Johanna more heroic frees his production from the leftist curiosity cabinet to which some critics would consign it. The juxta-position of the saint canonized even before her death with the still speaking woman's final reflections on her failure to change the world offers a critique that targets not merely capitalism but also the fearsome difficulty of fighting it.

To "post-Marxists" and other skeptics, however, Brecht appears to offer merely an illusion of insight into the "ewige Gesetze / Der menschlichen Wirtschaft" (*BFA* 3:187; eternal laws of / Human economy, *Plays* 3.1: 67), which remain for likely theater spectators, like the small-time speculators who utter this lament, "forever opaque." Opening at the Deutsches Theater in December 2009, Stemann's production used pop culture elements, especially the casual irony of the talk-show host and the image repertoire of a video game, shifting from unreal urban skylines in the boom to vertiginous arrays of zeros in the bust, to deconstruct not only plot and character but also the attempt by Brecht to analyze economics through drama.[30] While the program included Brecht on the economic plot, Knopf on cornering the market, and Wolfgang Engler on Johanna's embodiment, even in her naïveté, of a human remainder to commodification that might constitute the core of resistance to capitalist exploitation, the performance began with an alienated rather than critically dis-illusioned reading of the text and ended with a shrug.[31] Orange Suhrkamp playtexts in hand, three men in white suits opened with the Black Straw Hat hymn "Obacht, gib Obacht! / [. . .] / Mut, ihr versinkenden Leute, wir kommen, schaut her" (*BFA* 3:134; Watchful, be watchful / [. . .] we shall prevent you from sinking, *Plays* 3.1: 8). Behind them, the audience could see video images (manipulated by videographer Ekaterina Grizik seated at a console stage left) juxtaposing Berlin's television tower with buildings from the Chicago and Frankfurt skylines. The signature of the East Berlin skyline since the 1970s, this tower had been ironically deployed already in the twilight years of the GDR, as in Heiner Müller's revival of his own play, *Der Lohndrücker* (The Wagebuster, 1956) at the Deutsches Theater in 1988, but its appearance here, next to architectural elements from cities known for their stock exchanges and thus for capitalist speculation, scrambles the separate legacies of East and West, communist and capitalist. The characters are likewise scrambled, as the performances of the actors Felix Goeser, Matthias Neukirch, and Andreas Döhler show. Goeser reads both scene title and text, announcing aggressively that Mauler receives a letter from New York, and Neukirch responds to him hesitantly, on this occasion as Cridle; Döhler, in the first of several abject turns, follows with the workers' lament about lost labor. As Mauler rises, Goeser and Neukirch appear to compete for his role, dominated initially by the bullish Goeser, until Neukirch comes to the fore as the sensitive soul in retreat from the "bloody business" and the market crash. Katharina Marie Schubert joins the three men in the opening hymn but plays Johanna in evening dress as a talk-show hostess apparently unable to read her teleprompter, as she stumbles through her lines and waves a wooden cross at the audience. Although praised by *Theater heute* as a parody "Charity Girl" whose attachment to the microphone mocks the political aspirations of Brechtian theater as "die heilige Johanna des Theaterbetriebs" (Saint Joan of show business), she looks and acts like Sarah Palin, and like the American talk-show hostess appears both silly and dangerous, as she winks vainly — in both senses — in the limelight.[32]

This deconstructive strategy is not Stemann's invention but Castorf's, who has mixed canonical texts with mass cultural scraps for decades; his actors began his 2006 version of *Im Dickicht der Städte* by reading, with apparently random abandon, from several books, including some by Brecht. Stemann's direction suggests a tacit acknowledgment that this ironic gesture may have exhausted its capital. When Döhler plays the worker that Johanna confronts in the depths as a scruffy prole-with-Lidl-bag, his attire and abject mien reiterate what has become a cliché of (East) Berlin show-business since Castorf's version of Gerhart Hauptmann's *Die Weber* (The Weavers, 1892) in 1998. His shift from bagman to Mrs. Luckerniddle in drag may amuse but it does not pretend to enlighten. When Johanna steps away from her mike and confronts in Margit Bendokat a second Luckerniddle more angry than abject, the audience hears more clearly the voice of proletarian Berlin.[33] While the veteran GDR actress's appearance as Luckerniddle — and later as the union leader and other workers — in shapeless shift and sweatpants may repeat the cliché of the scruffy proletarian rather than express "authentic attitude," her voice commands attention. Even in pitiable moments, as when Luckerniddle signs away her right to pursue her husband's case only to vomit on the promised food when she is reminded how he died, she dominates the stage. In the final moments, Bendokat stands on stage as exemplary persona rather than singular character as she repeats with authority the statement she uttered in frustration several scenes earlier when she spoke in response to Johanna's failure to deliver the strike notice: "Die Kommunisten haben recht behalten. Die Massen hätten nicht auseinanderlaufen dürfen" (*BFA* 3:204; the communists were right; the masses should not have broken ranks, *Plays* 3.1: 86). An unseen machine gun fells Bendokat in mid-speech, and Schubert's Johanna offers only "huh" in response, the verbal counterpart to a shrug in talk-show mode.

Even in echo, however, Bendokat's voice stirs unquiet ghosts from the critical GDR repertoire, in particular her formidable *HO-Verkäuferin* (state shop saleswoman) from Müller's 1988 revival of *Der Lohndrücker* at the Deutsches Theater. Although *Theater heute*'s Christine Wahl prefers to see something other than effective realism in the "end of irony" and the eruption of "the real" effected by Bendokat's presence, she has to acknowledge that Bendokat's stage presence gives her the authority of a "hidden lead character," signaling a return to critical *Verfremdung* from the alienated dead-end of excessive irony.[34] This return from alienation, however, introduces an irony of an unexpected kind. So forceful is her performance that, despite Schubert's final shrug at theatrical and political illusion, Bendokat lends the last words of Stemann's production a heroic aspect that, in the face of capitalism's resurgence, is appealing but illusory. By contrast, while Peymann's production may indeed play with pathos in its concluding scenes, it places the focus firmly on capitalism's power to commodify pathos while profiting from misery. While the last stage image depicts Johanna's canonization, this scene comes after a long pause, as if it were an afterthought to Slift's sermon "Nun atmet auf, nun muß der Markt gesunden / [. . .] / Und noch einmal behaupten wir den Plan / Und läuft die Welt in uns genehme Bahn" (*BE Johanna* 75; *BFA* 3:216; Breathe easy now, the market *must* recover / [. . .] / Our calculations have again proved true / *And the world turns the way we want it to, Plays* 3.1: 98, modification in italics). This sermon ends the play's argument, to which the Black Straw Hats' celebration of their new power and Johanna's death and canonization provide merely the corollary.

Slift's sermon, delivered at the BE with cynical zeal by Veit Schubert, preaches "capitalism as religion," even though Brecht may not have read Walter Benjamin's unpublished 1921 fragment by that title. According to Benjamin, capitalism maintains the belief of its adherents in the unfettered market as the primary generator of wealth and well-being, along with their faith in its ability to correct itself after a crash. Paradoxically, it does so not by promising redemption from sin but by immersing its adherents in guilt, especially those at the bottom who have failed to profit from the market.[35] Eighty years after Benjamin's insight, after US government intervention gave the world's biggest banks capital for big bonuses but left the real economy in the Great Recession, the Washington consensus stands exposed as free-market fundamentalism, which critics would describe as the irrational belief in the rationality of markets and the rhetorical presentation of the interests of speculators as the common good.[36] Free-market fundamentalism has been decried even by market investors like George Soros, who first used the term to highlight the "danger to open society" of unfettered speculation, and by Nobel Prize-winning economist Joseph Stiglitz, who suggested that "the fall of Wall Street is to market fundamentalism what the fall of the Berlin Wall was to Communism." Yet the resurgence of speculation at the expense of social welfare suggests that free-market fundamentalism will be harder to dislodge than the Berlin Wall. Despite popular resentment in Germany, the US continues to defend this orthodoxy.[37] In keeping with Brecht's caution against official pressure for fictional or "phony solutions" (*Scheinlösungen*) to real problems (*BFA* 23:258; *BT* 267), *Johanna* ends without heroic resistance to capital. But, while Schubert and Stemann's final shrug leaves the hole between resistance and resignation simply gaping, Droste, Karge, Peymann, and the BE mark the critical distance between the power of capitalism to dominate through enforcing resignation through guilt on the one hand, and the refusal of the "human remainder," in Engler's phrase, to submit to that calculation on the other.[38] This refusal to submit to capitalist calculations of value has yet to give rise to the revolutionary overthrow of the system of the kind that Bendokat's communist might have invoked. Nonetheless, capitalist demands that the general population submit to austerity while transnational banks once again reap record profits have provoked dissent in the erstwhile heart of social democratic Europe (in France and Germany), on the European periphery, especially in Greece, among the poorest of the poor in Africa, and even in the United States.

The globalization of anti-capitalist agitation, as well as the growth of non-governmental organizations like the World Social Forum, challenge the capitalist consensus of corporations, the World Bank, and the International Monetary Fund, and may yet light the spark that, in an image accidentally but aptly relevant to Brecht's Chicago, "will set the prairie ablaze."[39]

Notes

[1] Only the formerly GDR daily *Berliner Zeitung* carried commentary on the *Communist Manifesto*. Wolfgang Engler, author of *Die Ostdeutschen: Kunde von einem verlorenen Land* (Berlin: Aufbau, 1998) discussed Brecht's interest in Marx and the manifesto's relevance to contemporary Europe in "So viel Hoffnung war nie: Gleiches Stück, wechselndes Personal," *Berliner Zeitung*, 21–22 February 1998. For discussion, see Loren Kruger, *Post-Imperial Brecht: Politics and Performance, East and South* (Cambridge: Cambridge UP, 2004), 171–214.

[2] Karl Marx and Friedrich Engels, *Manifest der kommunistischen Partei* (1848; Stuttgart: Reclam, 1999), 22; Samuel Moore, trans., *Manifesto of the Communist Party* [1888], ed. Engels, introduction by Eric Hobsbawm (London: Verso, 1998), 37, trans. mod.; hereafter cited as Marx/Engels, *Manifest/Manifesto*, with page numbers from the German and then the English edition. I follow Hobsbawm in attributing primary authorship to Marx; Hobsbawm, "Introduction," *Manifesto*, 4.

[3] John Willett and Ralph Manheim, "Introduction," in Brecht, *Collected Plays*, vol. 3, pt. 1: *Saint Joan of the Stockyards*, trans. Ralph Manheim (London: Methuen, 1991), xix; hereafter *Plays* 3.1 and page number in the text. Note: "stockyards" is a euphemistic translation of *Schlachthöfe*, literally: slaughterhouses.

[4] Fritz Walter, *Berliner Börsen-Courier*, 12 April 1932; reprinted in Gisela E. Bahr, ed., *Bertolt Brecht: Die heilige Johanna der Schlachthöfe; Bühnenfassung, Fragmente, Varianten* (Frankfurt a.M.: Suhrkamp, 1971), 218–20. The *Berliner Börsen-Courier*'s chief theater critic was Herbert Ihering, who had supported Brecht's work since 1924.

[5] The *Berliner Funkstunde* (April 1932) aired seven scenes out of eleven. Contacted by Brecht after the war despite his Nazi collaboration, Gründgens staged the play three years after Brecht's death; see Brecht, "Zu 'Die heilige Johanna der Schlachthöfe,'" *BFA* 24:488.

[6] Ernst Schumacher, "Zeitgenössiches Theater?," *Berliner Zeitung*, 21 August 1968.

[7] Robert Reich, US Labor Secretary in the Clinton Administration, notes in "The Root of Economic Fragility and Political Anger" (http://robertreich.

org/post/805148061/the-root-of-economic-fragility-and-political-anger, accessed 2 September 2010) that the extreme inequality of both 1928 and 2008, when 1% of the population received 24% of US income, as opposed to 9% in the 1960s, was harmful not only because it violated norms of equity or social justice, but also because it generated economic instability by denying the majority full access to the economy as producers or consumers while rewarding a tiny minority for short-term speculative bubbles, and by propping up that minority when the bubble burst, rather than focusing on long-term investment and steady returns. In other words, rising inequality is bad for capital as well as labor. For analysis of the links between the Great Depression and the Great Recession and the liabilities of the so-called Washington consensus, see the *Dollars & Sense* collective, ed., *The Economic Crisis Reader* (Boston: Economic Affairs Bureau, 2009).

[8] Mark Twain, "The German Chicago," in *The £1,000,000 Bank-Note and Other Stories* (1893; rpt. Freeport, NY: Books for Libraries, 1970), 200–232; Walter Rathenau, "Die schönste Stadt der Welt," *Die Zukunft* 26 (1899): 36–48.

[9] A 2010 survey commissioned by the conglomerate Bertelsmann reflected widespread skepticism in Germany about capitalism; see "Wachstumsskeptisch: Eine Umfrage zeigt: Die Deutschen zweifeln am Kapitalismus," *Die Zeit* (Hamburg), 18 August 2010, http://www.zeit.de/2010/34/Emnid-Umfrage, accessed 2 September 2010.

[10] Groys, "Die Revolution der Tugend," *Die Zeit* (Hamburg), 17 December 2009, http://www.zeit.de/2009/52/Armutsdebatte, accessed 2 September 2010.

[11] The several productions of *Johanna* by the Schauspielhaus Dresden invite research not only because the first GDR production was mounted there in 1961 but because its revivals in 1998 and 2009 were innovative, the former because it included dramaturgical material on Chicago labor history and the latter because it dramatized, in a vigorous physical performance, the dismemberment and commodification of human as well as beast, as some actors prodded others as though they were cattle and all grappled with precariously stacked metal boxes that represented cans of meat as well as the instability of the market.

[12] Bouck White, *The Book of Daniel Drew* (New York: Georgia Doran, 1910). The first German translation was by Maria Ewers aus'm Weerth, *Das Buch des Daniel Drew: Leben und Meinungen eines amerikanischen Börsenmannes* (Berlin: Bild- und Buchwelt, 1922).

[13] Frank Norris, *The Pit: A Story of Chicago* (New York: Doubleday, 1903); Upton Sinclair, *The Jungle* (New York: Doubleday, 1906). Norris's depiction of a wealthy capitalist ruined by his attempt to corner the future supply of wheat contrasts with Sinclair's focus on immigrant workers ground down (and ground up) by laboring in the slaughterhouses, but both highlight the violent sundering of social and personal bonds by capitalist speculation.

[14] Erich Mendelsohn, *Amerika: Bilderbuch eines Architekten* (Berlin: Rudolf Mosse, 1928); Egon Erwin Kisch, "Die Getreidebörse," in *Gesammelte Werke*, vol. 5, *Paradies Amerika*, 243–50 (1930; Berlin: Aufbau, 1991).

[15] George Bernard Shaw, *Major Barbara* (Harmondsworth: Penguin, 1960), 130.

[16] Käthe Rülicke-Weiler, "*Die heilige Johanna der Schlachthöfe*: Notizen zum Bau der Fabel," in *Wer war Brecht?*, ed. Werner Mittenzwei (East Berlin: Verlag das europäische Buch, 1977), 260–76.

[17] Rülicke-Weiler, *"Die heilige Johanna,"* 260.

[18] T. W. Adorno, "Engagement," in *Gesammelte Schriften*, vol. 11, *Noten zur Literatur* (Frankfurt a.M.: Suhrkamp, 1974), 409–30, here 417; "Commitment," trans. Shierry Weber Nicholsen, in *Notes to Literature*, vol. 2 (New York: Columbia UP, 1992), 70–96, here 83.

[19] Jan Knopf, ed., *Brechts "Heilige Johanna,"* (Frankfurt a.M.: Suhrkamp, 1986), 18, 9.

[20] Knopf, ed., *Brechts "Heilige Johanna,"* 110–11.

[21] The English "to spread the gospel" highlights the irony of using religion to rationalize exploitation, while the German asks only that the church should "für uns reden / Überall, daß wir gute Leute sind? Gutes planend in / Schlechter Zeit" (*BFA* 3:214; speak for us / Saying everywhere that we're good men).

[22] For former US Vice President Dick Cheney's connections to Haliburton and its war profiteering, see Russell Mokhiber and Russell Weissman, "The Ten Worst Corporations of 2003," *Multinational Monitor* 24 (2003): 12, http://www.multinationalmonitor.org/mm2003/122003/mokhiber.html; accessed 2 September 2010.

[23] Jean Ziegler, *Die neuen Herrscher der Welt und ihre globalen Widersacher* (Munich: Bertelsmann, 2003), cited in the program *Bertolt Brecht: Die heilige Johanna der Schlachthöfe* (Berlin: Berliner Ensemble, 2003), 28. Ziegler argues not only that Bill Gates of Microsoft owns more than the 100 million poorest Americans, but also that Gates and the other fourteen richest men in the world own more than the GDP of sub-Saharan Africa, with the exception of South Africa. Program notes and text cited hereafter as *BE Johanna*.

[24] Franz Wille, "Auf die Plätze. Fertig. Halt!" *Theater heute* 41, no. 3 (March 2006): 8, unfavorably compared Peymann's earnest treatment with Castorf's farcical deconstruction of leftist drama. In *Theatre is More Beautiful than War: German Stage Directing in the Late Twentieth Century* (Iowa City: U of Iowa P, 2009), Marvin Carlson acknowledged that the BE was "by some standards the most successful theatre in the capital," playing to "over 95 percent capacity" audiences, but still reiterated the fashionable dismissal of "old leftists" (70).

[25] Comments based on the edited text in the program and on the DVD; thanks to Laura Diehl for this material.

²⁶ Peter Hans Göpfert, "Der Scheinheilige von Chicago," *Berliner Morgenpost*, 7 September 2003.

²⁷ Despite Willett's familiar translation "alienation" (*BT* 91), *Ver-fremd-ung* is better rendered by the literal "e-strange-ment" or by *dis-illusion*; see Eric White's translation of Brecht's "An Essay on the Effects of Dis-illusion in Chinese Acting" (1936; *BFA* 22:960–68). Dis-illusion highlights critical *resistance* to the dispossession implied by *Entfremdung*, the term that Marx inherited from Hegel. *Entfremdung* is appropriately translated as alienation, which links the term also to Anglo-American legal history, as in the alienation of property. For comment, including the productive association of dis-illusion with Max Weber's *Entzauberung* or de-enchantment, see Kruger, *Post-Imperial Brecht*, 39–48.

²⁸ Esther Slevogt, "Der Karnevalkommunismus oder: der Kapitalist und das Mädchen," *Financial Times Deutschland* (Hamburg), 8 September 2003.

²⁹ In her review "Die Terroristin," *FAZ am Sonntag*, 7 September 2003, Johanna Adorján was moved by Droste's performance to argue that, had Johanna not died, her anger at social injustice would have led her to underground politics and thence to terrorism in the manner of the Red Army Faction. Juxtaposing the extreme politics of the RAF's rebellion against West German capitalism with the legacy of Brecht is not in itself new. In their staging of Heiner Müller's adaptation of Brecht's *Fatzer* in 1978 in Hamburg, former GDR directors Karge and Matthias Langhoff had, with Müller's active participation, inserted RAF texts into the performance (see Kruger, *Post-Imperial Brecht*, 148–50); further, an anonymous review of the 1997 BE revival of *Die Maßnahme* in *Der Spiegel* mentioned Ulrike Meinhof, chief theoretician of the RAF, as a real-life analogue for the militant comrades in Brecht's play (ibid. 200). In the light of this history, what is surprising here is not the mention of the RAF per se but the apparently positive tone of the analogy in this newspaper.

³⁰ Comments based on the program *Die heilige Johanna der Schlachthöfe*, ed. Sonja Anders (Berlin: Deutsches Theater, 2009), hereafter *DT*, the performance script, and the DVD; thanks to Gisela Tenor for this material.

³¹ Engler, "Der menschliche Rest," *DT*, 13–32.

³² Christine Wahl, "Der Gang in die Tiefe," *Theater heute* 45, no. 2 (February 2010): 28. The affinity with Palin is my observation.

³³ Dirk Pilz, "Bedenk' die Wirklichkeit," *Berliner Zeitung*, 18 December 2009, described Bendokat's as "die einzige authentische Haltung" (the only authentic attitude) in the production; in the Western leftist *Tageszeitung*, Katrin Müller wondered how seriously to take this shift in tone; see "Vermisstenanzeige für das revolutionäre Subjekt," *TAZ* (Berlin), 18 December 2009.

³⁴ Wahl (see n. 32), acknowledges Bendokat's performance as critique of the production's "postmodern simulation antics [*Mätzchen*]" but ties herself in knots to assert that this critique uses "Brecht against Brecht to get beyond

Brecht." Writing after Bendokat won the Berlin Prize for theater, Eva Behrendt lauded her as "Die Wahrhaftigkeitsherstellerin" (restorer of genuineness), in *TAZ* (Berlin), 8 May 2010.

[35] Walter Benjamin, "Kapitalismus als Religion (1921)," in *Gesammelte Schriften*, vol. 6 (Frankfurt a.M.: Suhrkamp, 1985), 100–103.

[36] In *The Crisis of Global Capitalism: Open Society Endangered* (New York: Public Affairs, 1998), Soros argued that the deregulation of speculation in the 1990s was a danger to markets as well as society. Although without any allusion to Brecht, Stiglitz's analysis of corporate malfeasance bears a striking resemblance to Brecht's. The key chapter, "The Great American Robbery," in his *Freefall: America, Free Markets, and the Sinking of the World Economy* (New York: Norton, 2010), showed how Wall Street bankers used their influence with allies and former colleagues in government to secure their income while millions of ordinary citizens — in "Maulerian" terms, "quite a few" — lost their jobs or homes, and "pretty near everyone" else lost income.

[37] Stiglitz, interview with Nathan Gardels, in *The Huffington Post*, 16 September 2008, http://www.huffingtonpost.com/nathan-gardels/stiglitz-the-fall-of-wall _b_126911.html, accessed 2 September 2010. The US Chamber of Commerce's celebration of German GDP growth, despite the evident failure of free-market fundamentalism to guide or interpret economic activity, demonstrates the tenacity of the Washington consensus. See Peter Rashish, "Germany's Economic Growth: from Headlines to Long-term Success," *American Institute for Contemporary German Studies*, 2 September 2010, http://www.aicgs.org/ analysis/c/rashish090210.aspx, accessed 2 September 2010.

[38] Engler, "Der menschliche Rest," 15.

[39] Michael Hardt and Antonio Negri, *Commonwealth* (Cambridge: Harvard UP, 2009), xiv.

CPSIA information can be obtained at www.ICGtesting.com
Printed in the USA
BVOW060139290212

284038BV00002B/2/P

9 781571 134929